D0760639

RETAINING
VALUED
EMPLOYEES

Advanced Topics in Organizational Behavior

The **Advanced Topics in Organizational Behavior** series examines current and emerging issues in the field of organizational behavior. Written by researchers who are widely acknowledged subject area experts, the books provide an authoritative, up-to-date review of the conceptual, research, and practical implications of the major issues in organizational behavior.

Editors: Julian Barling, *Queen's University*
                     Kevin Kelloway, *University of Guelph*

Editorial Board: Victor M. Catano, *Saint Mary's University*
                     Cary L. Cooper, *University of Manchester Institute
                         of Science and Technology*
                     Daniel G. Gallagher, *James Madison University*
                     Jean Hartley, *University of Warwick*
                     Denise Rousseau, *Carnegie-Mellon University*
                     Paul Spector, *University of South Florida*
                     Lois E. Tetrick, *University of Houston*

RETAINING VALUED EMPLOYEES

Rodger W. Griffeth / Peter W. Hom

Advanced Topics in
Organizational Behavior AT●B

Sage Publications
International Educational and Professional Publisher
Thousand Oaks ▪ London ▪ New Delhi

Copyright © 2001 by Sage Publications, Inc.

All rights reserved. No part of this book may be reproduced or utilized in any form or by any means, electronic or mechanical, including photocopying, recording, or by any information storage and retrieval system, without permission in writing from the publisher.

For information:

Sage Publications, Inc.
2455 Teller Road
Thousand Oaks, California 91320
E-mail: order@sagepub.com

Sage Publications Ltd.
6 Bonhill Street
London EC2A 4PU
United Kingdom

Sage Publications India Pvt. Ltd.
M-32 Market
Greater Kailash I
New Delhi 110 048 India

Printed in the United States of America

Library of Congress Cataloging-in-Publication Data

Griffeth, Rodger W., 1946–
    Retaining valued employees / by Rodger W. Griffeth and Peter W. Hom.
       p.   cm. — (Advanced topics in organizational behavior)
    Includes bibliographical references and index.
    ISBN 0-7619-1305-X (cloth: acid-free paper)
    ISBN 0-7619-1306-8 (pbk.: acid-free paper)
    1. Labor turnover. I. Hom, Peter W. II. Title. III. Series.
    HF5549.5.T8 G74   2001
    658.3—dc21   00-011617

01 02 03 04 05 06 07 7 6 5 4 3 2 1

Acquiring Editor:	Marquita Flemming
Editorial Assistant:	MaryAnn Vail
Production Editor:	Diana E. Axelsen
Editorial Assistant:	Cindy Bear
Typesetter/Designer:	Lynn Miyata
Indexer:	Mary Mortensen
Cover Designer:	Jane M. Quaney

Contents

Preface   vii

1. How Turnover Can Be Costly to Organizations   1

2. Job Enrichment   31

3. Realistic Job Previews   46

4. Socialization and Supervision   66

5. Employee Selection   94

6. Using Employee Surveys to Predict Turnover
   and Diagnose Turnover Causes   118

7. Compensation and Rewards   153

8. Reducing Turnover Among Special Groups:
   Minorities and Women   180

9. Managing Exiting Employees   203

Appendix A: The Job Rating Form   224

Appendix B: The Job Diagnostic Survey   230

Appendix C: Scoring Key for the Job Diagnostic Survey
and the Job Rating Form   244

Appendix D: Job Characteristics Overall National Norms   248

References   249

Index   268

About the Authors   277

Preface

In recent times, employee retention has become one of the leading challenges for organizations. Given today's extremely low unemployment rates and weak company loyalty (a response to pervasive downsizing by Corporate America), employees are increasingly "jumping ship" for better job opportunities elsewhere. Thus, employers are desperate for turnover remedies, and a growing number of consultants and authors are eager to offer solutions. We, too, have been increasingly approached by companies seeking advice on how to manage turnover. Yet, as scholars who have investigated turnover for more than 20 years, we have been frustrated by what academic writings offer in the way of suggestions for personnel retention. In our earlier book, we had reviewed the scholarly literature on turnover and found limited practical solutions. Most researchers have focused on predicting turnover or testing theories about why employees quit. Other than selection techniques, scholars rarely have validated organizational interventions to verify whether they truly can deter resignations.

For different reasons, we also are distressed by the popular business press, which often relies on anecdotal evidence or testimonials to substantiate loyalty-building methods. Journalists or consultants often contend that certain techniques can lower turnover, citing some organizational success stories. Yet, their claims are rarely backed by "scientific" data; that is, we would have greater confidence in their proposed solutions if independent research established that the facility receiving the intervention had lower quit rates than other facilities not given this treatment (presuming relatively comparable facilities) or that the turnover rate in a particular facility had decreased over time since implementing the treatment. We acknowledge that the gold standard of double-blinded, controlled experiments is often impractical. Still, we cannot put much faith in practitioner suggestions based on informal observations or subjective opinion. After all, other branches of psychology—of which we (as organizational psychologists) are offshoots—would not prescribe psychotherapies or educational programs that have not been evaluated rigorously.

Given our misgivings about academic and practitioner writings, this book strives to derive practical prescriptions from our own academic work and that of other turnover researchers. At the risk of offending our academic colleagues, we prescribe practical solutions that have not necessarily been field-tested in controlled experiments. Nonetheless, these suggestions have some foundation in research studies, even though the underlying research may not meet the most rigorous standards of scientific proof. To illustrate, turnover investigators have shown that certain work experiences (e.g., routine, boring work tasks) or attitudes (pay dissatisfaction) predispose employees to quit. We argue that organizations might reduce turnover by following such research (e.g., using job enrichment or improving compensation). Though often based on correlational—rather than experimental—evidence, practical solutions grounded in research are nonetheless more valid than what underpins practitioner recommendations

We believe that employers can derive useful prescriptions from turnover research methods and findings. Rather than allow practitioner writings to dominate advice-giving, this book attempts to bridge both academic and practitioner worlds. We hope to translate scholarly findings into practical suggestions for employers who face retention problems.

For my family, Jacqui and Justin
The two people who taught me most about loyalty

—Rodger W. Griffeth

Dedicated with love to my family, Cheree, Ernest, and Rose
No turnover there

—Peter W. Hom

1

How Turnover Can Be Costly to Organizations

E mployee turnover is assuming crisis proportions for many employers who struggle to retain people in the tightest labor market in recent memory. Indeed, 52% of companies in a national survey report that their turnover is increasing (Wilson, 2000), and quit rates are running at a 10-year high of 1.1% a month (Bernstein, 1998). Based on a survey of resignation rates by the Saratoga Institute, a workforce research firm, 17 million workers will quit to take other jobs in 1999, compared with only 6 million 5 years before (Clark, 1999). On average, companies nationwide will have to replace one seventh of their workforce this year (Clark, 1999). Put differently, 1 in 10 workers was a quitter 5 years ago. Today, 1 in 7 quit (Clark, 1999).

When the costs of a single incidence of turnover are considered, the growing number of quits is even more alarming. For example, a computer programmer who quits might incur as much as $20,080 to a company, and an exiting pharmaceutical salesperson can cost an employer $62,708 in total expenses (Hom & Griffeth, 1995). Generally speaking, human resources professionals and researchers project that the cost of one turnover incidence ranges from between 93% to 200% of a leaver's salary, depending on his or her skill and level of job responsibility (Cascio, 2000; Johnson, 1995). Similarly, 45% of 206 medium-to-large companies polled by William M. Mercer consultants report that turnover costs them more than $10,000 per exit ("Survey Confirms High Cost of Turnover," 1998). When accumulated across all turnover incidences experienced by a company, such costs can weaken its bottom line. Thus, a 1992 investigation of turnover in the Arizona mental health industry estimated that the combined costs of turnover for 23 agencies totaled $3,757,141 in 1999 dollars (Hom, 1992).

Of course, turnover is not always bad. For example, vacating employees can increase promotional opportunities for other employees or can infuse new ideas and technology when new employees replace those who left (Staw, 1980). More than this, certain kinds of job exits—quits among marginal performers or overpaid employees—are even desirable (Dalton, Krackhardt, & Porter, 1981). Indeed, a certain quit rate might be tolerated as a cost of doing business in a particular industry (Abelson & Baysinger, 1984). Nonetheless, organizational-level research and corporate studies report that high exit rates generally worsen organizational effectiveness (Alexander, Bloom, & Nuchols, 1994). For example, Ulrich, Halbrook, Meder, Stuchlik, and Thorpe (1991) found that financially successful Ryder Truck Rental districts had lower quit rates than unsuccessful districts, and Alexander et al. (1994) documented that hospitals experiencing higher turnover among registered nurses faced greater operating and personnel costs.

To manage turnover effectively, corporations must monitor not only the extent of turnover but also its costs (Wilson, 2000). Otherwise, they face the predicament described by an Intel manager: "We lose time, we lose productivity, we lose efficiency. How do you put a number on that? I don't know. But I know it's not good" (Ettorre, 1997, p. 51). Although cumbersome, tracking direct personnel costs of turnover is most feasible. Other costs that a personnel exodus incur are indirect or difficult to measure, such as former employees sharing trade secrets with other competitors or forming competing businesses (Hom & Griffeth, 1995). These costs are no less real but are harder to quantify or anticipate. Putting a dollar figure on turnover costs is valuable because it can help justify expenditures for turnover remedies or interventions. Thus, employers can determine whether potential solutions offset the financial costs of the turnover problem. Otherwise, "it may be far less expensive to cope with turnover than to prevent it" (Dalton & Todor, 1979, p. 226).

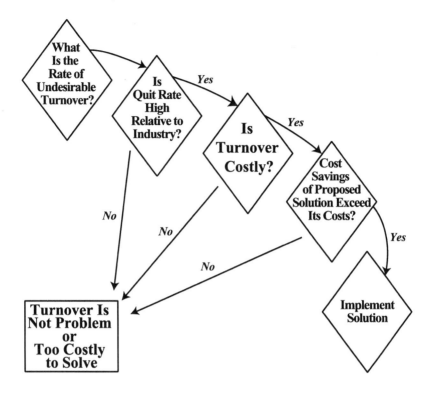

Exhibit 1.1. Diagnostic Model

Identifying Unwanted Turnover

We suggest answering the series of diagnostic questions in Exhibit 1.1 before attempting any proposed remedy. The first step requires that your firm calculate the actual rate of undesirable turnover, relying on personnel data. All too often, managers become alarmed when a few high-profile employees depart. Yet such "anecdotal evidence" may misrepresent whether turnover is truly a pervasive problem for your organization. Indeed, one of us had collaborated with an MBA team investigating turnover for an airline whose international hub was Hong Kong. Although the general manager believed that turnover was acute, the MBA team discovered that the actual quit rate was not dramatically different from that faced by other Hong Kong employers.

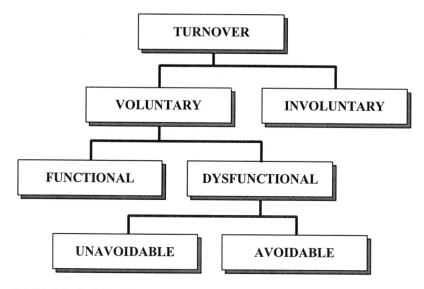

Exhibit 1.2. Defining Undesirable Turnover

Voluntary Quits

Before you can assess the extent of *undesirable* turnover in Exhibit 1.1, we must clarify what *unwanted* turnover means. According to Exhibit 1.2 (Hom & Griffeth, 1995), you should initially distinguish between *voluntary* and *involuntary* quits. Voluntary turnover means that employees freely choose to leave the job. In contrast, involuntary turnover represents employer-initiated job separations over which leavers have little or no personal say, such as dismissals or layoffs. Rather than measuring an overall quit rate that includes both voluntary and involuntary exits, we suggest focusing on the voluntary turnover rate. Voluntary quits are undesirable because employers did not request these departures, whereas involuntary exits are desirable because employers would not want to keep poor performers or excess manpower.

Determining whether employees leave voluntarily is relatively straightforward from interviews with the immediate superiors of exiting employees. For greater insight, voluntary exits can be classified further by exit interviews into more detailed reasons into why leavers quit. Derived from exit interviews, Exhibit 1.3 shows the various types of factors motivating nurses to quit a hospital voluntarily. (The hospital classified involuntary quits to include threaten-

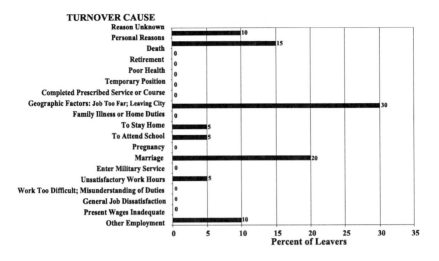

Exhibit 1.3. Types of Voluntary Turnover (Initiated by Employee)

ing or abusing patients or employees, defamatory statements about patients, insubordination, and property destruction.) This list of voluntary exit reasons is not unusual, although turnover researchers disagree over whether a particular reason is voluntary or not (Campion, 1991). For example, some scholars treat terminations due to poor health and retirement as voluntary departures (Campion, 1991; Hanisch & Hulin, 1990), whereas others regard exits due to childbirth and family relocations as involuntary (Hom & Griffeth, 1995; Price, 1977). For a preliminary classification, we prefer a broad definition of voluntary terminations to encompass all quits that employees initiate, including pregnancy- and relocation-induced turnover (the latter voluntary separations are further classified as unavoidable and removed; see subsequent discussion). After this determination, you would subtract the number of involuntary quits from the total number of employees quitting during the year.

Dysfunctional Quits

Among voluntary quits, we can further differentiate between *functional* and *dysfunctional* turnover. Functional turnover represents the exit of substandard performers, whereas dysfunctional turnover represents the exit of effective performers (or highly skilled or trained employees who are not easily replaced). Only the latter type of resignations disadvantage employers. Personnel records or interviews with supervisors can pinpoint which job exits are functional or dysfunctional (Campion, 1991). Deducting the number of functional quits from the total number of job quits may reveal much less severe turnover than imagined. To illustrate, a study of bank personnel exits discovered that high performers made up only 58% of all quits, making the gross 32% quit rate less alarming (Dalton et al., 1981). Besides involuntary exits, we therefore prescribe further reducing the overall number of quits by the number of functional exits.

Avoidable Quits

Finally, we can further divide dysfunctional exits into *avoidable* and *unavoidable* quits (Abelson, 1987). Unavoidable quits represent those employee separations that employers cannot control, such as terminations due to childbirth, full-time care for relatives, family moves, acute medical disability, and death (Abelson, 1987; Campion, 1991). Even so, many corporations are attempting to influence unavoidable exits by furnishing an assorted array of family- and lifestyle-friendly programs to help employees resolve work-family (or work-school) conflicts (Glover & Crooker, 1995; Hom & Griffeth, 1995). To illustrate, DuPont offers flextime, job-sharing, and telecommuting, and Eddie Bauer provides employees with lactation rooms, takeout dinners, and one paid "Balance Day" off a year (Hammonds, 1996). Thus, present-day companies are trying to control quits that historically have been deemed unavoidable (and private matters that are off-limits to employers). Consequently, your analysis should delete job exits that your company cannot truly control (or whose control is cost-prohibitive, such as offering on-site day care centers). In conclusion, your organization can more precisely derive the actual rate of undesirable quits by subtracting out involuntary, functional, and unavoidable quits.

Nursing Illustration

Exhibit 1.4 breaks down the overall quit rate of new nursing graduates working for an urban hospital into the three turnover classifications. The gross quit rate (number of leavers divided by number of new hires) was 14.6%. On closer inspection, 87% of these nursing quits were voluntary, and 13% were involuntary. Among voluntary nursing exits, 58% of the voluntary leavers rep-

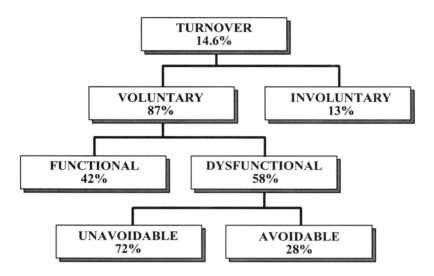

Exhibit 1.4. Turnover Classifications

resented dysfunctional exits (they attained favorable performance reviews during the probation period), whereas 42% were functional exits (ineffective performers who quit). Exit interviews further determined that 72% of dysfunctional quits were unavoidable—mainly marriages and family relocations (cf. Exhibit 1.3). Put differently, only 28% represented avoidable quits that the hospital could control. To summarize, once we remove involuntary, functional, and unavoidable exits, the true extent of unwanted nursing turnover for this hospital was merely 1.3%! This example is not far-fetched; another inquiry into job exits at a university also revealed that most turnover is voluntary and unavoidable (Campion, 1991).

Using Exit Interviews To Identify Turnover Avoidability

Admittedly, using exit interviews to ascertain whether resignations are avoidable or unavoidable is problematic (see Chapter 9). During interviews with superiors or other firm representatives, exiting employees may overstate unavoidable (and understate avoidable) reasons for why they leave to avoid "burning their bridges." After all, leavers may want favorable reference letters from former supervisors. Rather than blame poor supervision or work conditions, departing employees instead may attribute their exit to unavoidable reasons, such as family relocations or other personal motives (Campion, 1991). Despite the wisdom of identifying avoidable quits to focus "attention on reasons for turnover that an organization can control" (Campion, 1991, p. 210), conventional exit interviews may not easily disentangle unavoidable from avoidable quits (unless your firm carries out more accurate studies of turnover causes; see Chapter 9). Even if you cannot delete unavoidable quits, identifying and removing involuntary and functional quits still may produce sobering estimates of the turnover rate in your firm. In our nursing example, omitting only involuntary and functional quits yielded an undesirable quit rate of 4.4%, which is a fraction of the gross quit rate of 14.6%.

Benchmarking Turnover Rates

Following Exhibit 1.1, your organization should next ascertain whether your quit rates are significantly worse than industry rates. Just as other performance measures of company success (e.g., customer complaint rates, hiring effectiveness) are routinely audited, business enterprises should benchmark turnover rates. A benchmark study would analyze the turnover rates of your firm's competitors, including product and labor-supply competitors. Thus, the Arizona Council of Human Service Providers (a statewide association of 80 agencies that provide mental health care and other human services, such as drug counseling and crisis shelters) routinely collects turnover rates from its member agencies during annual salary surveys. To illustrate, Exhibit 1.5 shows quit rates for key positions in their industry. Similarly, salary surveys by the maquila industry—manufacturing plants along the U.S.-Mexico border that export products made or assembled in Mexico to the American market— often collect turnover rates from individual plants (Miller, Hom, & Gomez-Mejia, 1999). From a wage survey done in Mexicali, Mexico, Exhibit 1.6 shows the 1998 quit rates for assemblers—who represent the prime maquila workforce—for various manufacturing plants there.

All told, organizations must first ascertain whether their turnover rates truly exceed industry averages. Thus, a benchmarking study by the Ford Motor Company disclosed that the turnover rate among its exempt workforce was lower than that of the manufacturing industry (Exhibit 1.7; see Smith,

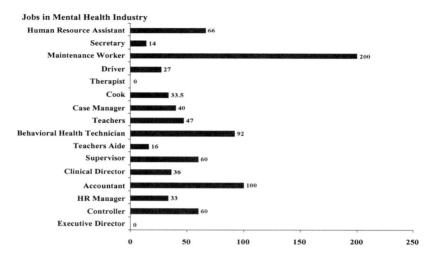

Exhibit 1.5. Turnover Rates for Various Jobs in the Mental Health Industry

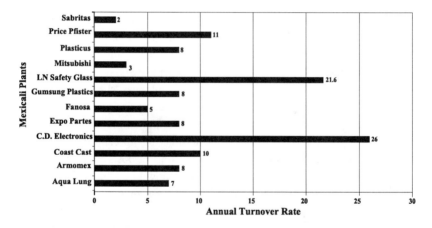

Exhibit 1.6. Overall Turnover Rates in the Electronics Industry (Mexicali, Mexico)

1999). Companies might thus carry out a special survey to assess industry-level quit rates or append additional questions on turnover rates to current wage surveys. A benchmarking investigation should sample both firms in one's industry as well as firms belonging to other industries that compete for the same manpower.

Exempt Employee Voluntary Attrition Rates (U.S. Industry, 1996)

	10%	*25%*	*50%*	*75%*	*90%*	*Average %*
Manufacturing	3.7	5.9	9.8	12.8	18.9	10.2
25,000+ employees	5.2	8.5	10.4	19.2	22.9	13.1
ALL	5.5	8.2	11.6	18.0	23.7	13.7

Ford rate . . . 4.8%

Exhibit 1.7. Benchmarking by Ford Motor Company
SOURCE: Saratoga Institute—1997 Human Resource Financial Report.

Personnel Costs

After assessing the turnover rate, your organization should gauge its cost (see Exhibit 1.1). Turnover costs can be broken down into three categories: *separation, replacement,* and *training* costs (Cascio, 2000; Flamholtz, 1985). As Exhibit 1.8 shows, separation costs refer to costs directly produced by quits, such as the expense of exit interviews with leavers. Replacement costs represent expenses incurred to replace exiting employees, such as the costs of advertising the vacated position. Training costs comprise company expenditures to orient and train new replacements for former employees. The following section describes the various elements making up each cost category, using an illustration from an investigation of turnover costs for mental health agencies (Hom, 1992). Our example describes how to compute the costs incurred when a manager (program coordinator) quits an agency. This position requires a master's degree in the behavioral health field and 3 years of experience. Agency managers typically supervise staff, make hiring and firing decisions, monitor program and contract compliance, and occasionally provide direct client services.

Separation Costs

As Exhibit 1.9 reveals, a key separation cost is the exit interview, whether done by a supervisor or human resources professional. Its cost is captured by estimating the amount of time to carry out the interview and the participants'

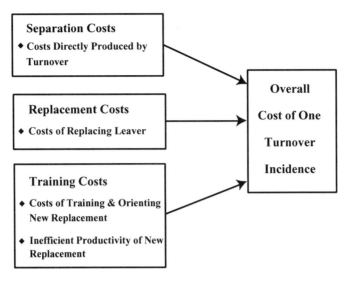

Exhibit 1.8. Turnover Costs

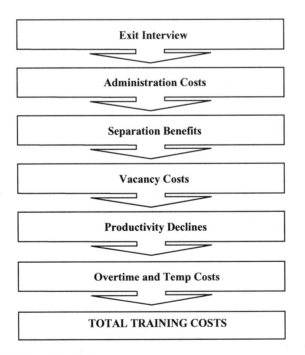

Exhibit 1.9. Separation Costs

hourly wages (i.e., total compensation, including base pay and fringe benefits). Exhibit 1.10 shows how to calculate the cost of the exit interview when a mental health manager quits (Hom, 1992). This cost (S1) is thus computed as the sum of two components: the cost of the leaver's time and the cost of the interviewer's time (Cascio, 2000; Hom & Griffeth, 1995). Each component cost is simply the time of the interview (in hours) multiplied by an interview participant's hourly compensation. In this example, we multiply the interviewer's ($10.77) and departing manager's ($17.85) hourly pay by the duration of the exit interview (3 hours) and sum the two product terms. As a result, we derive $85.86 as the cost of the exit interview with a departing manager (S1 in Exhibit 1.10).

Another separation cost is the administrative and paperwork cost of removing the leaver's name from payroll records (S2 in Exhibit 1.10). Hom (1992) asked human resources personnel to directly estimate this cost, and Cascio (2000) computed this cost by multiplying the time to delete leavers' names from personnel files by the personnel specialist's hourly pay. For our example, the administrative cost of processing a manager's exit was $185 in 1999 dollars (S2 in Exhibit 1.10).

Disbursement to leavers of separation benefits, such as unused vacation time, represents another separation cost (Hom, 1992). Because our goal is to estimate how costly voluntary turnover is, we would exclude severance pay, which is available for involuntary terminations (Cascio, 2000; Darmon, 1990). In our running example, the cost of unused vacation time for a quitting manager is $357, which is derived by multiplying the number of hours of unused vacation time (20 hours) by a manager's hourly pay ($17.85) (S3 in Exhibit 1.10).

Another separation cost associated with service organizations is the amount of client revenues lost when staff shortages—resulting from turnover—force companies to turn away customers (Darmon, 1990). For example, Hom (1992) operationalized "lost revenues" in his exploration of turnover costs in mental health agencies using the following formula:

Lost client revenues = Weeks a job remains vacant ×
Billable hours per week × Hourly rate charged for client services.

Of course, understaffed organizations might maintain the same client load with fewer personnel to avoid losing business. Still, an overworked workforce may provide inferior or delayed client services, alienating current customers

Separation Cost Factors	Formulas	Calculations For Exiting Manager	Estimated Cost
S1. Exit interviews	(Hours Spent on Exit Interview × Interviewer's Hourly Pay) + (Interview Time × Leaver's Hourly Pay)	($10.77 × 3 hours) + ($17.85 × 3 hours)	$ 85.86
S2. Administrative Costs	Direct estimate		$185.00
S3. Unused vacation time	Hours of Unused Vacation × Hourly Pay	20 hours × $17.85	$357.00
S4. Lost revenues due to vacancy	Weeks Job Is Vacant × Billable Hours per Week × Hourly Rate for Client Services	0	0
S5. Overtime costs for extra labor during job vacancy	Overtime Hours per Week × Weeks of Job Vacancy × Overtime Pay Rate × Average Hourly Pay	0	0
S6. Hiring temporary personnel during job vacancy	Weekly Hours Worked by Temp Workers × Weeks of Temp Work × Temp Worker's Hourly Pay	0	0
S7. Client assignment	Clerical Cost to Transfer Client Records + (Supervisory Time for Case Consultation × Supervisory Hourly Pay) + (Staff Time to Learn Client History × Staff Hourly Pay)	($128 Clerical Cost) + (4 Supervisory Hours × $18.88) + (4 Staff Hours × $17.85)	$274.92
Total separation costs	S1 + S2 + S3 + S4 + S5 + S6 + S7		$902.78

Exhibit 1.10. Estimating Separation Costs

and scaring away new ones (due to impaired reputations; Darmon, 1990; Hom & Griffeth, 1995). Because managers rarely service clients, Exhibit 1.10 reports no cost for this factor (S4) in our running example.

A related separation cost is the productivity loss that turnover may produce (Cascio, 2000). Specifically, leavers often are less efficient (less productive, more absent, etc.) just before they resign (Griffeth, Hom, & Gaertner, 2000; Hom & Griffeth, 1995; Rosse, 1988). In addition, resignations might diminish the productivity of remaining personnel, who must assume the leavers' job duties. Nonetheless, turnover cost analyses often omit productivity losses because they are difficult to assess (Cascio, 2000). Hom (1992), however, assessed this cost by computing the extra overtime pay given to coworkers who assume the leaver's duties and the expense of hiring temporary employees to do the leaver's job. (Arguably, these labor expenses do not represent pure costs because overtime and temporary work generate client revenues. They might thus be adjusted downward to take into account the revenues produced.) This cost is nonexistent for an exiting manager because colleagues who assume his or her responsibilities belong to exempt occupations (disqualifying them from mandatory overtime pay), and the mental health agency in our example did not hire temp employees to do managerial work.

Although Exhibit 1.9 outlines common elements underlying separation costs, certain costs are unique to a particular occupation or organization. For example, when a mental health professional leaves, his or her clients are reassigned to other professionals (Hom, 1992). As a consequence, the employing organization must assume the clerical costs of transferring client records, the cost of the time spent by a supervisor to explain the clients' background, and the cost of the time spent by other mental health professionals to learn the history of clients newly assigned to them. For a departing manager, the cost of client assignment was $274.92 (S7 in Exhibit 1.10). Finally, summing all separation cost elements yields an overall separation cost for the job (Cascio, 2000; Hom & Griffeth, 1995). For an exiting manager, the total separation cost is $902.78, which is derived from adding S1 through S7 in Exhibit 1.10.

Replacement Costs

Exhibit 1.11 shows the cost elements underpinning replacement costs, and Exhibit 1.12 describes how they are estimated. Quite obviously, advertising job vacancies (e.g., newspaper ads, mailings) is costly. Historical informa-

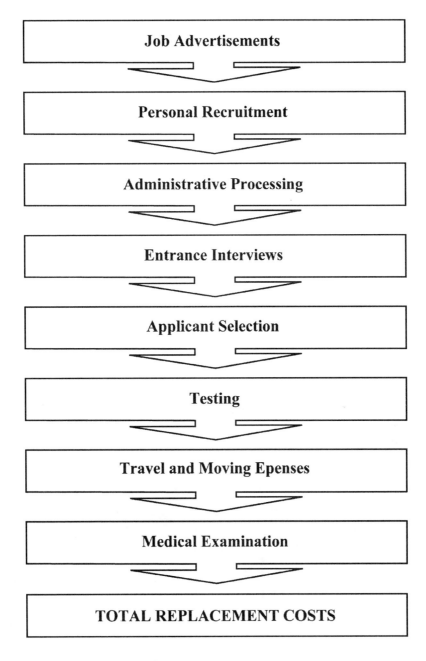

Exhibit 1.11. Replacement Costs

Replacement Cost Factors	Formulas	Calculations for Exiting Manager	Estimated Cost
R1. Advertising costs	Direct estimate		$ 306.00
R2. Job fairs and college recruitment	Hours at Job Fair or College Recruitment × Recruiter's Hourly Pay	10 Hours × $10.32	$ 103.20
R3. Application processing	(Hours Processing Resumes × HR Staff Hourly Pay) + (Hours Reviewing Resumes × Manager's Hourly Pay)	(6 Process Hours × $9.10) + (8 Review Hours × $22.36)	$ 233.48
R4. Applicant interviews	(No. of Interviewees × Interview Time × First Interviewer's Hourly Pay) + (No. of Interviewees × Interview Time × Second Interviewer's Hourly Pay) + etc.	(8 Interviewees × 1 Hour × $22.36) + (8 Interviewees × 1 Hour × $16.89) + (8 Interviewees × 1 Hour × $16.89) + (8 Interviewees × 1 Hour × $16.89)	$ 584.24
R5. Applicant selection	(Hours To Select Applicants × First Selector's Hourly Pay) + (Hours To Select Applicants × Second Selector's Hourly Pay) + etc.	(8 Hours × $22.36)	$ 178.88
R6. Miscellaneous costs	Tests + Substance-Abuse Test + Physical Exam + Reference Checks + Fingerprinting + Credentialing + Interviewee Travel Expenses + Relocation Expenses + Payroll Paperwork + Employment Agency Fees	$18 reference check + $28 fingerprinting + $150 credentialing + $90 agency fee	$ 286.00
Total replacement costs	R1 + R2 + R3 + R4 + R5 + R6		$1,691.80

Exhibit 1.12. Estimating Replacement Costs

tion on such costs might be gathered from accounting records. In our example, the cost of advertising for a managerial job was $306 (R1 in Exhibit 1.12).

Additional replacement costs include the cost of screening, interviewing, and selecting job applicants for the vacant position (R3 to R5 in Exhibit 1.12). These costs are generally computed by multiplying the time to perform these tasks by the hourly pay of employees doing these tasks. For instance, the cost of screening applicants (R3) is estimated as the amount of time spent processing and reviewing résumés multiplied by the processor's and reviewer's hourly compensation. As Exhibit 1.12 shows, this cost is $233.48 for a departing manager (R3).

The cost of entrance interviews is similarly calculated in the following fashion for each interviewer involved in the hiring process:

$$\text{Interview cost} = \text{Number of interviewees} \times \text{Typical length of}$$
$$\text{an interview} \times \text{Interviewer's hourly pay}$$

We then add up this interview cost for all interviewers participating in entrance interviews. For the exiting manager, the cost of interviewing prospective replacements is $584.24 (R4 in Exhibit 1.12). Likewise, we can estimate the cost of applicant selection by multiplying the time to make this decision by the hourly compensation of the decision makers. Exhibit 1.12 reports this cost (R5) as $178.88 for an exiting manager. In the agency in our example, only one individual made the final selection, but other firms might involve multiple participants (e.g., hold a special meeting for this purpose). In such cases, the time costs of multiple decision makers must be taken into account.

Finally, Exhibit 1.12 lists other "miscellaneous" replacement costs, which vary across organizations and occupations. These costs might range from $25 for simple drug testing to $45,000 for fully loaded moving expenses that include mortgage differentials, lease-breaking expenses, company purchase of the old house, costs of moving personal effects to the new locale, and utility hook-up fees (Cascio, 2000). For the particular profession and firm represented in our example, the relevant costs include the cost of reference checks ($18), fingerprinting ($28), credentialing ($150), and an employment agency fee ($90). Adding these miscellaneous costs yields $286 for an exiting manager. The total replacement cost is computed by adding the separate cost elements (R1 through R6 in Exhibit 1.12), which amounts to $1,691.80 when a manager leaves a mental health agency.

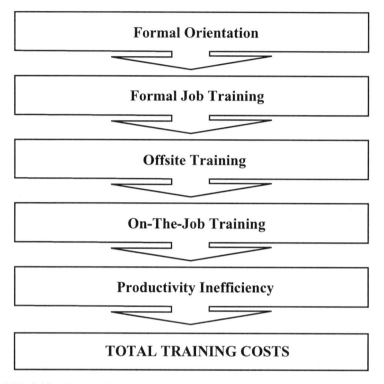

Exhibit 1.13. Training Costs

Training Costs

Orienting and training new replacements often account for a sizable turn-over cost (Hom & Griffeth, 1995). Exhibit 1.13 describes varied cost elements embodying this expense, and Exhibit 1.14 illustrates the formulas for comput-ing this cost when a manager exits an agency (Hom, 1992). Most costs are computed by multiplying the hourly compensation of trainers (including human resource specialists and supervisors) and new replacements (assuming they draw a paycheck during training) by the time to orient and train replacements.

Thus, we would compute the cost of formal orientation by multiplying the hourly pay of the orientation instructor and that of the newcomer by the duration of the orientation time (in hours) and sum these product terms (and include the cost of training materials). Exhibit 1.14 shows this cost (T1) as

Training Cost Factors	Formulas	Calculations for Exiting Manager	Estimated Cost
T1. Formal orientation	(Hours to Orient New Hire × Instructor's Hourly Pay) + (Orientation Hours × New Hire's Hourly Pay) + (Training Materials)	(2 Hours × $10.77) + (2 Hours × $17.85) + ($306)	$ 363.24
T2. Formal training	(Hours of Training × Instructor's Hourly Pay) + (Training Hours × New Hire's Hourly Pay)	(160 Hours × $22.36) + (160 Hours × $17.85)	$ 6,433.60
T3. Offsite training	(Hours To Attend Training × New Hire's Hourly Pay) + Tuition Charge	(8 Hours × $17.85) + $245	$ 387.80
T4. On-the-job training (OJT)	(OJT Hours × Supervisor's Hourly Pay) + (OJT Hours × New Hire's Hourly Pay)	(160 Hours × $22.36) + (160 Hours × $17.85)	$ 6,433.60
T5. Lost revenues during probationary period	(Experienced Incumbent's Billable Hours per Week – New Hire's Billable Hours per Week) × (Weeks During Probation Period That New Hire Serves Fewer Clients × Charge Rate for Client Services)	0	
Total training costs	T1 + T2 + T3 + T4 + T5		$13,618.24

Exhibit 1.14. Estimating Training Costs

Exhibit 1.15. Learning Curve for New Replacement

$363.24 for our example. Similarly, we estimate the cost of formal training by multiplying the trainer's and trainee's hourly pay by the number of training hours. In our example, the cost of training a replacement for a departed manager (T2) is $6,433.60 (T2 in Exhibit 1.14). The costs of offsite and on-the-job training are calculated in the same fashion (including tuition charges for courses and training material costs), being $387.80 (T3) and $6,433.60 (T4), respectively, for an exiting manager (see Exhibit 1.14).

Finally, many scholars have speculated that inefficient production by a new hire can be a prime training cost (Cascio, 2000; Flamholtz, 1985). Beginning employees may produce fewer goods or inferior service as they are mastering job duties (presumably, new replacements are less experienced or skilled than the leavers) (Cascio, 2000; Darmon, 1990). To illustrate, Exhibit 1.15 shows a hypothetical learning curve for new hires who attain standard production levels after a period of employment. Indeed, the *Journal of Accountancy* estimates that rookie inefficiency can cost as much as one third of the overall turnover cost (Johnson, 1995). Moreover, inexperienced employees may incur operating expenses by wasting raw materials or misusing equipment (Cascio, 2000). Though significant, this cost element is difficult to gauge and is often omitted from turnover costing studies (Cascio, 2000). Still, a consultant measured this cost by including the compensation paid to a replacement until that person gets "up to par" (Mercer, 1988).

For service positions, the cost of the substandard performance of new employees might be quantified as "foregone client revenues" (Hom & Griffeth, 1995). Incoming service workers may serve fewer clients as they are learning their job duties. For example, Sheridan (1992) estimated the gross profits per staff accountant in public accounting firms by subtracting the annual costs of employing the accountant from the annual revenues he or she produces during each year of employment. Using this approach, he projected that an accounting firm incurs an "opportunity loss of not retaining employees" of $47,000 when a new accountant (often college graduate) replaces a 3-year veteran.

Following Whiting (1989), Hom (1992) estimated "lost revenues during the probationary period" in the mental health agency to represent rookie productivity losses. Specifically, Hom (1992) estimated the difference in weekly "billable hours" between experienced and new mental health professionals (T5 in Exhibit 1.14). He then multiplied this amount by the number of weeks that the incoming employee sees fewer patients (during probation) and the charge rate for client services. Our example computes no cost for the departing manager who does not usually provide mental health services to clients directly.

Alternatively, one might derive some learning curve that plots how many billable hours are generated by beginning mental health professionals during the initial duration of employment (Whiting, 1989). Exhibit 1.16 shows a hypothetical example. The graph on the left plots the productivity (or weekly billable hours) during a new employee's probation period. The newcomer attains full proficiency during the fourth week, when he or she can generate 22.5 billable hours per week (the standard for a veteran employee). The right-hand graph reports the corresponding productivity losses during the probation period: the billable hours foregone by an inexperienced employee. Thus, when a newcomer generates only 5.6 billable hours during the first week (see the left-hand graph), the firm loses 16.9 billable hours for client services (see right-hand graph) (the standard 22.5 billable hours minus 5.6 hours = 16.9 hours). To estimate foregone revenues, one would multiply the lost billable hours per week by the charge rate for client services. If the charge (or billable) rate is $80, then the following calculations are done for the billable hours lost during the weeks that a replacement performs below par:

Week 1: 16.9 hours × $80 per hour = $1,352.00
Week 2: 11.25 hours × $80 per hour = $900.00
Week 3: 3.4 hours × $80 per hour = $272.00

and the results added (= $2,524).

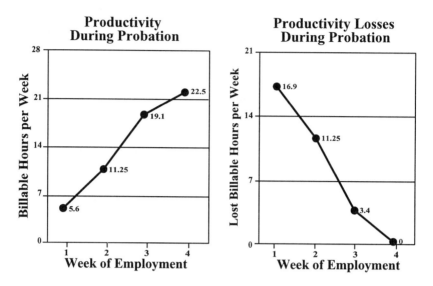

Exhibit 1.16. Lost Client Revenues When a Mental Health Professional Quits

Finally, the separation, replacement, and training costs are combined to derive an overall cost for one turnover incidence. In our example, the total turnover cost for an exiting mental health manager was $16,212.82. Because four managers left the agency in our example, the overall turnover cost for that position alone was $64,851.28 in 1999 dollars (= 4 × $16,212.82). Such information is quite revealing and shows how turnover can have an enormous economic impact on a company's bottom line.

Cost Savings of Retention Strategy

Once turnover's costs are estimated, organizations can more rationally judge the relative costs and benefits of various retention strategies (Cascio, 2000; Johnson, 1995). Thus, Merck & Company projected that an investment of 50% of an employee's salary in measures to reduce turnover produced a 1-year payback (Schlesinger & Heskett, 1991), and an Aetna Life & Casualty policy that allowed part-time return after family leave recouped $1 million in annual savings by cutting exits more than 50% among family leave-takers (Johnson, 1995). A cost-benefit analysis requires estimates of a prospective intervention's effectiveness as well as estimated turnover costs.

Control Group Evaluation

Comparison Groups	Turnover Rates (%)	Number of Leavers (No. of New Employees = 100)	Turnover Cost per Leaver ($)	Total Turnover Costs ($)
Control	17	17	6,018	102,306
RJP Recipients	5	5	6,018	30,090
Cost Savings (Difference)				72,216

Pretest-Posttest Evaluation

Comparison Groups	Turnover Rates (%)	Number of Leavers (No. of EAP Participants = 67)	Turnover Cost per Leaver ($)	Total Turnover Costs ($)
Before EAP	31	21	2,775	58,275
After EAP	9	6	2,775	16,650
Cost Savings (Difference)				41,625

NOTE: RJP = realistic job preview; EAP = employee assistance program.

Exhibit 1.17. Cost Savings of Retention Strategy

Companies can evaluate how well a program deters turnover by using control groups or pretest-posttest comparison (or rely on past research on intervention success). A control-group research design compares quit rates between a group of employees that receives the retention strategy and a group that does not (the control group). A pretest-posttest comparison assesses how the turnover rate changes before (pretest) and after (posttest) an intervention. Exhibit 1.17 describes cost-benefit analyses with these research designs. The top chart illustrates how to calculate cost savings of an intervention tested with a control-group design. The bottom chart depicts how to compute this savings with a pretest-posttest methodology.

The top chart shows how to compute the cost savings of a *realistic job preview* (RJP), which is a comprehensive preview of a job for new recruits that fully discloses its positive and negative qualities (see Chapter 3). Hom, Palich, and Bracker (1990) designed a preview of the accountant job in public accounting firms and used a control-group design to evaluate its efficacy for reducing quits among new accounting graduates. Their study established that incoming accountants who received the RJP quit public accounting firms at a lower rate (5%) than did a control group who did not receive the RJP (17%).

Given this information about RJP effectiveness, suppose a public accounting firm hires 100 staff accountants during a year. Typically, 17 of them (those not exposed to an RJP) would quit during the first year. Yet, if this firm presents a job preview to entering accountants, only five would exit. Next, we multiply the projected number of quits in each group by the turnover cost per incidence. Using an estimated cost of $6,018 in 1999 dollars (Hom, Bracker, & Julian, 1988), the total turnover cost incurred when a realistic preview is withheld from incoming personnel is thus $102,306 (= 17 × $6,018). By contrast, the total turnover cost for newcomers exposed to the RJP is only $30,090. The difference between these cost figures ($72,216) represents the "cost savings" of the RJP intervention. Similarly, Roth and Roth (1995) project that an RJP program could conservatively save a regional firm with five offices $300,000 if it reduces quits by one senior and one staff accountant each year at each office for 5 years. This analysis allows managers to answer the question in Exhibit 1.1 as to whether cost savings of the treatment for the problem exceed the treatment's costs—namely, developing and implementing the RJP (see Chapter 3).

Alternatively, companies may measure a program's impact by comparing quit rates before and after its implementation. The bottom chart in Exhibit 1.17 shows how to derive the cost savings of an employee assistance program (EAP) from a pretest-posttest design (Cascio, 2000). Before the EAP program, the historic rate of employee terminations was 31%. After its implementation, 6 of 67 EAP participants quit—a turnover rate of 9%. If these (67) participants had not enrolled in EAP, 21 of them would have quit the job (31% × 67). Given a cost of $2,775 per exit, the total cost of turnover before EAP implementation is $58,275 (= 21 × $2,775), whereas this cost is $16,650 (= 6 × $2,775) after EAP introduction. The cost savings for EAP is thus $41,625 (or $58,275–$16,650). Thus, this program is cost-justified presuming its cost savings surpass the cost of EAP.

Benchmarking Turnover Costs

Apart from tracking quit rates, companies might benchmark turnover costs. Such benchmarking would prove instructive because an organization's

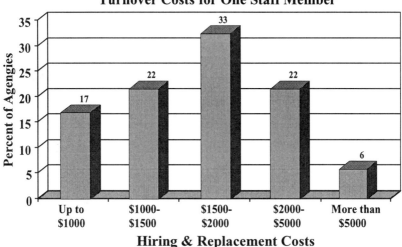

Exhibit 1.18. Benchmarking Turnover Costs

quit rate might exceed the industry average but not its turnover costs. Elevated quit rates are not alarming when quits are not costly. A firm's turnover costs might fall below industry costs because this firm can readily find replacements by drawing from a particular labor market (reducing replacement costs) or obtain more qualified replacements than competitors (lowering training costs) (Cappelli, 2000; Cascio, 2000).

To illustrate such benchmarking, the Arizona Council of Human Service Providers asks agencies participating in its wage survey to roughly estimate the costs of hiring and replacing one staff member. Exhibit 1.18 reveals how these turnover costs vary across agencies. Although simple, this approach does supply benchmarks. A more comprehensive approach was followed by Hom (1992), who circulated an elaborate questionnaire to Arizona mental health agencies (see Hom & Griffeth, 1995). To compare turnover costs across firms, this survey assessed the various elements that went into the computation of separation, replacement, and training costs (see Exhibits 1.10, 1.12, and 1.14). Exhibit 1.19 shows how turnover costs for Behavioral Health Technician III—a position in which incumbents plan and facilitate client activity, maintain client records, and carry client caseloads—fluctuate across 14 mental health agencies.

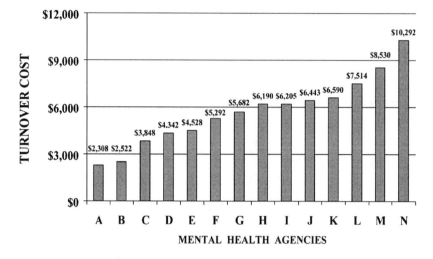

Exhibit 1.19. Cost of Turnover of Behavioral Health Technician III

Other Turnover Costs

There are other turnover costs that are harder to gauge than economic costs and that occur even when the overall quit rate for a given job is small (e.g., loss of a key scientist or executive) (Hom & Griffeth, 1995). Thus, it is worth bearing in mind such costs even if their consideration is subjective or qualitative (Johnson, 1995). To make such hidden costs salient, we suggest that managers check off a list of potential costs in Exhibit 1.20 whenever a particular turnover occurs. The following section reviews these additional turnover costs.

Impaired Service Quality

Turnover—especially among frontline service workers—may harm customer service (Schlesinger & Heskett, 1991). Clients may encounter delayed or interrupted service—due to staff shortages resulting from turnover—or less competent service by inexperienced replacements. As a result, customers may spend fewer consumer dollars or even defect to competing businesses. Moreover, the departure of experienced service workers disrupts the transmission of service values and norms that are essential for quality service to new generations of workers (Bowen & Schneider, 1988; Lytle, Hom, & Mokwa, 1998).

Potential Negative Effects Created When an Employee or Group of Employees Quits	*Mark a Check for Each Possibility*
1. Lose trade secrets to competitors?	
2. Leavers might form competing business?	
3. Loss of personnel jeopardizes production or introduction of new product or service?	
4. Personnel exodus impairs quality of customer service?	
5. Inspire more turnover among remaining employees?	
6. Endanger succession planning or demographic diversity?	

Exhibit 1.20. Checklist for Negative Ramifications of Turnover

As an example, Sears designed a business model that directs managers' attention toward how personnel exits can impair customer service (Cascio, 2000). Based on internal research, this road map positions employee attitudes and behaviors (including retention) as crucial underpinnings of corporate effectiveness. In this model, positive worker attitudes about the Sears organization drive financial success because satisfied (and loyal) sales personnel serve customers more effectively. Customers thereby form favorable impressions about Sears, making them repeat shoppers and more willing to endorse Sears to other shoppers. Sears becomes a more "compelling place to shop," and its return on assets, operating margins, and revenue growth thus improve. Similarly, Marriott Corporation projected that a 10% abatement in the quit rate among its workforce diminishes customer defection by between 1% and 3% and boosts revenues by between $50 million to $150 million (Schlesinger & Heskett, 1991).

Lost Business to Competitors

According to journalist accounts, turnover among key personnel can threaten a company's business and market share. For one, the exodus of scientists and engineers can delay or prevent introduction of new products or threaten future profitability in new markets (Gomez-Mejia, Balkin, & Milkovich, 1990). Similarly, the loss of information technology personnel can hamper firms' ability to implement e-commerce strategies to compete in changing markets (Wilson, 2000). For another, departing employees can take clients they serve away from their former employer. When a president of one of their units joined a competitor, PaineWebber lost one quarter of the portfolio managers and some key accounts (Lopez, 1993). Furthermore, firms that lose employees to competitors risk losing their intellectual property along with their personnel. As an Intel manager sees it, "The most important part of turnover is the loss of intellectual capital" (Ettorre, 1997, p. 51). A series of highly visible lawsuits attest to this turnover cost. Thus, Motorola filed a lawsuit claiming that Intel targeted its employees for recruitment to acquire sensitive information about its chip technology ("Motorola Sues Intel," 1999), and Volkswagen settled out of court with General Motors for $1.1 billion for luring away several top GM executives to steal secrets ("Keeping Secrets," 1997). Such "strategic poaching" has become widespread as corporations raid talent from other firms to expand into new markets quickly or to launch new businesses (Cappelli, 2000).

Yet, poaching even rank-and-file workers can hurt the companies being raided. Thus, Dow Chemical sued General Electric for recruiting junior-level engineers to learn about high-tech plastics, and Informix sued Oracle for hiring key members—including low-level engineers—from its research team developing extended parallel servers ("Keeping Secrets," 1997). Although corporations require employees to sign "noncompete" agreements that bar them from working for competitors, these agreements are usually short-lived (for 6 months to 3 years) and are difficult to enforce (Lopez, 1993). Finally, many Silicon Valley start-ups created by former employees of high-tech firms have spawned into formidable competitors (Mandel & Farrell, 1992).

Increase Turnover Among Remaining Employees

Employee exits might worsen the morale and retention of employees who stay behind. According to social information processing theory (Salancik & Pfeffer, 1978), leavers may disparage the present job and undermine other employees' attitudes toward the firm (prompting them to exit later). Also, personnel instability within a workgroup threatens cohesion among members, leading to more turnover (Mueller & Price, 1989; Sundstrom, De Meuse, & Futrell, 1990). When an employee's friends leave, he or she may feel less attached to the organization owing to fewer personal ties to colleagues (Cappelli, 2000; Price & Mueller, 1981, 1986). When teaching in Asia, one of the authors learned how departing Taiwanese and Hong Kong employees would recruit away entire groups of workplace friends for their new employers. That employees would quit a job to follow their friends may reflect

Asians' strong in-group allegiance and collectivism. The "snowballing" phenomenon, in which resignations occur in clusters within a company, suggests that employees can be influenced by leavers who are not necessarily their friends (Krackhardt & Porter, 1986). Exiting employees can thus inspire other employees to quit if they belong to the same occupational role and share similar communication patterns.

Jeopardize Future Leadership and Demographic Diversity

The business press reports many celebrated cases about how exiting top executives, such as Lee Iacocca of Chrysler and J. Ignacio Lopez de Arriortua at Volkswagen, have raided executives from their former employer (Lopez, 1993). The drain of managerial talent disrupts not only a firm's performance but also its succession planning. Given that executives are changing jobs more often than they did 10 years ago (Lopez, 1993), "companies are starting to sense that they don't have the bench strength they need" according to an Indiana University professor (Ettorre, 1997, p. 50). Indeed, "most traditional corporations are ready, willing and able to ruthlessly take their senior talent wherever they can find it, " a labor law expert contends ("Keeping Secrets," 1997).

Minority and women professionals and managers also quit Corporate America at higher rates than do white men, according to journalistic accounts and research studies (Cohen, 1999; Cox & Blake, 1991; Greenhaus, Collins, Singh, & Parasuraman, 1997; Stroh, Brett, & Reilly, 1996). Their exodus undermines the ability of corporations to achieve greater workforce diversity in occupations that have been traditionally reserved for white men.

Summary of Suggestions

To summarize, we suggest following the steps outlined in Exhibit 1.1 to diagnose the severity of the turnover problem:

1. Determine the voluntariness, functionality, and avoidability of turnover cases.
2. Subtract out involuntary, functional, and unavoidable quits from the overall quit rate to ascertain the rate of undesirable turnover.
3. If possible, benchmark turnover rate to industry rates.
4. Estimate the personnel costs of turnover.

5. Determine whether potential retention strategies are cost-justified.
6. Attempt to benchmark turnover costs.
7. Evaluate the potential for other kinds of turnover costs.

In conclusion, fact-finding and analysis are essential for correctly diagnosing turnover's existence and severity. Only after pinpointing the turnover
rate (especially the extent of undesirable quits) and whether this rate surpasses
some industry benchmark can organizations determine if turnover is an actual
problem. Otherwise, firms would be implementing solutions where no problem exists. Only by assessing how much turnover costs can we appreciate how
turnover is damaging to a company's bottom line and whether any proposed
solution is costlier to execute than the problem itself.

2

Job Enrichment

David looked at his watch. "Holy Cow," he thought. "It's only 10 a.m.! It feels like I've been doing this boring job all day rather than 3 hours. I don't understand why they don't change the way this job is done around here. I've made several suggestions to management on how to improve the work environment, but no one ever does anything. I just don't understand. Stefan quit the other day because the work is so boring, and I can't wait until my lunch break so I can look at the newspaper's job listings again so I can find a new, less boring job." As David was thinking this, he failed to tighten a bolt to its recommended torque. "Oh what the hell," David thought, "no one cares anyway, so why should I."

We've all experienced boredom in something we've done, and we know how it feels. The clock seems to stop, and we feel tired and listless, which may affect the quality of our work, as it did David's. This chapter looks at the notion of job redesign and job enrichment (JE). It describes to managers what they can do to redesign the work to make it more meaningful to employees, build responsibility into the work, provide employees with knowledge of the actual results of their work activities, and ultimately reduce turnover.

Research indicates that enriching work is a potentially useful intervention for reducing turnover (Griffeth, 1985; McEvoy & Cascio, 1985). The model of JE we recommend is one that was proposed more than 20 years ago, with dozens of empirical studies testing and supporting most of the model's basic premises. Titled the *task characteristics model,* its creators (Hackman & Old-ham, 1976, 1980) based it on sound principles of internal motivation. They went to considerable lengths to describe a very rich model with conditions or psychological states needed for creating internal motivation. They proposed job or task characteristics that influence or foster these states; created a summary index for determining the overall potential of job norms for a large number of occupations; and described useful principles that managers can use for enriching work. Since then, a great deal of empirical research has been devoted to testing most of the basic tenets of the model. The result is a reasonably robust model of the JE process. In this chapter, we describe each component of the model and show how you can use it to increase a job's intrinsic motivation and retain valued employees.

Overview of the Task Characteristics Model

The basic model is relatively simple. By increasing a job's scope or complexity, viewed subsequently as the *task characteristics,* employees will find work more motivating and attractive (work outcomes) because the critical psychological states are enhanced. It proposes the following basic relations:

Core Job Characteristics → Critical Psychological States → Work Outcomes

Thus, work outcomes are enhanced to the extent that the job has "critical psychological states." Hackman and Oldham (1980) proposed three states that are an essential component of each job. Employees need to learn from the job by knowing the results that they themselves were personally responsible for creating and on a job they felt was meaningful. These states are derived from basic task characteristics of a job: *skill variety,* or using various skills and talents to perform the work; *task identity,* or doing a whole and identifiable piece of work; and *task significance,* or doing work that substantially affects the work or lives of others. Moreover, jobs should have a certain degree of *autonomy* or freedom to schedule work and work procedures, and there should be *job feedback* or the obtaining of direct and clear information about

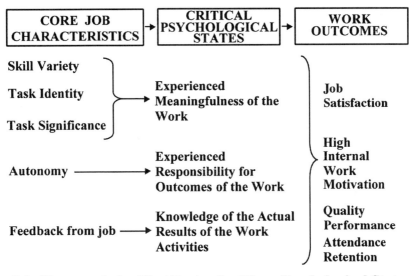

Job Characteristics That Foster the Three Psychological States

Exhibit 2.1. The Job Characteristics Model

performance (Hackman & Oldham, 1980). If these task characteristics and critical psychological states are generally present in work at relatively high levels, then important work outcomes are enhanced.

Specifically, employees report higher internal work motivation, satisfaction with growth and development, satisfaction with the work itself, improved quality of work performance, and lower absenteeism and turnover. If task characteristics and critical psychological states are relatively low in a particular job, then these work outcomes are also low, and the employee is less likely to behaviorally participate in the job or the organization. A more complete description of the model can be seen in Exhibit 2.1.

As you can see from this exhibit, task characteristics are rather specific in the critical psychological states they influence. Skill variety, task identity, and task significance influence the experienced meaningfulness of work; autonomy solely influences the perceived responsibility for outcomes of the work; and feedback from the job influences knowledge of the actual results of the work activities.

Research indicates that JE can curb turnover. Some studies find that employees holding complex jobs are less likely to quit (Griffeth, 1985; Katerberg, Hom, & Hulin, 1979; Price & Mueller, 1981, 1986). McEvoy and Cascio's (1985) meta-analysis revealed that field experiments enriching jobs reduced turnover more effectively than did realistic job previews (RJPs), an intervention described in Chapter 3. Thus, the effect of JE ($r = .17$) exceeded the effect of RJPs ($r = .09$). However, the former estimate was based on only five studies, and only two of them randomly assigned participants to treatments (one experiment found no impact on turnover; Locke, Sirota, & Wolfson, 1976). Nonetheless, one of the authors of this book (Griffeth, 1985) did randomly assign part-time university employees to enriched or unenriched work conditions. Following Hackman and Oldham's (1980) implementing principles (described in more detail subsequently), he enriched the job— upgrading skill variety, task significance, and job feedback—and found that enriched work did indeed reduce turnover.

Using the Task Characteristics Model

As we mentioned earlier, one of the more appealing aspects of this model is that Hackman and Oldham (1980) described how managers could use the model to analyze jobs that do not motivate employees. To do this, we describe several steps managers would follow to diagnose a job. (Note: For managers who are seriously considering JE, we highly recommend reading several chapters from Hackman & Oldham, 1980. For all intents and purposes, the material presented here is a brief synopsis of more detailed and relevant material presented in that book.)

Step 1: Select the Job

One way to select a job for JE is to identify a job with a high turnover rate. Because a high turnover rate has many causes, it is necessary to use an additional method to determine whether JE is a cause. Because job incumbents are a valuable source of information, we recommend communicating with them about the job. You could assemble a focus group of employees whose sole purpose is to discuss problems with the job. If comments like "The job is boring" or "I don't feel like I'm accomplishing anything" or "It contains no variety" or "It is unimportant" surface, then this could be indicative of a job low in scope or one that is too simple. It could indicate that the job may need JE because internal work motivation is not present or present at low levels.

A manager also could administer the Job Rating Form (JRF) to supervisors (or outside observers familiar with the job) of employees performing the job. The JRF is a questionnaire Hackman and Oldham developed to evaluate if others also perceive the job as having low work motivation. It measures the model's job characteristics and critical psychological states (see Appendix A).

An alternative method is to conduct exit interviews of quitting employees to see if any of these comments are mentioned. However, we prefer the former methods over the latter for a variety of reasons, but certainly the exit interview could be a supplemental method.

Step 2: Administer the Job Diagnostic Survey

How much does the job need to be enriched? Or, what components of the job need to be enriched to create higher internal work motivation? Do most of the employees performing the job have low internal work motivation? These are questions that a manager would probably ask after identifying a job or family of jobs needing enrichment. To answer them, Hackman and Oldham (1976) developed and validated a survey called the Job Diagnostic Survey, which measures all components of the model that are presented in Exhibit 2.1. It can be used to diagnose the existing job(s) prior to work redesign, as well as after a job is redesigned, to determine how much the job has changed and to assess the work outcomes presented in the model. The survey is not copyrighted and is presented in Appendix B, with the scoring key for both the Job Diagnostic Survey and the JRF presented in Appendix C.

The Job Diagnostic Survey also assesses two job characteristics not presented in the model but that may by useful, depending on the job, such as sales. They are feedback from agents and dealing with others. The former assesses the degree to which an employee receives information about his or her performance from supervisors or coworkers, and the latter assesses the extent to which employees work with other organizational members or external organizational "clients" or customers (Hackman & Oldham, 1980). Although not specifically stated, feedback from agents likely influences the critical psychological state of knowledge of results, and dealing with others likely influences experienced responsibility for the outcomes of the work.

Step 3: Score the Job Diagnostic Survey

As mentioned earlier, the scoring key provides managers with specific instructions on how to score the Job Diagnostic Survey. Many useful spreadsheet programs can be used to aid you in computing the averages for each component of the model for your problem job. (Note: Several items need to be "reversed-scored" before the averages are computed. These items are noted in the scoring key. Be sure to reverse-score these items before you compute the averages.) Once you complete the computational chores, you could compare the results from your job to extensive norms developed for this reason. But we believe the norms may be outdated. They were developed more than 20 years ago and may no longer be representative of jobs. (Note: We present the job characteristics norms in Appendix D anyway.) We therefore recommend another basis for comparison, which we describe in Step 4.

Step 4: Compare Your Job to the Scale Midpoint

How do you know which aspects of the job need the most improvement? It is possible that not all job characteristics need redesign—perhaps only one, two, or three of them. We recommend making this comparison graphically. In this way, you can more easily see which characteristics need improvement.

Several years ago, the authors were asked if they would study a clerical job to see if turnover could be reduced. After several focus groups and individual interviews with employees to determine why employees were leaving, it became apparent that the job was very boring and not very motivating, causing employees to look for more challenging, interesting work. In other words, it had many of the problems that David had with his job in the opening case. We decided that job redesign would be appropriate for this job because, during the interviews, employees stated a number of things that could be done to improve their job.

Shortly after obtaining permission from management to continue, the Job Diagnostic Survey was administered to the employees. Exhibit 2.2 shows the averages of the task characteristics before the redesign effort was completed.

As can be seen from this exhibit, skill variety, task identity, autonomy, and feedback from the job itself were lower than the scale midpoints. Task significance was higher than the midpoint. This latter finding appears to be a fairly common result because most people perceive their jobs as important.

However, even though task significance is typically high, we assess it prior to a redesign effort because after a typical redesign effort employees perceive their jobs as more important, and we would like to see this as an additional improvement. As the next step illustrates, obtaining all necessary information at the same time would greatly benefit the redesign effort. One may even improve characteristics that are not low, like task significance.

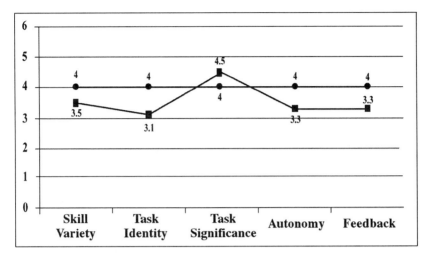

Exhibit 2.2. Job Diagnosis Survey Scores Compared to Scale Midpoints

Hackman and Oldham (1980) also developed an overall score for jobs they called the Motivating Potential Score. All jobs have some degree of Motivating Potential Score, which can range from a low of 1 to a high of 343, with an average of 128 for U.S. firms (including managerial, professional, and technical jobs, which tend to be higher than most jobs). The Motivating Potential Score is the overall motivating potential of a job to foster internal work motivation. It is calculated from the first five task characteristics using the following formula:

$$\text{Motivating Potential Score} = \frac{[\text{Skill Variety} + \text{Task Identity} + \text{Task Significance}]}{3} \times \text{Autonomy} \times \text{Feedback}$$

As you probably noticed from the formula, autonomy and feedback are given more importance in determining a job's Motivating Potential Score than are skill variety, task identity, and task significance. A low score on either autonomy or feedback can directly lower the Motivating Potential Score, and skill variety, task identity, and task significance are averaged in the formula. This is because, according to the theory, both experienced responsibility and knowledge of results must be present if internal work motivation is to be high, and autonomy and feedback, respectively, are the characteristics that directly influence those two states. Thus, a low score on either of these two characteristics would lower one's Motivating Potential Score.

On the other hand, a low score on either skill variety, task identity, or task feedback would not necessarily lower experienced meaningfulness of the work because it is possible that one of the other two characteristics could compensate for it. In addition, because low autonomy and feedback from the work itself contribute more directly to a low Motivating Potential Score, it is necessary to focus our attention on improving these aspects of the work. For the job described in Exhibit 2.2, the average Motivating Potential Score was a mere 81, low by anyone's standards.

Step 5: Obtaining Input for Redesigning the Work

We believe the best way to accomplish this step, and the way also recommended by Hackman and Oldham (1980), is to convene focus groups of employees. Because the intent, this time, is on redesigning the work, the job incumbents represent one of the most knowledgeable groups in the organization. It is important to recognize this early and use this resource. Moreover, it is our experience that most employees, when asked to participate in ways to improve their jobs, are usually ready and willing to comply. They are usually ignored during the job's creation anyway, and they usually have a lot of good ideas on how to improve the work. Also, because it is actually their jobs being changed, they are usually motivated to help.

Once the focus group is convened, and the purpose of the meeting is explained, this step is very similar to a group brainstorming session, with more direction. Direction is provided by showing the group the results of the Job Diagnostic Survey (as in Exhibit 2.2), defining the task characteristics (see Exhibit 2.3 for formal definitions of the task characteristics), and presenting the implementing principles, which are described in the next step.

Step 6: Using the Implementing Principles

Another reason we like and recommend using this model is that Hackman and Oldham (1980) have described several principles that managers can use to redesign work. Briefly, they are (a) combining tasks, (b) forming natural work groups, (c) establishing client relationships, (d) vertically loading the job, and (e) opening feedback channels.

- **SKILL VARIETY:** The degree to which a job requires a variety of different activities in carrying out the work, involving the use of a number of different skills and talents of the person.

- **TASK IDENTITY:** The degree to which a job requires completion of a "whole" and identifiable piece of work; that is, doing a job from beginning to end with a visible outcome.

- **TASK SIGNIFICANCE:** The degree to which the job has a substantial impact on the lives of other people, whether those people are in the immediate organization or in the world at large.

- **AUTONOMY:** The degree to which the job provides substantial freedom, independence, and discretion to the individual in scheduling the work and in determining the procedures to be used in carrying it out.

- **JOB FEEDBACK:** The degree to which carrying out the work activities required by the job provides the individual with direct and clear information about the effectiveness of his or her performance.

Exhibit 2.3. Definitions of Task Characteristics

Exhibit 2.4 shows that each of the implementing principles is designed to influence one or more of the job characteristics directly.

Combining Tasks. As can be seen from Exhibit 2.4, both skill variety and task identity are increased when we combine tasks to form new and larger modules of work. Thus, rather that several people doing small parts of the job, separate tasks can be combined into a whole, more meaningful piece of work. In this way, the variety of skills needed to do the work increases. In addition, because the employee is now better able to identify with this whole meaningful piece of work, task identity, too, increases.

In thinking about how to combine tasks, Hackman and Oldham (1980) recommended the use of a flow chart to answer the following questions: How does the work get to the employee, and where does it go when he or she is finished working on it? Do the separate tasks that are performed relate to one another? Does it make sense to combine these separate tasks into a single, larger job? What happens when there is a problem? More specifically, to whom does the employee go, or what does the employee do if there is a problem?

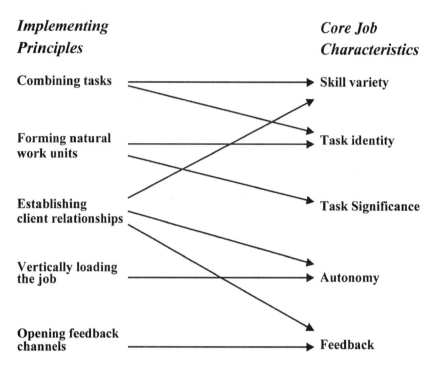

Exhibit 2.4. Links Between the Implementing Principles and the Core Job
                 Characteristics

As an example, Hackman and Oldham (1980) used the redesign of an electric toaster assembly line. In this situation, an employee's main responsibility might be attaching the 6-foot cord to the toaster and passing it to the next employee who does an additional small, routine task. If the toaster setting were redesigned, each employee would be responsible for assembling a complete toaster, plugging it in, and testing it. This latter task usually is reserved for another department, such as quality control. In this way, the variety of skills needed is increased, and it is also easier for the employee to identify with a completed and shining new toaster than with the electrical cord attached to an empty toaster chassis.

Forming Natural Work Units. The idea behind this principle is to form work into logical or inherently meaningful groupings. As Exhibit 2.4 shows, when natural work units can be formed, task identity and task significance are improved. Hackman and Oldham (1980) suggested several bases for forming natural work units.

The first basis is *geographical.* Here a salesperson would be assigned a particular section of the city, state, or country as their "turf." By identifying with this area, salespeople would experience greater meaningfulness of their work. Many salespeople already have their natural workgroups formed in this way.

The second basis for forming natural work units relates to the *type of business.* Insurance claims adjusters might be assigned or allowed to select which type of business in which they wanted to work, such as utilities, manufacturing, or residential property.

Rather than create typing or word processing pools, employees would be given responsibility for typing in particular departments like accounting or human resources. This type of natural unit is called *organizational.*

Sales people, clerks, and other occupations could be assigned clients via *specific alphabetic or numerical groups* such as T-Z, as another way to form natural units.

A fifth way is assign employees to *specific types of accounts,* such as institutions, individuals, or businesses.

Establishing Client Relationships. As noted previously, natural work units can be formed around specific groups of "clients" who receive the work. In some cases, it may be possible to put the employee in direct contact with clients and give him or her continuing responsibility for managing relationships with them.

As a case in point, several years ago, one of the authors bought some bookcases via a mail-order company. These required some assembly, and relevant hardware (a bag of wood screws and some brackets) was provided. Inside each carton was a small slip of paper that stated

> Your shipment was packed by *Joan.* If any hardware is missing or shelves are damaged, please contact her at *(800) xxx-xxxx.*

Usually, I discarded this paper because every carton was packed with the exact amount of screws and brackets needed to assemble the bookcase. However, one carton was missing a few pieces. Although it would have been easy to replace them from a hardware store, I decided to call "Joan" to see if this was a valid note and an attempt at establishing a client relationship. I dialed the number and someone answered with the company's name. I asked to speak to Joan. I was then asked to hold and, almost immediately, a friendly sounding woman picked up the phone and said "Joan speaking. May I help you?" When I explained the nature of the problem, she sincerely apologized for the oversight and said she would put the missing screws in the mail that very day. Within a few days, I received a small padded envelope containing an entire package of the hardware with a handwritten note, again apologizing and letting me know if I had other problems with the bookcases to be sure to call her. I was very impressed with the professionalism and promptness with which this situation was handled. And, although originally annoyed by the missing screws, I decided I would still purchase products from this company, especially after the way this problem was handled.

From this example and Exhibit 2.4, establishing client relationships would improve skill variety, autonomy, and feedback. Skill variety is improved because employees would have to develop skills for dealing directly with clients such as interpersonal relations, a useful skill for employees to develop when dealing with annoyed clients.

Autonomy increases because employees have more responsibility for deciding how to manage the relations with clients. Feedback also increases because establishing client relations means that employees have opportunities to receive direct and indirect praise or criticism about their work.

Vertically Loading the Job. As Exhibit 2.4 shows, vertically loading the job improves autonomy. Vertically loading means to "push down" to the employee responsibility and authority that were reserved for higher levels of supervision or management. There are several ways a job can be vertically loaded. For one, employees can be given more discretion in how, when, and even sometimes where to do their work. Telecommuting is a good example of this. Although some employers have adopted telecommuting to reduce inter-role conflict (Hom & Griffeth, 1995), due to office space requirements, or even due to the rigors of commuting, the results are in many ways an informal or formal way employers have unwittingly redesigned the work. Telecommuting—working at home and electronically transferring the results to the office (Hom & Griffeth, 1995)—meets most of the requirements of vertically loading the job. In addition to giving employees more discretion for how, when, and where they do the work, it also gives them opportunities to make decisions about when to start and stop, even when to take breaks. Telecommuting employees also would be encouraged to seek solutions to problems they encounter rather than immediately to seek supervisor assistance, also an aspect of vertically loading the work. As Hackman and Oldham (1980) conceived vertical loading, it "is to advance employees from a position of highly restricted authority to one of reviewed authority and, eventually, to near-total authority for their work" (p. 139).

Opening Feedback Channels. The object of this principle is to provide employees with additional feedback directly from doing their work, which indirectly influences their performance. As Exhibit 2.4 shows, this principle directly increases feedback about the work. Barriers, whether natural or artificial, are removed that isolate employees from existing information about their job performance. In so doing, employees are provided with direct, immediate, and regular feedback about their performance. Although employees generally receive feedback from supervisors in the form of annual reviews or appraisals, this method is not as effective as daily feedback about performance. Moreover, the annual appraisals themselves are fraught with problems.

An example of how employers have unwittingly opened feedback channels is by ascribing to the principles of Total Quality Management. In many cases, this means feedback from customers as well as from the job itself.

Hackman and Oldham (1980) described several ways feedback can be improved. These are described subsequently:

1. *Establish direct relationships with clients.* This may be as easy as providing a phone line through which a client could speak directly to an employee about a product or service, as in the previous example. Or it may be provided through naturally occurring data about how well a product or service meets the needs of those who receive it. Or, it may be necessary to develop a survey of clients to provide this information.

2. *Place quality control (QC) close to the workers.* This could mean having employees perform their own QC checks or tests—usually tasks performed by a separate department or individual. Indeed, if QC tests are provided in a separate department, then employees may not immediately learn of a mistake they are making. By conducting their own QC checks and finding their own mistake, employees will learn to improve their performance.

3. *Provide summaries of the work.* This ensures that employees have the data they need to improve their performance. Many organizations may collect this information and communicate it to higher management, but not to the employees who do the work. By providing it to employees, you provide them with information they need to improve their performance.

Today, computers can provide employees with information that was once inaccessible to them. Because most clerical operations are performed on computers today, programs could be modified to let employees know when they have made an error and to provide a positive feedback message when a period of error-free performance has been sustained. This is much less controversial than using programs that enable supervisors to monitor employee performance.

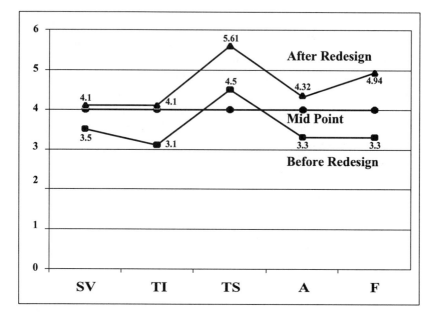

Exhibit 2.5. Results of a Job Redesign

An Example

In this section, we provide a brief summary of how the task characteristics model was used to enrich an impoverished job. Recall, in Exhibit 2.3, we presented the results of a job needing redesign. As mentioned, we were able to redesign the job, and the process we used was described in the preceding six steps. The results of the redesign effort are presented in Exhibit 2.5. As is apparent, the job was successfully redesigned. Although skill variety and task identity averages did not exceed the scale midpoints—our goal—the job was enriched on these two dimensions based on the pre-redesign averages.

The two most important dimensions increased considerably after redesign, an outcome we hoped would happen. Furthermore, task significance was increased, as incumbents saw their work as even more important—obviously a favorable perception. Finally, the Motivating Potential Score increased to 101 (from 81), indicating an overall perception of a more enriched job. Although it was still below the national average, the job was improved.

Was it improved enough to affect the job's outcomes? First, all three critical psychological states increased, as did job and work satisfaction, internal work motivation, and several dimensions of employees' subsequent performance ratings (attendance, initiative, accuracy of work, and adaptability). More important for us, employee turnover was reduced, as well.

This chapter is intended to introduce the reader to a relatively direct way to improve employee turnover by redesigning the work itself. We have provided enough information here to illustrate how truly easy the procedure is. If one wishes to redesign a job, we encourage the reader to obtain a copy of Hackman and Oldham's (1980) excellent and easily readable book in which they provide much more detail for the procedures and give helpful advice.

Summary of JE Suggestions

We summarize this chapter with the following:

1. Assemble focus groups of employees working in the job in question to discuss problems with the work itself, and potential ways to improve it.
2. Administer the JRF to supervisors familiar with the job to determine if they also see the job as "boring," "too simple," or "unimportant."
3. If the job in question is described in these terms, administer the Job Diagnostic Survey to employees doing the job.
4. Score the Job Diagnostic Survey, according to the key.
5. Compare this job to scale midpoints for each dimension of the task characteristics.
6, Compute the job's Motivating Potential Score. If it is below 128, and the two most important dimensions, autonomy and feedback, are below their scales' midpoints, the job will probably benefit from systematic redesign.
7. Convene another focus group of employees examining ways the job can be changed that would result in improvements in the work itself. Use the implementing principles to guide the focus group's discussion;
8. Redesign the job based, in part, on the input from employees.

3

Realistic Job Previews

George Coffey was sitting at his desk reading a company report when the department manager, Bill Nutley, knocked on his door and stuck his head in.

"George, I just got off the phone with the head of the Gregory Group, and they don't seem to understand some aspects of the new contract. I told them you would fly out right away and explain it to them."

"What? Bill, this is Joanna and my—this is our anniversary. We are driving up the coast for the weekend, right after work tomorrow. Can't you get someone else to go? This is very important to us."

"Well, the Gregory account is important to *us*, too, George," Bill said, somewhat irritated now. "Do you think we can afford to lose it? It represents a lot of money to the firm. I'm sure Joanna will understand."

George wasn't so sure Joanna *would* understand. After all, for the last month, he had spent 60 to 70 hours a week drawing up this contract. "I really don't understand the problem," he said. "I've been in contact with them on *every* point, spending a ton of hours on the phone explaining the dozens of faxes I've sent them. Plus, I was just there last week."

"They said something about the language wasn't clear," Bill responded. "Maybe they just need some hand-holding before they sign. It is a lot of money they're going to pay us."

"Maybe if I just called them again and explained it to them over the phone. Maybe that would work," George said, thinking out loud.

"No. I don't think that would work . . ."

"Oh, good grief, Bill," George interrupted. "This is just boilerplate stuff. Almost anyone could take care of it—Bob, or Eleanor, for example. They were involved in the project from the beginning, and know all about it."

"No, George. They specifically want you to come. I believe they've come to really trust you. Stop by Caren's office and she'll give you the flight information. I'm truly sorry, George, but this is really important," Bill said and closed the door.

"Damn," George thought. "This constant short or no-notice travel is really starting to irritate me. That, and other things, too. If I'd known when I interviewed that I'd be traveling so much, I never would have accepted this position. Maybe it's time to think about finding a job with a lot less travel."

Clearly, George is dissatisfied with the amount of travel he perceives in the job. Perhaps, if some of the features of the job had been communicated to George, he probably would not have accepted this position. His expectations about the job, the travel involved, and possibly other things are probably not being met by the company, his boss, and so forth. Had Bill or others been honest with George and presented the job in realistic terms, his dissatisfaction with the job might not have occurred. More important, he might not have started thinking about changing jobs—an intermediate step in the turnover process.

Realistic job previews (RJPs) represent a proven technique for reducing turnover among new employees. Job previews represent comprehensive profiles of a job, describing both its positive and negative features to new hires during employment interviews or orientation. Job previews presumably reduce quits among new hires by preventing them from experiencing "reality shock." Generally speaking, a new job is typically oversold to newcomers, creating inflated job expectations. Once they begin work, newcomers often find that their job does not live up to their lofty expectations. As a result, they become disenchanted and leave. If, instead, newcomers are forewarned by RJPs about undesirable job features before starting work, they will avoid disillusionment. Previewing a job makes their entry expectations more accurate and thereby lowers the chances that those expectations will be disconfirmed at work.

Providing Job Candidates With Accurate and Complete Information About the New Job Reduces Turnover

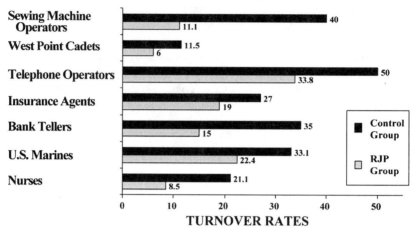

Exhibit 3.1. Realistic Job Previews

Organizational research has firmly established that delivering RJPs to beginning employees during hiring or orientation can (modestly) improve their retention in a wide range of jobs (Hom & Griffeth, 1995; Wanous & Collela, 1989). Exhibit 3.1 illustrates results from experimental tests that presented RJPs to one group of new hires and withheld them from others (a "control" group). After a passage of time, entering employees given RJPs often quit at lower rates than those not given RJPs. On average, RJPs (used in private industry) boost job retention rates by 8% (Wanous, 1992). In the following section, we consider guidelines for RJP design and administration.

RJP Medium and Content

You can communicate realistic information about a particular job through various means, including booklets, audiovisual media (films, videotapes), live presentations (during interviews or orientation), and work samples (that are meant to assess applicants' qualifications by having them complete a small version of a job). Surprisingly, RJP booklets are as effective as other media, including more sophisticated films or videotapes, for reducing turnover among new hires (Premack & Wanous, 1985). Similarly, a more comprehensive review of different modes of RJP presentations recently concluded that verbal or written RJPs are superior to audiovisual RJPs (though oral presentations are best; Phillips, 1998). Unlike booklets, videotapes or films better prepare newcomers on how to cope with impending frustrations on the new job by providing vivid, visual illustrations (i.e., role models) of how they can successfully handle such frustrations (Phillips, 1998; Wanous, 1992).

Regardless of which communication modes you decide for RJPs, your previews should be comprehensive and valid; that is, avoid basing your RJPs on the impressions of a few job incumbents and supervisors, who might furnish biased or incomplete descriptions. Moreover, effective RJPs convey the impressions of incumbents in that job—what they typically like and dislike about their job duties—as well as objective work conditions. Indeed, *subjective reality*—as seen through the eyes of veteran incumbents—may most help new incumbents (Wanous, 1989). After all, new recruits are usually less informed about the intrinsic qualities of a job's content (such as how mundane or tedious tasks are or how rarely incumbents get performance feedback) than they are about its extrinsic work features (e.g., pay rates, office setting) (Wanous, 1980). Because booklet RJPs are relatively simple to design, we next illustrate their development following a procedure to promote valid job descriptions.

The Nuts and Bolts of RJP Design

With the help of the Arizona Society of Certified Public Accountants (CPA), we recruited 27 Phoenix firms to participate in developing a generic RJP brochure about auditing work in public accounting firms (Hom, Palich, & Bracker, 1990). We followed the steps set out here.

Interviews

We interviewed 48 senior and staff accountants about the audit staff job, asking questions about job duties as well as (satisfying and dissatisfying) work experiences.

Editing Statements

We then transcribed their comments and generated 686 statements descriptive of staff work. Next, we edited the statements to improve clarity

1. INTERVIEWS
- Identify job content
  - ♦ 48 staff and seniors
  - ♦ 12 firms

2. RJP SURVEY
- Verify interview comments
  - ♦ 108 staff and seniors
  - ♦ 484 statements

3. STATISTICAL ANALYSIS
- Identify shared descriptions
  - ♦ 70% consensus
  - ♦ 252 statements

RJP SURVEY

Which of the following statements accurately describes the staff job?
Circle a TRUE or FALSE:

1. Staff find it difficult to see a finished product in auditing work because they do only bits and pieces.	TRUE	FALSE
2. During the first year, new staff's activities are mundane and monotonous.	TRUE	FALSE
3. Staff sacrifice quality for speed to complete their jobs.	TRUE	FALSE
4. Staff have little opportunity to influence the ways things are done in this firm.	TRUE	FALSE

Exhibit 3.2. RJP booklet design

and avoid redundancy. This editing process yielded 484 statements, which we compiled into a survey. Exhibit 3.2 shows sample questions from this survey.

Survey Validation

We next circulated this survey to 108 staff and senior accountants from various firms. Ideally, survey participants should include a representative cross-section of the population of incumbents in a given job. Each respondent independently verified whether each statement accurately or inaccurately described staff work. We thus relied on judgments by job incumbents to decide whether comments from the earlier interviews were valid and portrayed a relatively common work experience.

Booklet Development

After collecting the surveys, we statistically analyzed the responses to the questions. Specifically, we computed the percentage of the survey participants

Statistical Analyses
Compute Percentage Choosing Each Answer

Descriptions of Auditing Work	*Answering "True" (%)*	*Answering "False" (%)*
1. Staff find it difficult to see a finished product in auditing work because they do only bits and pieces.	85	15
2. During the first year, new staff's activities are mundane and monotonous.	73	27
3. Staff sacrifice quality for speed to complete their jobs.	60	40
4. Staff have little opportunity to influence the way things are done in this firm.	91	9

Exhibit 3.3. Statistical Analyses

who thought each statement was true and the percentage who deemed it false. Following past practice, we decided that a statement was "realistic" if at least 70% of job incumbents regard that statement as "true" (Reilly, Tenopyr, & Sperling, 1979). Exhibit 3.3 reports how incumbent accountants rated a set of descriptors about audit work. Because 85% of them endorsed "Staff find it difficult to see a finished product in auditing work because they do only bits and pieces" (Statement 1), we considered this comment an accurate job description and included it in the RJP booklet. By contrast, only 60% of respondents endorsed Statement 3: "Staff sacrifice quality for speed to complete their jobs." We rejected this comment because it did not achieve sufficient agreement among job incumbents about its validity. After this screening, the RJP booklet comprised 252 "validated" statements. Exhibit 3.4 shows sample statements from this RJP. This RJP therefore communicates "workplace reality" as experienced by most staff accountants.

   We later evaluated this realistic portrayal of the accounting profession. Specifically, we presented this RJP to one group of newly hired accounting graduates during orientation and withheld it from another group. We monitored their employment for a year, finding that those not given the RJP quit employment more readily than did those given the RJP (see Exhibit 3.4). Exhibit 3.5 further shows that the accountant RJP increased job longevity. This graph is derived from a survival analysis, a statistical method that considers whether the RJP can influence employment duration (Meglino, DeNisi, & Ravlin, 1993; Morita, Lee, & Mowday, 1993). The separate "survival" curves

RJP BROCHURE

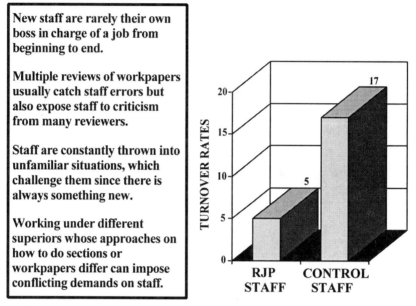

New staff are rarely their own boss in charge of a job from beginning to end.

Multiple reviews of workpapers usually catch staff errors but also expose staff to criticism from many reviewers.

Staff are constantly thrown into unfamiliar situations, which challenge them since there is always something new.

Working under different superiors whose approaches on how to do sections or workpapers differ can impose conflicting demands on staff.

Exhibit 3.4. Realistic Job Previews for New Staff in Public Accounting

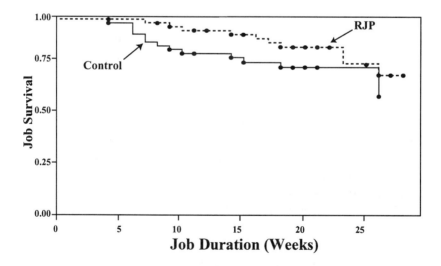

Exhibit 3.5. RJPs Increase Employment Duration Among New Accountants

for the control and RJP groups indicate the proportion of beginning accountants who stay employed at various times during the first year of work. This proportion declines for both RJP and control groups but more so for the control group (a Wilcoxon chi-square test was marginally significant at .08), indicating that the RJP prolongs job tenure. When the RJP variable is introduced as a predictor in a Cox regression analysis, this survival analysis method suggests that RJP recipients resign at a rate that is 58% of that of the control group. Put another way, newcomers not shown the RJP are 1.74 times more likely to quit than those given the RJP. Public accounting firms should welcome the fact that RJPs can enhance job longevity. Although most staff accountants eventually exit public accounting (given the limited partnerships available), public accounting firms still prefer that accountants remain employed long enough to recoup the investment in their training (Sheridan, 1992).

Caveats

For the Arizona Society of CPAs, we designed a generic RJP that describes what this occupation is like in many accounting firms. Quite obviously, your RJP booklets would be limited to one company, although you might solicit perceptions and opinions from job incumbents scattered across multiple facilities; that is, job content and duties may vary across different locales. Input from these multiple sources would help ensure that your RJP booklet about a given job pertains to all facilities.

Sampling Representativeness and Cross-Checks

We suggest that participants in the RJP design be somewhat representative of your population of job incumbents; that is, do not include only veteran employees who might have forgotten what it was like to be a rookie trying to master the ropes. Short-tenure employees can provide a unique perspective, sharing insights into the particular difficulties they recently confronted when adjusting to a new job. After all, recipients of your RJP would endure similar adjustment pains when they begin work. Thus, previewing the impressions of employees who had survived the first year of work might be especially valuable to entering employees. Moreover, we suggest cross-checking incumbent perceptions of the job with senior management and personnel executives for additional verification (Dean & Wanous, 1984).

Booklet Content

You might supplement your RJP with results of ongoing opinion surveys of your workforce, listing areas that employees find satisfying and dissatisfying (Dean & Wanous, 1984; Wanous, 1992). Moreover, adding "critical incidents" to the RJP helps communicate stressful circumstances at work more vividly. Critical incidents represent incumbents' reports of actual events they have experienced or witnessed at work and furnish concrete details about typical frustrations and stresses at work (Dugoni & Ilgen, 1981).

In another project that produced an RJP brochure for nurses, we asked nurses to describe in their own words (using an open-ended survey) something that happened while working that made them feel good about their job (Hom, Griffeth, Palich, & Bracker, 1998). We also asked them to describe negative critical incidents. One RN reported the following incident:

> A nursing aide did not keep a close watch on a post-op patient's urine output and did not inform me of the inadequate amount. The patient went into renal failure and had to receive temporary dialysis. I felt it was my fault because I was team leading and the final responsible nurse on that shift.

Although the details surrounding this particular event are unique, portraying this and similar kinds of medical mishaps in the nursing preview clearly illustrates that such accidents are relatively common for nursing graduates. In the same manner, a Prudential RJP booklet includes situations that "typically" confront insurance agents. Examples include "how an agent plans to attend an eagerly anticipated social event . . . but must postpone it because it is the only night a prospect can meet" and "an agent pays a call on a prospect to discuss insurance, only to be subjected to uncomplimentary . . . even though unwarranted . . . remarks about sales personnel" (Wanous, 1992, p. 66). Of course, critical incidents should be certified by job incumbents and managers as being universal rather than isolated, idiosyncratic experiences.

Apart from covering objective and subjective realities, your RJP booklet should provide balanced coverage of the job: What are its good and bad sides? RJPs are realistic profiles of the job, not simply negative portraits. Indeed, military recruits, when shown an excessively pessimistic film about basic training, actually left the Army at a higher rate than others not shown this film (Meglino, DeNisi, Youngblood, & Williams, 1988). Rather, a balanced film describing both positive and negative aspects of basic training most improved retention among Army trainees.

Finally, your RJP might portray the performance standards for a job, such as the precise work behaviors and results that clearly define high and low standards of job performance (Naffziger, 1985). If such performance expectations are communicated during recruitment, less able (or less self-confident) job applicants might screen themselves out of the job. Given clear descriptions of performance standards, they might decide that they could (or would) not meet the job's performance expectations and decline your job offer (assuming your screening procedures failed to identify them as marginal performers). In this way, previewing performance standards might decrease how many poor performers enter the organization.

For example, Exhibit 3.5 shows special rating scales created by Hom, DeNisi, Kinicki, and Bannister (1982) for students to judge the teaching effectiveness of college instructors. Known as Behaviorally Anchored Rating Scales (BARS), these scales show a series of behavioral incidents that illustrate various performance levels for each performance dimension. Based on interviews with college students (who would be the prime users of this rating instrument), Hom et al. (1982) identified 10 aspects or dimensions of teaching effectiveness, such as grading fairness and lecturing ability. With the aid of students, they generated vertical rating scales for each performance dimension. Each scale comprises a set of behavioral incidents representing a particular performance dimension (according to consensual judgments of students) that are positioned at various points on the scale (also based on student judgments). These behavioral incidents help clarify what high and low performance means (and illuminate the meaning of the performance category). As Exhibit 3.6 reveals, college students consider an instructor highly organized if he or she "gives out and explains the syllabus" and "makes a point of summarizing a previous lecture before beginning the present one." By contrast, they define a disorganized instructor as one who "is rarely prepared for class" or who "ends class early because she or he was not prepared."

Prospective college instructors might benefit from a realistic preview that includes such teaching-effectiveness rating scales. BARS information would provide beginning instructors with more precise knowledge of what constitutes effective teaching, helping them make more informed decisions about whether to accept a position with a particular college and whether they can meet that college's teaching standards—or even if they want to do so. Being forewarned, incoming instructors are also better prepared to cope with those challenging standards (cf. Hom et al., 1998).

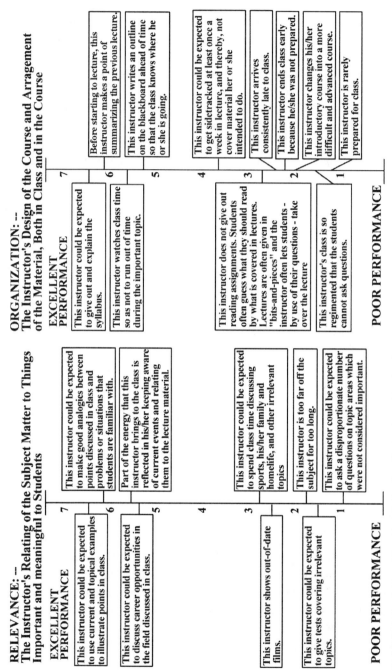

RELEVANCE: ―
The Instructor's Relating of the Subject Matter to Things Important and meaningful to Students

EXCELLENT PERFORMANCE

7
- This instructor could be expected to use current and topical examples to illustrate points in class.
- This instructor could be expected to make good analogies between points discussed in class and problems or situations that students are familiar with.

6
- Part of the energy that this instructor brings to the class is reflected in his/her keeping aware of current events and relating them to the lecture material.

5
- This instructor could be expected to discuss career opportunities in the field discussed in class.

4

3
- This instructor could be expected to spend class time discussing sports, his/her family and homelife, and other irrelevant topics
- This instructor shows out-of-date films.

2
- This instructor is too far off the subject for too long.

1
- This instructor could be expected to give tests covering irrelevant topics.
- This instructor could be expected to ask a disproportionate number of questions on topic areas which were not considered important.

POOR PERFORMANCE

ORGANIZATION: ―
The Instructor's Design of the Course and Arragement of the Material, Both in Class and in the Course

EXCELLENT PERFORMANCE

7
- Before starting to lecture, this instructor makes a point of summarizing the previous lecture.
- This instructor could be expected to give out and explain the syllabus.

6
- This instructor writes an outline on the blackboard ahead of time so that the class knows where he or she is going.
- This instructor watches class time so as not to run out of time during the important topic.

5

4
- This instructor could be expected to get sidetracked at least once a week in lecture, and thereby, not cover material her or she intended to do.

3
- This instructor arrives consistently late to class.
- This instructor does not give out reading assignments. Students often guess what they should read by what is covered in lectures. Lectures are often given in "bits-and-pieces" and the instructor often lets students - by use of their questions - take over the lecture

2
- This instructor ends class early because he/she was not prepared.
- This instructor changes his/her introductory course into a more difficult and advanced course.

1
- This instructor is rarely prepared for class.
- This instructor's class is so regimented that the students cannot ask questions.

POOR PERFORMANCE

Exhibit 3.6. College Teaching Behaviorally Anchored Rating Scales

Guidelines for RJP Delivery

In this section, we discuss some recommendations on how to deliver RJPs.

RJP Timing

Most experts prescribe giving RJPs early to job candidates before they actually enter the company, when their preemployment expectations about the job are most inaccurate and inflated (Breaugh, 1992; Wanous, 1992). Delivering RJPs during recruitment also allows prospective employees to make a more informed choice about whether to accept your job offer. Organizational researchers believe that those who decide to choose your offer will better fit with the rewards and demands available in this job (Wanous, 1992). Such person-job fit, in turn, will lead to higher satisfaction and job retention. Applicants rejecting your job offer know "it's not for them" and avoid becoming costly turnover problems for your firm.

Nonetheless, a potential side-effect of disseminating good and bad news about a job during recruitment is that more qualified job candidates might be driven away (Rynes, 1990). Consider a research study by Bretz and Judge (1998) documenting "adverse self-selection." They found that college graduates with superior academic achievement and work experience are less willing to pursue jobs for which negative information has been presented by recruiters. Indeed, one reason why RJPs might work is that only less-qualified job applicants would accept a job whose deficiencies had been previewed. Unlike those not shown RJPs, RJP recipients who decide to join the company comprise more inferior job candidates who remain loyal precisely because they are less employable elsewhere. All the same, a comprehensive review concludes that new hires "receiving RJPs just before hiring were less likely to withdraw from the application process than those not receiving RJPs" (Phillips, 1998, p. 684). Still, there remains the possibility that those (fewer) RJP beneficiaries who do exit the recruitment process are superior job candidates (Hom & Griffeth, 1995).

Alternatively, you might deliver your RJP later—after job applicants have accepted the job offer—to avoid the potential loss of quality prospective employees. Several research reviews support this suggestion, failing to establish that early RJP administration is superior to late RJP administration (Hom & Griffeth, 1995; Phillips, 1998; Premack & Wanous, 1985). Posthire RJPs

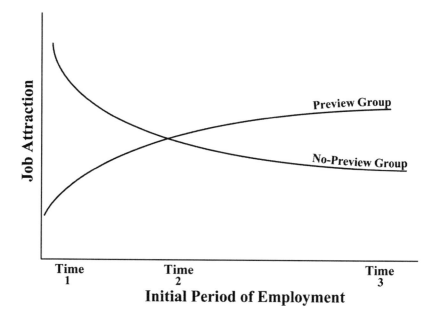

Exhibit 3.7.   Relative Attraction to Job Among Newcomers

work as well as prehire RJPs! Even so, some experts believe that distributing previews late jeopardizes their effectiveness because newcomers are forewarned too late and are not given the chance to make informed job decisions (Breaugh, 1983; Suszko & Breaugh, 1986). Indeed, presenting RJPs after prospective employees have joined the company may lead them to believe that the company misled them into accepting the job (Horner, Mobley, & Meglino, 1979). In conclusion, trade-offs exist for early and late RJP timing. Perhaps a conservative approach would be to disseminate previews early only when your job attracts many applicants or when other benefits for assuming the job can offset the negative job qualities depicted in the RJPs (Meglino & DeNisi, 1987).

Binding Newcomers to the Job

Sometimes, realistic previews can actually prompt newcomers to leave prematurely (Dean & Wanous, 1984; Meglino, DeNisi, & Rawlin, 1993). To explain this effect, Exhibit 3.7 shows how job attraction changes over time for beginning employees given RJPs and those not given RJPs, drawing from

Meglino and DeNisi's (1987) theory. New hires without RJPs initially view the new job as highly attractive when starting work (Time 1). After time has elapsed, their naïveté eventually develops into reality shock as they discover unexpected faults with their job. Their job attraction falls, and they are motivated to quit (Time 3). By contrast, newcomers exposed to job previews (that reveal the job's shortcomings) initially find the position less attractive (Time 1). Given weaker job attraction, they are more prone to exit after they begin working at Time 1 than are newcomers not shown RJPs. However, if RJP recipients stay during the time they are disaffected, they ultimately will develop stronger job attraction (and higher retention at Time 3) than those not given RJPs. This is because RJPs do not assist newcomers immediately (Time 1) but require time to work, according to Meglino and DeNisi. Over time, they help "inoculate" new hires against reality shock and better prepare them to deal with work frustrations.

Given this scenario, Meglino and DeNisi (1987) recommend "binding" RJP recipients to the job during the critical period when their job attraction is weakest (between Times 1 and 2). Otherwise, they are more likely to resign than those not given RJPs (Meglino et al., 1993). To bind RJP recipients to the job, Meglino and DeNisi suggest using employment contracts. For example, your firm might obligate incoming employees to stay for a certain duration of time (e.g., a year). If they meet that condition, they might receive a retention bonus or avoid having to repay the firm for expenses incurred in their training. Alternatively, you might create a psychological contract with RJP recipients. When organizations invest considerable time and effort in newcomers, they create a psychological contract that is repaid through employee loyalty. Special training, liberal relocation costs and services, as well as mentorship programs, also can imbue feelings of reciprocity among newcomers (Meglino & DeNisi, 1987).

Incumbent Presentations

According to research by Colarelli (1984), having trained job incumbents deliver the job previews can enhance their persuasiveness and impact. Thus, we recommend that experienced employees present the RJP to job candidates and be prepared to answer their personal questions. Incumbent presentations are compelling for several reasons (Colarelli, 1984). First, new recruits may consider job incumbents to be more trustworthy and more knowledgeable about the position than managers or recruiters. Second, job applicants feel less inhibited about asking questions of employees who resemble them in social status. Third, incumbents may provide additional information that your firm might hesitate to include in an official brochure or film. That is, they can "speak off the record" and inform prospective employees about aspects of the job that your company may not wish to acknowledge formally.

Work Samples

Besides evaluating applicant qualifications, work samples—in which job applicants are required to perform the requirements of the job they seek—can provide them with a realistic "in-the-trenches" view of what the job is about (Farr, O'Leary, & Bartlett, 1973). For example, the life insurance industry has found that having prospective agents experience the sales process—from prospecting and securing an interview to fact-finding and designing a plan— can dramatically enhance job survival (Ragaglia, 1991; Raphael, 1975). In one experiment, 40% of new agents participating in a work sample survived 12 months versus 5% of new agents not participating in a work sample (Raphael, 1975).

Who Should Get RJPs?

We next describe the types of newcomers who would benefit most from RJPs and what positions warrant realistic portrayals.

New Labor Force Entrants

Job previews may most help new entrants to the workforce, those graduating from high school or college. Vocational scholars point out that student and work roles contrast markedly in authority relationships (teachers vs. bosses), performance feedback (frequent tests vs. annual performance reviews), time discretion (freedom to "cut" classes vs. rigid daily work hours), and autonomy (schools praise autonomous intellectual work, whereas business firms expect greater compliance to work rules and regulations) (Feldman, 1988; Taylor, 1985, 1988). Because these roles are so different, graduating students would find the transition from school to work to be especially stressful. As a consequence, RJPs may prove especially beneficial for new graduates.

New Professionals

Along these lines, RJPs may aid students graduating from professional schools, such as education and nursing schools. Although often exposed to their future occupation from coursework and internships, professional students' understanding of professional life is still limited and unrealistic. Why is this so? For one thing, professional education emphasizes abstract systems of knowledge rather than practical applications in specific cases—the predicaments working professionals usually face (Abbott, 1988; Blanchard, 1983). For another, school-bred professional standards and ethical codes often clash with business norms of efficiency and control (Andersen, 1989; Von Glinow, 1988; Wallace, 1995). What is more, practicing professionals typically do many nonprofessional tasks (e.g., new auditors carry audit bags for senior auditors and do "grunt" tasks) and also give up expected professional duties (Abbott, 1988; Dear, Weisman, & O'Keefe, 1985; Van Maanen & Barley, 1984). It is not surprising, then, that beginning professionals all too often experience reality shock during their initial employment (Blanchard, 1983; Dean, Ferris, & Konstans, 1988; Ferguson & Hatherly, 1991). Indeed, even student internships may not dispel workplace misconceptions because interns often work under ideal conditions (Blanchard, 1983; Murnane, Singer, & Willett, 1988). To illustrate, nursing students may care for one patient as opposed to an unmanageable number typically borne by nurses working evenings (Huey & Hartley, 1988; Medved, 1982). Supporting their value, several tests demonstrate that professional previews can decrease quits among new entrants to the nursing, accounting, and teaching professions (Hedley, 1985 reported in Wanous, 1992; Hom et al., 1998).

Previous Job Exposure

RJP theorists universally contend that naive newcomers unfamiliar with a job are the ones who would most benefit from RJPs (Breaugh, 1992; Wanous, 1992). Although doubtlessly true in most cases, this principle does not always hold. For example, Meglino et al. (1993) found that RJPs most reduced exits among incoming corrections officers who passed their probation period and had prior correctional experience. Meglino and his associates argue that people who have previous experience with a given job develop a mental framework for the job. Prior knowledge of the general outlines of a job then helps newcomers more readily comprehend and recall the specific information contained in RJPs. Better understanding and memory of RJP materials, in turn, increase their impact on turnover. These findings are heartening, implying that firms can distribute RJPs to all newcomers, including those who had been employed in a similar line of work (who would process the RJP information better). RJPs might educate even "experienced" newcomers. Although they had worked a similar job, they had not necessarily worked in the particular place of employment depicted in the RJP.

Individual Differences

Certain types of people are more receptive to RJPs (Meglino et al., 1988). In particular, more intelligent newcomers benefit from RJPs because intelligent people can better attend to and understand the content of RJPs. For example, military research shows that a videotaped RJP most reduced attrition among more intelligent Army trainees (Meglino et al., 1988). Moreover, realistic previews most deter exits among newcomers who are initially committed to an organization (Meglino & DeNisi, 1987). According to Meglino and DeNisi, high organizational commitment prevents new hires who are discouraged by the RJP from leaving during the initial period of employment when their job attraction is low (see Exhibit 3.7). Over time, the committed newcomers will develop higher job attraction as the RJP inoculates them against reality shock and enhances their ability to manage stress (e.g., they are less upset when they encounter anticipated stresses; Dugoni & Ilgen, 1981).

"Invisible" Jobs

RJPs are also more suitable for certain jobs—namely, occupations that are not externally visible to outsiders. For such jobs, prospective employees—outsiders who may become insiders—cannot learn about job qualities through direct observation and would benefit from previews about those positions. By contrast, RJPs are less informative for jobs whose characteristics are externally visible to outsiders, such as bank tellers and salesclerks (Wanous, 1992). Job candidates learn about these jobs in the course of interactions with these firms as customers. By the same rationale, RJPs are not as useful for positions that are filled internally from the current workforce rather than externally from outsiders (Wanous, 1992). After all, new entrants to jobs—attained through promotions or job transfers—are insiders who already know the company, though not necessarily the new position. RJPs for internal job candidates would thus prove superfluous.

High Turnover Jobs

RJPs work best for jobs in which most incumbents quit (Wanous, 1992). For example, if the typical job survival rate (percentage of newcomers who stay throughout the initial employment) is 80% for a job, Premack and Wanous (1985) project that the RJP can only improve survival rates by 6% (given their estimate of RJP strength). That is, RJPs would raise the job survival rate from 80% to 84.8%. By comparison, if the typical job survival rate is 20%, then RJPs can boost the survival rate by 24% (increasing this rate to 24.8%)! Thus, it is important to consider the historic quit rate in a position before investing the time and effort to design and implement a preview for this position.

Using RJPs To Improve Job Performance

Besides retention, certain RJPs can improve job performance. Specifically, RJPs that emphasize the development of coping skills might have performance-enhancing effects (Meglino et al., 1988; Waung 1995). Your preview would not only describe typical frustrations for newcomers but also furnish advice and/or behavioral models for how they might overcome those frustrations. Job performance improves because RJP recipients have clearer expectations of their work role (allowing them to target their efforts toward meeting job requirements) and better manage stressful events that otherwise would impair perceived self-efficacy and persistence (Horner et al. 1979; Wanous, 1978). As mentioned previously, audiovisual RJPs develop coping skills better than other kinds of RJPs (Phillips, 1998; Premack & Wanous, 1985).

Deflating Expectations Without RJPs

Buckley, Fedor, Veres, Wiese, and Carraher (1998) demonstrated that an "Expectation Lowering Procedure" (ELP) can reduce newcomer expectations and quits without using job-specific content information. They propose that ELPs are often more feasible than RJPs because they do not require expensive and time-consuming job analyses. What is more, RJPs may poorly describe jobs that are increasingly less well-defined in many corporations (Bridges,

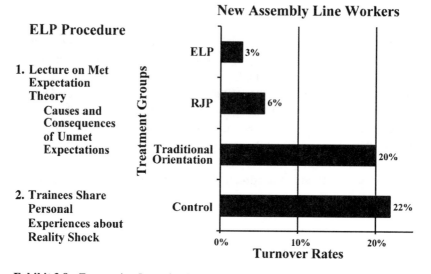

Exhibit 3.8.   Expectation Lowering Procedure (ELP) Can Improve Retention
SOURCE: Adapted from Buckley, Fedor, Veres, Wiese, and Carraher (1998).

1994). Indeed, job analysis (the basis for sound RJPs) may no longer be applicable to jobs that are continually changing due to market demands, technology, and ongoing improvement efforts.

During this special orientation program, new hires learn (a) how important it is for their expectations to be realistic when beginning a new job, (b) how the typical organizational socialization process often promotes the development of unrealistic job expectations, and (c) how entry expectations—when inflated—are often violated, resulting in dissatisfaction, turnover, and other negative outcomes. New hires are also asked to think of situations in which their expectations were disconfirmed in previous jobs and to share their experiences with others in the session.

Buckley et al. (1998) provided an ELP to a group of new assembly line workers and gave a conventional RJP to another group. A third group of new hires received a traditional orientation, and a fourth group represented a control group (receiving no orientation program). After the first 6 months of employment, the control and traditional orientation groups exhibited higher quit rates than the RJP and ELP groups (see Exhibit 3.8). What is more, new workers in the RJP and ELP conditions reported lower initial job expectations than those in the control and traditional conditions. Therefore, preemployment expectations and turnover among beginning employees can be reduced without job-specific RJPs. In sum, when jobs are continually changing, as they are in many team-based and quality-oriented environments, ELPs are preferable to RJPs.

Summary of RJP Suggestions

We now summarize the key suggestions discussed thus far for RJP development and implementation:

1. Ensure that RJP content is comprehensive, balanced, and valid.
2. Use written or oral presentations. They are superior to audiovisual RJPs, though oral presentations are most effective (Phillips, 1998).
3. RJPs should describe the subjective realities of job incumbents: how those in the trenches view and experience work tasks and demands.
4. Trained incumbents should deliver the RJPs.
5. Distribute RJPs early—during the recruitment of job applicants, because RJPs do not necessarily increase applicant attrition from the recruitment process. If there is reason to believe that the RJP might drive away more qualified applicants, deliver the RJP soon after job acceptance (Phillips, 1998).
6. Bind newcomers to the job if the RJP appreciably depresses their attraction to the job.
7. Deliver RJPs to new entrants to the organization, not insiders.
8. Use RJPs for jobs that are not externally visible to outsiders.
9. Use RJPs for high-turnover jobs.
10. Consider ELPs for generic jobs lacking clear definitions, for jobs occupied by few incumbents (and when thorough job analysis would prove prohibitive), and for continuously evolving jobs.

Finally, bear in mind that RJPs cannot substitute for good jobs (Wanous, 1980).

Socialization and Supervision

New employees often exit an organization because they did not successfully adapt to the organization's values and culture, becoming fully assimilated members (Hom & Griffeth, 1995; Wanous, 1992). Historically, beginning employees are most likely to quit during their initial period of employment before they have accumulated much job tenure (Griffeth et al., 2000; Mobley, 1982). Indeed, higher job quits among short-tenure employees continue today, as the Bureau of Labor estimates that employees remain employed for 3.6 years on average ("Workers Switch Jobs," 2000). Because inadequate organizational socialization likely underlies their greater quit propensity, this chapter considers the various ways to facilitate the transition of newcomers from outsiders to established job incumbents. We also examine how certain supervisory practices can improve job retention, as supervisors are often responsible for orienting and socializing entering employees (Bauer, Morrison, & Callister, 1998; Louis, Posner, & Powell, 1983; Saks & Ashforth, 1997).

Organizational Socialization

In this section, we consider those socialization practices and policies that have the most promise for increasing job tenure among new hires, according to organizational research.

Socialization Tactics

Organizational socialization research has identified certain tactics for assimilating newcomers that can strengthen organizational commitment and job retention (Ashforth & Saks, 1996; Jones, 1986; Van Maanen, 1978; Van Maanen & Schein, 1979). Specifically, socialization thinkers have identified two types of socialization tactics used by companies: *institutionalized* and *individualized* socialization. Institutionalized tactics encourage newcomers to conform to preexisting definitions of the work role, whereas individualized tactics inspire newcomers to innovate and redefine their work role (Ashforth & Saks, 1996; Jones, 1986). Institutionalized tactics most enhance job loyalty and commitment by helping newcomers cope with the anxiety and uncertainty of the new job. By contrast, individualized tactics encourage newcomers to challenge the status quo, which increases creativity but not necessarily firm loyalty.

Exhibit 4.1 describes the specific tactics differentiating institutionalized from individualized socialization. *Collective* tactics socialize new recruits together in one group (which develops an "in-the-same-boat" collective consciousness), whereas *individual* tactics assimilate new recruits individually (Jones, 1986; Van Maanen, 1978). Lock-step MBA programs that require graduate students to complete course work as a cohort illustrate the former approach, whereas doctoral training assigning Ph.D. students to professors as research apprentices exemplifies the latter approach. Institutionalized and individualized socialization also differ in formality of socialization. In particular, formal tactics provide specific training programs to new recruits outside the normal work setting, whereas informal tactics require that new recruits learn the new role on a trial-and-error basis, aided by experienced coworkers (Jones, 1986). Thus, the police academy represents a formal tactic for assimilating new police officers, whereas new assistant professors at universities typically learn the "ropes" informally from colleagues.

Sequential tactics represent an institutionalized form that puts new recruits through a series of well-defined developmental experiences that pre-

INSTITUTIONALIZED SOCIALIZATION	INDIVIDUALIZED SOCIALIZATION
Collective Group newcomers and put them through common set of experiences	Individual Manage newcomers individually and put them through unique set of experiences
Formal Segregate newcomers from regular employees during socialization	Informal Not differentiating newcomers from experienced incumbents
Sequential Newcomers assume job after following a fixed sequence of steps	Random Newcomers experience ambiguous or changing sequence
Fixed Have a timetable for assumption of new job by newcomers	Variable No timetable for newcomer assumption of job
Serial Experienced employees socialize newcomers	Disjunctive No role model is provided for newcomers
Investiture Affirm incoming identity and personal traits of newcomers	Divestiture Deny or abolish past identity of newcomers

Exhibit 4.1. Socialization Tactics

pare them for the new position. By comparison, *nonsequential*—or random—tactics represent individualized socialization, for they do not lay out a sequence of learning experiences before entering employees assume their new roles. Thus, management training programs in some corporations that rotate trainees across various functions represent a sequential tactic (Van Maanen, 1978). Illustrating a random tactic, one of the author's former Ph.D. students became an associate dean at a small college (where he was an associate professor) without ever having served as chairman, normally a stepping stone for higher administrative posts.

Fixed versus *variable* tactics further distinguish institutionalized from individualized socialization. Fixed tactics furnish new recruits with timetables about the duration of various steps in their assimilation into the organization, whereas variable tactics do not communicate precise schedules for completion of various steps (Van Mannen, 1978). Thus, medical school graduates who undertake training for advanced specialties follow a fixed socialization tactic. They know in advance the timing and duration of their developmental steps: internships, residencies, and fellowships. In comparison, trade apprenticeships prescribe a minimum number of years of training for apprentices but do not predetermine when they advance to journeymen (Van Maanen, 1978).

Institutionalized socialization also involves *serial* tactics that assign regular employees the responsibility for grooming new hires. On the other hand, *disjunctive* tactics further individualize socialization, for they provide recruits no role models, leaving them on their own to discover the demands of the new work role. Thus, police recruits are assigned to veteran officers after the police academy (a serial tactic), whereas a sole woman law graduate joining an all-male law firm may have to decipher work role requirements alone (a disjunctive tactic; Van Maanen, 1978). Finally, *investiture* tactics of institutionalized socialization value the personal attributes of new hires, preferring to capitalize on their personal qualities rather than mold them (Ashforth & Saks, 1996). By contrast, *divestiture* tactics of individualized socialization deny or strip away newcomers' incoming characteristics. Applying investiture, corporations hiring senior executives presumably seek their particular skills and talents and want them to keep their former identity. In contrast, the Marine Corps uses divestiture to erase basic recruits' former civilian identity to forge a new Marine identity.

After identifying how institutionalized differs from individualized socialization, researchers have shown that institutionalized socialization tactics lessen stress symptoms and quit decisions among beginning employees (Ashforth & Saks, 1996). All told, this body of work offers broad guidelines on the *structural* features of socialization programs that increase newcomer retention. Companies should use collective, formal, sequential, fixed, serial, and investiture tactics to assimilate new hires, enhancing their job loyalty. Nonetheless, socialization tactics investigations have not identified the content of effective programs. The next section reports specific orientation programs that improve newcomer assimilation and retention.

Socialization Learning

Socialization researchers have identified the kinds of knowledge that newcomers must learn to become successful job incumbents (Saks & Ashforth, 1997). In the most advanced research on newcomer learning, Chao, O'Leary-Kelly, Wolf, Klein, and Gardner (1994) specified six domains of learning that promote organizational assimilation: performance proficiency (the knowledge and skill to do the job), people (the right persons from whom to learn about the organization), politics (the power structure inside the com-

- Performance proficiency
  Learn about job requirements and skills and knowledge to perform those
  requirements

- People
  Establish effective and satisfying work relationships

- Politics
  Learn who are the most influential people in the firm and how politics work

- Language
  Learn the acronyms, slang, and jargon that are unique to organization

- Organizational goals and values
  Learn company goals and values

- History
  Learn company traditions, customs, myths, and rituals

Exhibit 4.2. What Should Newcomers Learn To Become Successful Employees?
SOURCE: Adapted from Chao, O'Leary-Kelly, Wolf, Klein, and Gardner (1994).

pany), language (the technical language and jargon that is unique to one's profession and company), organizational goals and values (the mission and
means of the company), and history (the firm's customs, traditions, and stories) (see Exhibit 4.2). Their investigation revealed that entering incumbents
who master these content domains during their socialization phase become
more successful incumbents.

Following this approach, Klein and Weaver (2000) designed an organization-wide orientation program to instruct newcomers on various content areas
of socialization learning. Their program presented information about corporate goals and values, history, and language that would pertain to new hires in
any position (see Exhibit 4.3). This training omitted descriptions about the
informal political structure, work performance requirements, or social networks that are unique to a particular work setting or job. According to Klein
and Weaver's evaluation, beginning employees who attended this orientation
learned more about the organization's history and goals and values than did
those not attending orientation. Those attending this program developed
higher organizational commitment. In short, an organizational-level orientation that covers company traditions and principles can help to assimilate newcomers and perhaps improve their retention (due to increased company commitment; Hom & Griffeth, 1995).

- Focus on certain socialization content
  - Company goals and values
  - Company history and traditions
  - Company language
    - Acronyms, slang, and jargon

- Orientation program
  - Videotaped welcome from president
  - Exercise to familiarize with firm traditions and language
  - Videotape and discussion
    - Firm mission and history
  - Lecture/discussion of workplace principles

Exhibit 4.3. Instructional Goals and Structure of Orientation Program
SOURCE: Adapted from Klein and Weaver (2000).

Realistic Shock Programs

Socialization studies have uncovered a family of orientation programs that address reality shock (Kramer & Schmalenberg, 1977; Wanous, 1992). Like RJPs, these programs forewarn newcomers about impending frustrations on the new job. Unlike RJPs, which simply communicate information, these orientation programs more actively train newcomers to cope with upcoming stressors (Wanous, 1992).

Bicultural Training. Kramer and Schmalenberg (1977) pioneered an orientation program for nursing graduates called "bicultural training" (see Exhibit 4.4). After a "honeymoon" phase, new nurses attend weekly "rap sessions" (lasting 90 minutes) during the sixth week of hospital employment, when they most experience reality shock. In these sessions, they share problems and ways for coping with them. At the same time, new nurses read Kramer and Schmalenberg's workbook about stressful events typically faced by nursing graduates (e.g., infrequent performance feedback, feelings of incompetency) and complete workbook exercises on how to handle those events. About the 18th week, beginning nurses and head nurses attend workshops on conflict resolution—first alone in their groups and later together.

SOCIALIZATION PHASES FOR NEW NURSES

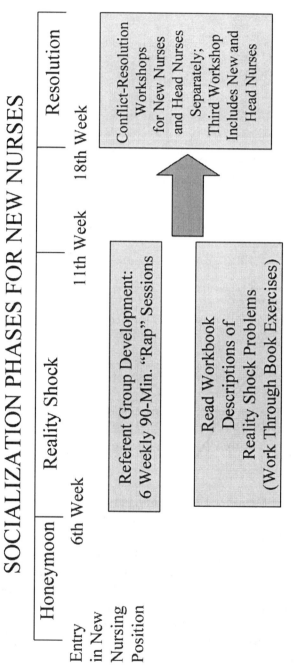

Honeymoon	Reality Shock	Resolution
6th Week	11th Week	18th Week

Entry
in New
Nursing
Position

Referent Group Development:
6 Weekly 90-Min. "Rap" Sessions

Read Workbook
Descriptions of
Reality Shock Problems
(Work Through Book Exercises)

Conflict-Resolution
Workshops
for New Nurses
and Head Nurses
Separately;
Third Workshop
Includes New and
Head Nurses

Exhibit 4.4. Bicultural Training
SOURCE: Adapted from description in Kramer and Schmalenberg (1977).

- Include realistic information

- Provide general support and reassurance

- Use role models to demonstrate coping skills

- Discuss role model's actions

- Provide opportunity for rehearsal

- Teach self-control of thoughts and feelings

- Target specific stressors to different new hires

Exhibit 4.5. Realistic Orientation Programs for New Employee Stress Guides
SOURCE: Adapted from discussion in Wanous (1992).

Nurses role-play how to manage interpersonal conflicts, which aids adjustment and empowers them to challenge their hospital for better nursing care. Besides allaying reality shock, bicultural training thus transforms entering nurses into change agents who would champion superior nursing care at hospitals. When compared with traditional orientation programs, bicultural training was found by several studies to improve job loyalty among new nurses (Holloran, Mishkin, & Hanson, 1980; Kramer, 1977).

ROPES. Wanous (1992) endorsed a similar socialization program called ROPES, an acronym for Realistic Orientation Programs for New Employee Stress. He based ROPES on medical investigations, showing that stress preparation programs help patients cope with impending medical treatments, such as surgery or childbirth (Wanous, 1992). Exhibit 4.5 summarizes his recommendations for effective ROPES programs. Like job previews, ROPES should forewarn new employees about stressful conditions on the new job.

Going beyond forewarnings, ROPES programs would provide emotional support and reassurance to newcomers. For example, they might reassure newcomers that their fears and anxieties are normal during early employment and that such feelings would decline over time. Moreover, ROPES orientation would present live or videotaped role models that demonstrate coping skills.

New hires would thus observe how a role model actually copes with a particular stressor. Furthermore, ROPES participants would discuss the model's actions, because group discussion facilitates learning. Trainees in ROPES programs would have opportunities to practice the coping behavior they witnessed.

In addition, ROPES would instruct newcomers on how to control their thoughts and feelings when confronted with stressful events. For example, they might learn relaxation or self-talk techniques to claim anxiety. Finally, ROPES orientation would address not only general stressors that affect most newcomers but also those affecting some newcomers. Such specificity improves ROPES credibility to entering employees, suggesting that an orientation program that considers common and unique stressors must have been designed with great care and time.

Given its origin in stress preparation for medical patients, ROPES has great promise for increasing new recruits' job survival (Wanous, 1992). As expected, several examinations have verified that orientation programs comprising elements of ROPES (e.g., observation of videotaped role models, small group discussion, general support and reassurance) do indeed lower tension and quits among new employees (Gomersall & Myers, 1966; Meglino et al., 1988; Wanous, 1992).

Self-Management Training. An emerging perspective in socialization theory and research, *proactive socialization* regards newcomers as assertive agents who can actively lower uncertainty in the new work role through their own initiatives (Bauer et al., 1998; Saks & Ashforth, 1997). By contrast, traditional viewpoints focus on "what organizations do to newcomers, and on how newcomers respond, without addressing ways in which newcomers may take a proactive role" (Morrison, 1993, p. 557). This new philosophy suggests that newcomers can manage their socialization experiences and diminish stress and anxiety as they adapt to their new workplace rather than simply rely on external agents (Saks & Ashforth, 1996).

Beginning employees can proactively cope with reality shock using self-management techniques (Tsui & Ashford, 1994). Specifically, Manz (1992, Manz & Neck, 1998) identifies three types of self-management techniques in his comprehensive framework for self-leadership, which prescribes that employees should lead themselves in the workplace (see Exhibit 4.6). These approaches help new hires better structure the new work setting and thereby reduce the uncertainty and anxiety of early work experiences (Saks & Ashforth, 1996).

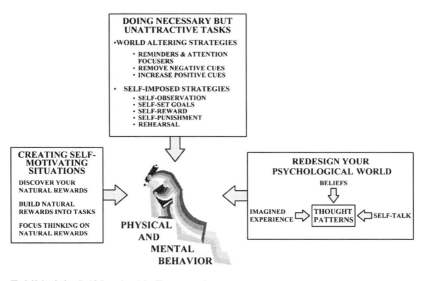

Exhibit 4.6. Self-Leadership Framework
SOURCE: Adapted from Manz and Neck (1998).

To illustrate, Manz (1992; Manz & Neck, 1998) suggests that newcomers can rely on *world-altering* and *self-imposed* strategies to motivate themselves to do necessary but *unattractive* work tasks. The former strategies include efforts to change the environment, and the latter strategies represent attempts to change one's behaviors. World-altering strategies would include reminders and attention focusers (listing daily tasks), removal of negative environmental cues that prompt undesirable behaviors (e.g., delete computer games from the personal computer), and introduction of positive cues that increase desired behaviors (e.g., associate with colleagues who do desired behaviors) (Manz, 1992; Manz & Neck, 1998).

Besides altering the workplace, new hires might control themselves with self-imposed strategies. Exhibit 4.7 outlines these "self-regulating" strategies and how they are performed. Self-observation thus involves determining when and under what conditions one's behavior occurs, and self-goal-setting requires one to set personal goals to guide one's efforts. Self-reward represents ways for rewarding oneself for doing desired behaviors, whereas rehearsal entails practicing desired behaviors—both physically and mentally.

Finally, *self-punishment* comprises ways to penalize oneself for doing undesired acts. Manz and Neck (1998) suggest that self-punishment should be done sparingly (e.g., for only the most egregious acts) because people normally would cheat rather than punish themselves for engaging in undesired

- Self-observation
  - Record behavior frequency
  - Note conditions: Antecedents and consequences of your behavior
- Self goal-setting
  - Identify long-term goals
  - Identify short-term goals that serve long-term goals
  - Set specific goals
  - Set challenging but attainable goals
- Self-reward
  - Identify what motivates you
  - Consider enjoyable activities
  - Consider intrinsic rewards (self-praise)
  - Develop habit of self-reinforcement
- Self-punishment
  - Remove rewards supporting negative acts
  - Reward alternative, positive acts
- Rehearsal
  - Break down challenging task into parts
  - Physically practice key parts
  - Mentally practice key parts
  - Reinforce your practice

Exhibit 4.7. Self-Imposed Strategies
SOURCE: Adapted from Manz and Neck (1998).

behaviors. People who punish themselves would not develop intrinsic satisfaction for the desired alternative behavior. For example, employees who apply sanctions to themselves when they are absent from work would not necessarily become more positively motivated toward work attendance—the opposite, desired behavior. Instead, Manz and Neck recommend removing rewards that maintain the undesired act (e.g., absence) and delivering rewards for performing a desired act that substitutes for the undesired act (e.g., attendance) (cf. Saks & Ashforth, 1996).

Apart from inducing themselves to do required but undesirable tasks, newcomers can *redefine* work tasks—to transform them into desirable activities or "self-motivating" situations (Manz & Sims, 1989). To do so, new hires must build *natural rewards* into their work activities. What are natural rewards? They are incentives build into the activity itself and derive from doing the task (Manz, 1992). Natural rewards differ from *extrinsic rewards,* such as pay and recognition, which are byproducts of task performance. Rather, natural rewards come from doing the task itself and are not separate from tasks themselves. More precisely, a *naturally rewarding* activity provides the doer with greater personal competence and self-control (or self-determination) as well as a sense of purpose (Deci, 1975; Hackman & Oldham, 1980). To make work more naturally rewarding, Manz and Neck (1998) advise that employees build natural rewards into work activities— "turn work into play"—or mentally focus on available natural rewards in those activities. For example, a management consultant might follow up his or her suggestions to a client firm by soliciting feedback on how those suggestions improved business operations, and a hospital housekeeper might focus his or her thoughts on the significance of maintaining a clean, sterile environment for recovering patients.

Finally, new employees can change how they think—how they interpret frustrations (or challenges) that confront them—besides acting on their environment or their own behaviors (Manz, 1992, Manz & Neck, 1998). Manz and Neck identify two types of thought patterns: *opportunity* and *obstacle* thinking. Opportunity thinkers interpret a problem as an opportunity to grow and develop, whereas obstacle thinkers view a problem as an obstacle that can set them back or defeat them. Professor Martin Seligman, a psychologist at the University of Pennsylvania, has documented how opportunity thinking can enhance career effectiveness (Manz & Sims, 1989). His study of insurance agents found that the manner in which agents deal with failure to make a sale determined whether they became outstanding sales personnel or quit the company. Sales personnel with an optimistic outlook—opportunity thinkers—sold 37% more insurance in their first 2 years than did agents with pessimistic views—obstacle thinkers. Moreover, obstacle thinkers were twice as likely to quit in their first year.

Although such thinking may well reflect a personality disposition (Judge, 1992), Manz and Neck (1999) contend that people can "redesign their psychological world." They argue that one can move from obstacle thinking to opportunity thinking by addressing belief systems, self-talk, and imagined experiences. Belief systems represent how functionally or dysfunctionally one thinks about a problem. One's beliefs about a problem determine how one emotionally responds and behaves toward the problem (Burns, 1999a, 1999b).

- All-or-nothing thinking
- Overgeneralization
- Mental filter
- Discounting the positives
- Jumping to conclusions
  - Mind-reading
  - Fortune-telling
- Magnification or minimization
- Emotional reasoning
- *Should* statements
- Labeling
- Personalization and blame

Exhibit 4.8. Cognitive Distortions
SOURCE: Adapted from Burns (1999a).

For example, an individual's fear of public speaking may be fueled by dys-functional beliefs, such as "my audience will dislike my speech." Exhibit 4.8 describes the various ways beliefs can be dysfunctional, according to David Burns (1999a, 1999b), a Stanford psychiatrist:

1. "All or Nothing Thinking"—viewing things as black or white.
2. "Overgeneralization"—seeing a specific failure as an endless pattern of defeat.
3. "Mental Filter"—overly dwelling on a single unfavorable detail.
4. "Disqualifying Positives"—downplaying positive aspects of an event.
5. "Jumping to Conclusions"—drawing negative conclusions without concrete evidence.
6. "Magnifying and Minimizing"—exaggerating the importance of negatives but minimizing positives.
7. "Emotional Reasoning"—interpreting reality through negative emotions.
8. "Should Statements"—using "should" or "must" to motivate oneself.
9. "Labeling and Mislabeling"—describing oneself or others with negative labels.
10. "Personalization"—blaming oneself for negative events even when one is not primarily responsible.

1. Describe distressing situation
   - New staff receives negative feedback from a senior's written review points of her work papers

2. Describe "automatic" thoughts
   - Thought No. 1: "My senior thinks I am an incompetent auditor"
   - Thought No. 2: "I was a top student in college; I should have done the job correctly"
   - Thought No. 3: "This is awful. I did a terrific job"

3. Classify thoughts using list of cognitive distortions
   - Thought No. 1: Mind-reading
   - Thought No. 2: *Should* statement
   - Thought No. 3: Magnification and all-or-nothing thinking

4. Develop rational response

   Substitute automatic thoughts with realistic, positive thoughts
   - Rational response to Thought No. 1: "It's the senior's job to detect errors. He writes critical comments on all new staff's work papers"
   - Rational response to Thought No. 2: "Don't expect your first audit job to be perfect. School doesn't teach you everything"
   - Rational response to Thought No. 3: "I should view this feedback as an opportunity to learn, not as a condemnation of me personally"

Exhibit 4.9. Dealing With Dysfunctional Thoughts
SOURCE: Adapted from Burns (1984).

Used with Burns's (1999a, 1999b) technique, this classification scheme can help one deal with dysfunctional thinking (see Exhibit 4.9). To illustrate Burn's four-step program, we describe a common problem encountered by accounting graduates joining public accounting firms: excessive "negative" detailed feedback from superiors about their work papers for their first audit job. New accountants would first describe events that upset them, such as unfavorable work paper reviews, on paper. In the second step, they would identify and record all thoughts that this performance feedback *automatically* prompts. According to Burns (1999a), people's feelings of emotional distress are rooted in—or aggravated by—their inappropriate interpretations of a stressful event, which he calls "automatic thoughts." In our running example, the negative feedback might have produced the following automatic thought among the accountants: "This is awful, I did a terrible job" (Thought 3 in Exhibit 4.9).

After listing all automatic thoughts, distressed accountants would categorize their thoughts according to Burn's categories of cognitive distortions (see Exhibit 4.8). Step 3 is crucial, because classifying automatic thoughts helps people understand *how* their beliefs are irrational. To overcome dysfunctional thinking, people must first identify how their automatic thoughts are dysfunctional. Thus, new accountants might judge that Thought 3 represents "magnification" or "all-or-nothing thinking" (see Exhibit 4.9).

Finally, distressed accountants would challenge those dysfunctional, automatic thoughts and substitute more rational beliefs for them (Step 4 in Exhibit 4.9). For each automatic thought, then, they would generate (and record on paper) a "rational" response. These alternative thoughts represent counterarguments and must be *sufficiently* persuasive to defeat and replace the initial "distorted" beliefs. For instance, distressed accountants might write this response to counter Thought 3: "I should view this feedback as an opportunity to learn, not as a condemnation of me personally" (see Exhibit 4.9).

Besides developing functional thinking, imagined experiences can help newcomers become opportunity thinkers (Manz & Neck, 1999). People often imagine the consequences of an act before they act. If they imagine their behavior will lead to negative consequences, this imagery can undermine their performance. If, however, they imagine positive outcomes, they will feel more confident about their performance and perform better. Thus, a speaker who envisions a receptive appreciative audience for his or her upcoming speech would perform better than a speaker who imagines a hostile audience. To enhance imagery, Manz and Neck prescribe mentally practicing step-by-step the successful execution of a challenging behavior before attempting the behavior, much like athletes before an athletic trial.

Finally, speaking to oneself positively can promote opportunity thinking, whereas self-defeating talk can undermine one's ability to solve problems. To upgrade self-talk, Manz and Neck (1999) recommend that people analyze their current self-talk tendencies (e.g., "Is the talk constructive?"), practice constructive self-talk ("Talk aloud positively and then internalize it"), and talk themselves through challenges (talk positively when preparing for and meeting challenges).

Despite limited research, several studies affirm that self-management training can improve how new hires become assimilated into an organization.

● **Week 1:** Introduction to Self-Management Principles

● **Week 2:** Self-Assessment
          Identify Reasons for Sick Leave

● **Week 3:** Goal-Setting

● **Week 4:** Self-Monitor Attendance
          Record Attendance & Reasons for Missing Work

● **Week 5:** Reinforcers

● **Week 6:** Behavioral Contract
          Identify Rewards for Achieving Goals

● **Week 7:** Maintenance

Exhibit 4.10. Self-Management Training To Improve Work Attendance
SOURCE: Adapted from discussion by Frayne and Latham (1987).

For example, Saks and Ashforth (1996) found that entry-level accountants who set specific goals for themselves (i.e., self-goal-setting) and observe their behaviors and what cues cause them (i.e., self-observation) better coped with the new job and felt less anxiety during their first months at work. A few investigations have shown that self-management training can yield positive dividends. To illustrate, Frayne and Latham (1987) designed a training program to reduce absenteeism among government employees, comprising seven weekly 1-hour group sessions (see Exhibit 4.10). During the first week, the trainer explained self-management principles. In the second week, trainees learned self-assessment: They identified reasons for absences and circumstances prompting absences. During the third week, trainees learned to set goals for higher attendance and discussed how they would meet these goals. In the fourth week, they learned to record their own work attendance using charts and diaries. For the fifth week, they were taught to identify rewards (and sanctions) to give to themselves as a result of achieving (or not achieving) attendance goals. The sixth session required trainees to write a behavioral contract with themselves. In writing, they spelled out their attendance goals, the time

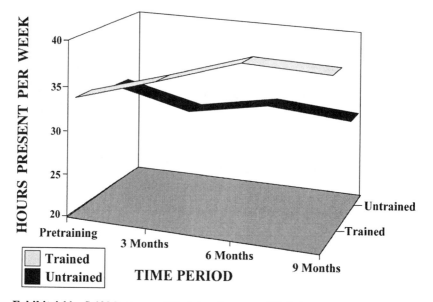

Exhibit 4.11. Self-Management Training: Impact on Work Attendance
SOURCE: Adapted from discussion by Frayne and Latham (1987).

frame for goal attainment, the consequences for meeting (or not meeting) the goals, and the behaviors needed to reach the goals. Finally, trainees considered conditions that might provoke a relapse in work attendance and how to plan for and cope with relapses. Exhibit 4.11 shows how this training elevated attendance relative to a control group not trained in self-management.

Similarly, Neck (1992) designed a program—"thought self-leadership" (TSL)—to promote opportunity thinking. Comprising six weekly 2-hour sessions (see Exhibit 4.12), this TSL training helped airline employees cope with the stress of their company's bankruptcy. During the first week, Neck introduced trainees to self-leadership theory. During the second week, he instructed trainees on Burn's classification scheme for dysfunctional thinking and had them practice identifying and overcoming dysfunctional thoughts. During the third week, Neck explained Butler's (1981) advice on how to internalize positive self-talk and had trainees participate in a self-talk exercise. During the fourth week, Neck described the steps to successful mental imagery from Orlick (1986). For the fifth week, Neck instructed trainees on opportunity versus obstacle thinking and had them complete Manz's (1992) personality test, which provided feedback on their thinking pattern. The last session dealt with relapse prevention, wherein trainees identified situations that might

- Overview of TSL
  - Factual accounts of famous people using TSL
- Managing dysfunctional beliefs
  - David Burns's categories of dysfunctional thinking
  - Practice "daily mood" log (Burns, 1984)
- Adopting positive self-talk
  - Discover negative self-talk exercise (Pamela Butler, 1981)
- Mental imagery
- Though patterns: Opportunity vs. obstacle thinking
  - Identify thinking pattern (Manz, 1992)
- Relapse prevention

Exhibit 4.12. Thought Self-Leadership Training (TSL)
SOURCE: Adapted from Neck (1992).

trigger regression to old pessimistic mental habits. Trainees also identified coping strategies to deal with relapses into obstacle thinking. Exhibit 4.13 shows that TSL training increased job satisfaction and job affect among airline employees.

Finally, Dutch researchers developed an intervention program to train mental health professionals in certain self-management techniques to reduce burnout (Van Dierendonck, Schaufeli, & Buunk, 1998). Often experienced by human services professionals, burnout is a syndrome of three symptoms: emotional exhaustion (depleted emotional resources), depersonalization (negative, cynical attitudes toward recipients of behavioral services), and diminished personal accomplishments (feelings of performance inadequacy) (Maslach, 1982). Van Dierendonck et al. (1998) claim that dysfunctional beliefs about the equity of the relationship between helping professionals and recipients of their care underlie burnout feelings. Given high emotional investment in caregiving, human services professionals may perceive that they get insufficient rewards for the care, empathy, and attention they give others. Despite holding ideals of unselfish giving, helping professionals may still feel "shortchanged" because care recipients often do not (or cannot if they are mentally disabled) reciprocate with something in return (e.g., gratitude).

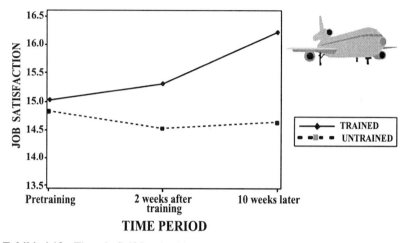

Exhibit 4.13. Thought Self-Leadership: Impact on Employee Morale During Air-
         line Bankruptcy
SOURCE: Adapted from Neck and Manz (1996).

Van Dierendonck et al. (1998) designed a burnout intervention that
focused on ways for helping professionals to restore equity in professional-
recipient relationships, using cognitive restructuring exercises. First, their
program described how professionals could reestablish equity by adjusting
their contributions or outcomes, explaining how inequity arises when one
party in a relationship between two parties receives rewards that are not pro-
portionate to his or her contributions to that relationship. This training also
instructed professionals to change their perceptions of relationship investments and outcomes, such as lowering expectations of rewards from care
recipients. Finally, this burnout intervention stimulated participants to
actively pursue another career if equity could not be achieved in the job
because leaving an inequitable situation is one means to reestablish equity.
With these goals in mind, Exhibit 4.14 outlines the specific techniques in this
burnout intervention. Mental health professionals whose superiors were supportive (motivating them to restore equity without leaving) *and* who participated in this burnout training expressed lower quit intentions than those not
attending this program.

By contrast, Waung (1995) instructed new hires in a quick-service food
chain and hospital on cognitive restructuring (learning to convert threats into
challenges) and self-talk, but they did not quit at lower rates than others given
(posthire) realistic job previews. (Both orientation programs communicated
the stressful aspects of the new job and what behaviors can effectively deal

- **Five Weekly Group Sessions by Psychologist**

- **Cognitive Restructuring**

  Look at Personal Situation in Different Way

  See Opportunities for Growth, Not Hindrances

- **Lecture on Burnout Theory**

  Its Relevancy to Participants

- **Relaxation Training**

- **Plans to Realign Job With One's Expectations**

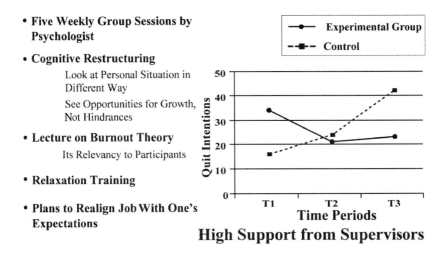

High Support from Supervisors

Exhibit 4.14. Burnout Intervention (Dutch Mental Health Professionals)
SOURCE: Adapted from Van Dierendonck, Schaufeli, and Buunk (1998).

with stressful situations.) Unlike programs described previously, this self-management instruction lasted only 30 minutes and omitted essential ROPES components, such as group discussion and rehearsal, by using a lecture format (Wanous, 1992).

All told, self-management training—especially when delivered over multiple sessions and adopting modeling, group discussion, and practice—can help newcomers better manage the stress of adapting to a new workplace and ultimately improve their retention. Though not specifically addressing newcomer stress, these empirical demonstrations are sufficiently compelling that their programs merit adoption for the transition stress experienced by new hires (Frayne & Latham, 1987; Neck, 1992; Van Dierendonck et al., 1998). After all, these studies revealed how intensive training in self-management can lower absences, dissatisfaction, and quit decisions, which are well-established precursors to turnover (Hom & Griffeth, 1995).

Supervision

Management researchers long have blamed bad supervision as a prime culprit of turnover (Hom & Griffeth, 1995; Mobley, 1982). Despite widespread journalist accounts about how tyrannical bosses can drive out employees (Marano, 1995), existing research yields little practical suggestions for "loyalty-building" supervision. Rather, turnover studies primarily have established that *satisfaction* with supervision promotes job retention without necessarily identifying specific behaviors by supervisors that commit employees to the company (Griffeth et al., 2000). A few investigations have shown that superiors who are participative in their leadership style, communicate often about work-related matters, and expressed consideration toward employees can build a stable workforce (Fleishman & Harris, 1962; Hom & Hulin, 1981; Price & Mueller, 1981, 1986). Though hard to discern, we nonetheless derive guidelines from the available sparse research on loyalty-inducing leadership practices.

Leader-Member Exchange

A leadership theory by George Graen and his associates holds greater promise for specifying supervisory actions that sustain job loyalty (Dansereau, Graen, & Haga, 1975; Graen, Liden, & Hoel, 1982). According to this perspective, superiors develop different types of working relationships with subordinates. With some subordinates (a "cadre"), they participate in high "leader-member exchanges" (LMX) and offer them inducements that go beyond the formal employment contract, such as job discretion, participation in department-wide decisions, detailed news and feedback, and social support. In return, this cadre is expected to work harder, express greater commitment, and assume more responsibility for the work unit. With other subordinates (known as "hired hands"), superiors rely on formal authority rather than special transactions to extract their compliance with job requirements and orders. Exhibit 4.15 shows diagnostic questions that managers can ask to decide whether their relationships with particular subordinates are effective (characterized by high LMX). In support, various investigations have disclosed that newcomers who form high LMX with their new superior develop higher job satisfaction, company commitment, and retention (Dansereau et al., 1975; Ferris, 1985; Gerstner & Day, 1997; Graen & Ginsburgh, 1977; Graen, Novak, & Sommerkamp, 1982).

Graen and his associates designed a leadership program to instruct managers on how to form high-quality social exchanges with subordinates (Graen et al., 1982; Scandura & Graen, 1984). Exhibit 4.16 describes this training program, which uses lecture, discussion, and role-playing to instruct trainees. Trainees learn how to implement LMX with subordinates with active listening, ways to exchange mutual expectations and resources, and one-on-one

- Does your subordinate know where she or he stands with you?
- How well do you understand your subordinates' problems and needs?
- How well do you recognize your subordinates' potential?
- Would you use your authority to help your subordinate solve problems in her or his work?
- Can your subordinate count on you to "bail him or her out" at your expense when she or he needs it?
- Does your subordinate have sufficient confidence in you that he or she can defend and justify your decision if you were not present to do so?
- Would your subordinate describe her or his working relationship with you as effective?

Exhibit 4.15. Leader-Member Exchange
SOURCE: Adapted from Scandura and Graen (1984).

sessions. In another session, trainees meet with their subordinates and follow a prepared script to communicate their concerns and expectations about each other's job and their working relationship. Several evaluations have documented that LMX training can increase subordinate morale and productivity. LMX training might boost personnel retention because other research has established that subordinates having effective working relationships with their superiors are more committed and loyal (Gerstner & Day, 1997).

Reducing Role Stress

Turnover researchers long have concluded that role stress is a major determinant of why people quit jobs (Griffeth et al., 2000; Hom & Griffeth, 1995; Netermeyer, Johnston, & Burton, 1990; Thomas & Ganster, 1995). Incumbents quit their work roles if they face excessive role conflict (i.e., when they perceive incompatible demands from others about how to meet their role requirements), role ambiguity (e.g., when they are unclear about the organization's expectations for their work role), role overload (e.g., role occupants face too many expectations or demands), or work-family conflict (otherwise known as *interrole conflict,* in which compliance with the work role is incompatible with full compliance with another—family—role; Thomas & Ganster, 1995).

- Training format
  - Six 2-hour sessions
  - Lecture
  - Discussion
  - Role-playing
- Posttraining application
  - One-to-one conversation between manager and subordinate
  - Follow special interview guidelines
- Training topics
  - Leader-exchange model and how to use it (2 hours)
  - Active listening skills (2 hours)
  - Exchanging resources (2 hours)
  - Practicing one-on-one sessions (4 hours)

Exhibit 4.16. Leader-Member Exchange Training

Exhibit 4.17 describes the various ways that superiors might affect role stress. Several investigations have documented that certain actions by superiors can reduce role conflict and ambiguity and thereby turnover (Johnston, Parasuraman, Futrell, & Black, 1990; Jones, Kantak, Futrell, & Johnston, 1996). Similarly, Thomas and Ganster (1995) report that supervisors who empathize with employees' family responsibilities can diminish their work-family conflicts, and Kossek and Nichol (1992) observe that supportive first-line supervisors are essential for successful family-friendly policies. Based on these findings, Exhibit 4.18 illustrates how superiors can alleviate role ambiguity and conflict, and Exhibit 4.19 describes supervisory behaviors that can reduce work-family conflict.

Abusive Supervision

According to Tepper (2000), abusive supervision refers to the extent to which "supervisors engage in the sustained display of hostile verbal and nonverbal behaviors, excluding physical contact" (p. 178) toward subordinates. Despite widespread anecdotal reports about its pervasiveness and destructive-

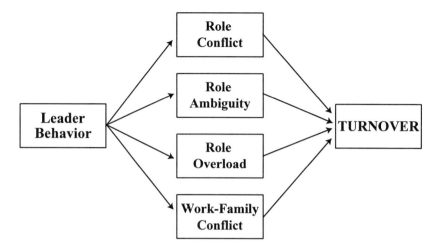

Exhibit 4.17. The Role of the Supervisor in Alleviating Role Stress

- Reducing Role Conflict
  - Assign tasks to your subordinates with adequate materials and resources to execute the tasks
  - Reduce incompatible requests that your subordinates receive from two or more people
  - Reduce conflicting job requirements for your subordinates
  - Assure that your subordinates can do their job duties without "bucking" company rule or policy
- Reducing role ambiguity
  - Ensure that your subordinates' authority matches the responsibilities assigned to them
  - Clearly define your subordinates' responsibilities
  - Clarify the criteria for pay raises and promotions
  - Give clear directions and expectations
  - Ensure clear policies and guidelines
  - Clarify the opportunities for career advancement
  - Provide clear performance feedback

Exhibit 4.18. How To Reduce Role Stress
SOURCE: Adapted from House, Schuler, and Levanoni (1983).

- Switch schedules to accommodate employee's family duties
- Let employees decide when their work day begins and ends
- Permit personal phone calls to check on family members
- Listen to employee's problems
- Help employee solve work-family conflicts
- Show understanding of employee's needs as a working parent
- Juggle tasks to accommodate employee's family responsibilities

Exhibit 4.19. Supervisory Support That Reduces Work-Family Conflict
SOURCE: Adapted from Thomas and Ganster (1995).

ness (Marano, 1995), unfair or abusive supervision has only recently come under academic scrutiny (Aquino, Griffeth, Allen, & Hom, 1997; Donovan, Drasgow, & Munson, 1998; Tepper, 2000). This line of inquiry shows that abusive supervisors are often responsible for many forms of workplace injustice that can instigate resignations (see Chapter 7). As Exhibit 4.20 shows, abusive superiors do not fairly distribute rewards (distributive injustice), do not follow fair methods for allocating rewards (procedural injustice), and do not justify their allocation decisions to employees (interactional justice). As a result, employees exposed to such injustice are prone to quit. Upholding this theory, several investigators have affirmed that abusive supervision prompts job exits because they create unjust working conditions (Aquino et al., 1997; Dittrich & Carrell, 1979; Donovan et al., 1998; Price & Mueller, 1981, 1986; Tepper, 2000). Exhibit 4.21 lists some of the typical behaviors of abusive supervisors and helps organizations identify abusive bosses in their midst.

Data-Based Supervisory Intervention

Because academic research offers little guidance on retention-inducing supervision, Krackhardt, McKenna, Porter, and Steers (1981) developed a program that instructs bank supervisors on how they can reduce teller quits based on initial research into why tellers quit. First, they investigated the particular supervisory behaviors that induce tellers to leave. Specifically, they interviewed tellers and branch managers to identify what supervisory actions (or inaction) might influence teller resignations. Next, they surveyed a larger sample of bank tellers, who described the extent to which their superiors performed those behaviors (as well as their intentions to remain in the bank).

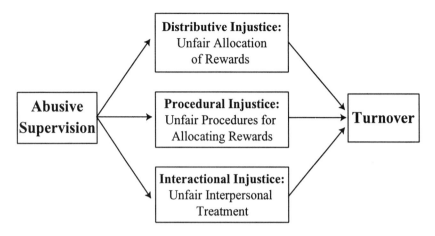

Exhibit 4.20. How Abusive Supervision Increases Turnover
SOURCE: Adapted from Tepper (2000).

- Do supervisors ridicule employees?
- Do supervisors criticize employees in front of others?
- Do supervisors lie to employees?
- Are supervisors rude to employees?
- Do supervisors break promises they make to employees?
- Do supervisors express anger at employees when they are mad for another reason?

Exhibit 4.21. Detecting Abusive Supervision
SOURCE: Adapted from Tepper (2000).

They then analyzed the survey data, relating teller perceptions of supervisory behaviors to teller decisions to stay or leave. This analysis identified those supervisory acts that could affect turnover (see Chapter 6). To illustrate, tellers who saw that their superiors "made life easier" planned to remain employed in the bank longer.

Next, Krackhardt et al. (1981) derived a turnover-reduction intervention based on this inquiry into the supervisory causes of turnover. To test its efficacy, they randomly assigned this intervention to some bank branches—the "experimental" group—but withheld it from other branches (control group). (The branches were first matched by size, location, and average depositor

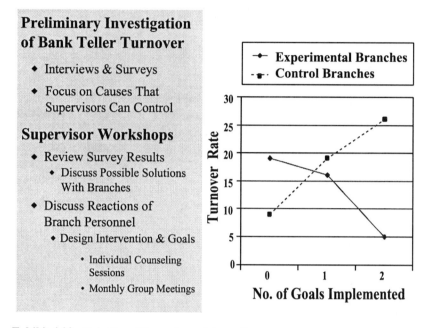

Exhibit 4.22. Data-Based Supervisory Intervention
SOURCE: Adapted from discussion by Krackhardt, McKenna, Porter, and Steers (1981).

income before group assignment.) The intervention included two workshops with first-line supervisors. In the first session, supervisors from experimental branches reviewed the survey findings and discussed potential solutions. Afterward, they returned to their branches to discuss possible solutions with tellers and managers. In the second meeting, supervisors decided on the particular actions they would undertake to improve teller retention. In particular, they planned to hold individual counseling sessions and monthly group meetings. During counseling sessions, supervisors would meet with each teller at least once during the next 3 months and focus on the teller's needs and offer performance feedback. Supervisors also would try to meet with tellers as a group at least four times during the next 3 months and exchange information and questions as well as resolve work group problems.

Exhibit 4.22 shows results of this data-based intervention. Experimental branches implementing *both* individual counseling *and* group meetings had the lowest quit rates compared to a matched group of control branches. All told, though current research may not determine what supervisory acts work, organizations can carry out their own self-study to identify the kinds of supervisory behaviors that can affect employee turnover. Based on such internal research, organizations can design intervention programs that encourage certain supervisory behaviors (e.g., more coaching sessions with employees) or train supervisors to develop specific skills (e.g., counseling skills).

Summary of Suggestions

To summarize, we suggest the following socialization and supervision practices to improve retention:

1. Use institutionalized socialization tactics—collective, formal, sequential, fixed, serial, and investiture tactics—to structure socialization experiences for newcomers.
2. Ensure that organization-wide orientation programs for newcomers cover these topics: corporate goals and values; company history and tradition, and corporate jargon and language.
3. Design reality shock programs that incorporate ROPES features, such as realistic job preview, role models, group discussion, and rehearsal.
4. Teach newcomers self-management techniques, including how to manage environmental cues and their own behaviors, how to enrich their job content, and cognitive restructuring.
5. Instruct supervisors on how to develop high leader-member exchange with their subordinates.
6. Teach superiors how to alleviate role stress for employees.
7. Identify and remove abusive supervisors or abusive supervisory practices.
8. Design data-based interventions that target supervisory behaviors that affect turnover.

Employee Selection

Mike looked at his watch. He had about 15 minutes before his meeting with his boss. He was relieved that his exit interview with Susan Jameson went well, considering this was her last day on the job. This was the third voluntary quit this month, which put the company's turnover rate at about 25%, if this trend continued. She really didn't say much, as he looked at his notes. She was generally very unhappy with her job. She said she didn't fit into the job or maybe the organization. He shrugged. Whoever felt "they really fit in with a job"? I mean, it was just a job, he thought. But as HR Director, he was supposed to find out why these employees were quitting, but he didn't have a clue. Maybe better selection would help, but that is costly. But so is this constant turnover. He estimated that, all things considered—separation, replacement, and orientation and training costs—it cost nearly $5,000 to replace each employee who left, more if they were a high performer, like Susan, and the other two this month. Well, he didn't have any more time to think about this right now, he had to go to his meeting and, unfortunately, offer some suggestions for improving this situation.

The concept of person-organization or person-job fit is at the very heart of employee selection. Without appropriate and valid methods, employers are doomed to high turnover. What Mike was facing is a very common situation among HR managers and others today: high turnover of good employees who give vague reasons for their exit. Employees themselves may not really know why they are quitting, just that they do not like the job or the organization and never really fit in. In Chapter 3, we described realistic recruiting as a way to help employees develop coping skills and to show that the employer is honest and concerned about their well-being. In this chapter, we explore several possible selection strategies employers can use to retain valued employees with the idea of improving fit. We start with the strategy that typically has resulted in extremely high retention over the years—biographical predictors, also known as *weighted application blanks*. We end the chapter describing an innovative methodology with promising results.

Weighted Application Blanks

To ensure a more stable workforce (Kinicki, Lockwood, Hom, & Griffeth, 1990), employers typically would like to screen out job applicants if they show signs of the "hobo syndrome" (Ghiselli, 1974; Hulin, 1991)—the frequent changing of jobs. To date, the weighted application blank (WAB) has yielded the most accurate predictions of turnover (Bernardin, 1987; Cascio, 1976; Cotton & Tuttle, 1986; Schmitt, Gooding, Noe, & Kirsch, 1984). WABs rely on the broader field known as biodata, which is the attempt to use life experiences to predict job performance. It is based on the notion called the "consistency principle"—the best predictor of future behavior is past behavior (Wernimont & Campbell, 1968), and it remains a viable method of selection today (Gatewood & Feild, 1998). In the next section, we describe procedures for developing and validating WABs.

Prediction of Employee Turnover Using Weighted Application Blanks

WABs are fairly detailed application forms converted into tests. An overview of this conversion starts with an examination of current and former employees' past answers to items on an application blank completed during their hiring. We seek items that elicited different responses from long- and short-term employees (Gatewood & Feild, 1998)—*stayers* and *leavers*. After identifying the discriminating items, we derive a key that assigns different

Table 5.1 Response Categories

Previous Salary	Education	Years of Formal Education
Less than $15,000	Grade school	1–6 years
$15,000 – 20,000	High school	7–9 years
$20,000 – 25,000	Some college	10–12 years
$25,000 – 30,000	College graduate	13–14 years
Over $30,000	Graduate work	15–16 years
		More than 16 years

NOTE: For ease of presentation, we have selected only three items to create response categories. In reality, and with the use of today's powerful database programs and computers, many more items could be collected from personnel records. Indeed, it is recommended to use as many items as possible in the initial analyses because many items will not differentiate between stayers and leavers. Practically any item that can be converted into response categories like those set out previously could be used for Weighted Application Blanks development. However, it is a good practice to use items derived from a thorough job analysis (Gatewood & Feild, 1998).

scores to the two groups' dissimilar answers. Summing scores on these particular items generates a test score indicating quit propensity. After the WABs are developed, candidates fill them out, and those whose computed WAB scores suggest job instability would be screened out.

An Example

In this section, we take the practicing manager through the steps in developing and validating a WAB, using turnover as the behavior.

1. Define two groups of employees. In this case, we are interested in stayers and leavers; however, different groups could be used (e.g., *high performers* vs. *low performers, employees with high attendance* vs. *employees with low attendance*). Almost any behavior could be used, as long as it is objectively identifiable.

2. Select items from application blanks for analyses (avoid sensitive items that could be considered obviously illegal or invasive of job applicants' privacy, such as age, gender, race, or national origin). For this example, we use previous salary, education level, and years of formal education.

3. Specify response categories for each item (see Table 5.1).

4. Identify from personnel records past and present employees who are stayers and leavers. About 75 from each category are the minimum needed to establish stable weights. Thus, we need 75 stayers and 75 leavers.

Table 5.2 Response Categories, Percentage Responding, and Integer Weights

Number Responding	Number Responding		Percentage Responding		Percentage Difference	Integer Weight
	Stayer	*Leaver*	*Stayer*	*Leaver*		
Previous salary						
Less than $15,000	30	8	40	11	+29	+3
$15,000 – 20,000	15	22	20	29	–9	–1
$20,000 – 25,000	15	15	20	20	0	0
$25,000 – 30,000	7	15	9	20	–11	–1
Over $30,000	8	15	11	20	–9	–1
Total	75	75	100	100		
Education						
Grade school	17	11	23	15	+8	+1
High School	26	19	35	25	+10	+1
Some College	22	12	29	16	+13	+1
College Graduate	6	26	8	35	–27	–3
Graduate Work	4	7	5	9	–4	0
Total	75	75	100	100		
Years of formal education						
1-6 years	17	11	23	15	+8	+1
7-9 years	10	10	13	13	0	0
10-12 years	16	9	21	12	+9	+1
13-14 years	11	8	15	11	+4	0
15-16 years	17	30	23	40	–17	–2
More than 16 years	4	7	5	9	–4	0
Total	75	75	100	100		

5. Determine item weights:

   A. Examine application blanks of stayers and leavers

   B. Examine how the two groups responded to questions on the application blank. Place these numbers in tabular form.

   C. For each response category, compute the percentage of stayers and leavers choosing that response category.

   D. For each response category, compute the percentage difference between the stayers and leavers.

   E. Convert the percentage difference to an integer weight.

These five steps are depicted in Table 5.2 for each of our three items.

Leavers	WAB Score
Mary	0
Joan	10
Karl	20
Bob	30
Chuck	40
Sum	100

Stayers	WAB Score
Peter	50
Angelo	40
Vida	30
Rodger	60
Lynn	70
Sum	250

Number of leavers $(N_1) = 5$

M_1 = Mean of Leavers' WAB scores

$M_1 = 100/5$

$M_1 = 20$

Number of Stayers $(N_2) = 5$

M_2 = Mean of Stayers' WAB scores

$M_2 = 250/5$

$M_2 = 50$

We would then use the following formula to calculate the point-biserial correlation (r):

1. $r = (M_2 - M_1)\sqrt{\dfrac{N_1 N_2}{sd}}$

2. $r = \dfrac{(50 - 20)}{20.62}\sqrt{\dfrac{5*5}{10*9}}$

3. $r = 30\sqrt{\dfrac{.27}{20.62}}$

4. $r = \dfrac{30*.527}{20.62}$

5. $r = \dfrac{15.81}{20.62}$

6. $r = .766*$ or $.77*$

NOTE: The correlation is large and statistically significant; thus, the WAB can predict turnover accurately. So, if the results of cross-validation supported this finding, we could use this WAB to predict stayers. WAB = weighted application blank.
$* p < .05.$

Exhibit 5.1. Calculating a Point-Biserial Correlation

6. Now that you have the weights from the sample, estimate the predictive accuracy of the WABs.

A. For each stayer and leaver, find the response to each item and its corresponding weight from the scoring key.

B. Add up the weights for an employee's responses to compute a total score for each employee.

C. Compute a point-biserial correlation between the employees' WAB scores and their membership in the stayer or leaver group. (Note: A formula for calculating a point-biserial correlation is provided in Exhibit 5.1.)

In a separate step, shown subsequently, we used a spreadsheet program to calculate the standard deviation of the sample.

Computing the Standard Deviation

Employee	*Status*	*WAB Score*	*Gender*
Mary	Leaver	0	Female
Peter	Stayer	50	Male
Joan	Leaver	10	Female
Angelo	Stayer	40	Male
Karl	Leaver	20	Male
Vida	Stayer	30	Female
Bob	Leaver	30	Male
Rodger	Stayer	60	Male
Chuck	Leaver	40	Male
Lynn	Stayer	70	Female

NOTE:　$SD = 20.615528$ or 20.62

D. If the correlation is sizable and statistically significant, WABs may be used to hire potentially stable employees.

However, to increase our confidence in the results, it is necessary to cross-validate our findings. Cross-validation helps us to determine if the predictive power of the WAB is a chance finding or if it is truly predictive of turnover. Step 7 describes this process.

7. Cross-validation.

A. Identify another sample of 50 stayers and 50 leavers from the same employee population.

    B. Examine their completed application blanks.

    C. Compute WAB scores for these employees using the scoring key developed from the first sample.

    D. Compute a point-biserial correlation between their WAB scores and their employment status, as in Step 6 (stayers vs. leavers).

    E. If the second correlation is statistically significant and similar in value to the first correlation, then you have confirmation of the predictive power of your WABs.

  8. If WABs have predictive power, use them to screen new job applicants.

    A. After job candidates complete the application blank, examine each applicant's response to each item.

    B. Find the corresponding weights for these responses from the scoring key.

    C. Add up the weights for a particular candidate to derive a total WAB score.

    D. Hire only job candidates with the highest WAB scores.

In the previous example, job candidates will receive a high WAB score if his or her application responses are similar to responses made by stable employees. Periodically, every 3 to 5 years, depending on whether the job or labor market has changed, the scoring key for the WABs should be updated. You would do this by repeating Steps 1 through 7. Another thing managers can do to be certain they are not discriminating unfairly is to compare the WAB scores for groups of employees. For example, while collecting the data from applications to develop the WAB scores, managers also can collect data regarding age, gender, race, and so forth. Then they can make group comparisons using the WAB scores to determine if any differences exist. If no statistically significant differences exist, then the WABs could be used to select members of that group. For example, by coding gender into the database, we can check to see if our WAB discriminates unfairly against women.

Problems With Weighted Application Blanks

WABs are not without their problems, however. Fearing charges of discrimination, few companies actually use WABs, despite their predictive validity (Gatewood & Feild, 1998). Inquiries about some demographic traits violate state fair-employment statutes, and screening based on certain background attributes (such as residence) may disproportionately reject minority or female applicants (Gatewood & Feild, 1998). Besides, the apparent irrelevance of certain questions and potential invasion of privacy may prompt dis-

To determine if our WAB is biased and discriminates against women, we also can compute a biserial correlation between genders using our WAB scores.

Females	WAB Score		Males	WAB Score
Mary	0		Peter	50
Joan	10		Angelo	40
Vida	30		Rodger	60
Lynn	70		Bob	30
			Chuck	40
			Karl	20
Sum	110		Sum	240
M	27.5		M	40
$N_1 = 4$			$N_2 = 6$	

Then, using the formula we used earlier, we can calculate the point biserial correlation (r).

1. $r = \dfrac{(M_2 - M_1)}{sd^1} \sqrt{\dfrac{N_1 N_2}{N(n-1)}}$

2. $r = \dfrac{(40 - 27.5)}{20.63} \sqrt{\dfrac{24}{90}}$

3. $r = \dfrac{12.5}{20.62} \sqrt{.27}$

4. $r = \dfrac{12.5 * .52}{20.62}$

5. $r = \dfrac{6.5}{20.62}$

6. $r = .32$

NOTE: This correlation is not significant, indicating that gender and WABs are unrelated; therefore, bias due to gender discrimination does not appear to be a problem with this WAB. Unfortunately, this is a very small sample. If these exact data were found in a larger sample ($N > 40$), then the correlation would have been significant, indicating that males were more likely to be selected than females using this WAB. Clearly, then, one would not want to use this WAB for the purposes of reducing turnover in this job. Similar analyses should be conducted with minority applicants.

Exhibit 5.2. Is the Weighted Application Blank (WAB) Biased Against Women?

crimination lawsuits (Breaugh & Dossett, 1989; see Exhibit 5.2 to see if the WAB discriminates against women). In a survey of practitioners, Gatewood and Feild (1998) report that only about 7% had ever used biodata. Companies may face impaired public relations and sizable litigation costs to defend so-called unfair questions. In spite of evidence that the questions are related to the job, some federal courts have overturned WABs because firms failed to defend them as the *best* selection device by proving that alternative selection methods with less adverse impact do not exist (Arvey & Faley, 1988; Breaugh & Dossett, 1989).

To overcome traditional problems with WABs, Breaugh and Dossett (1989) advanced a rational basis for choosing biographical data. Traditional empirical approaches provide little understanding about the reasons that biodata items predict turnover, and they require large samples from which scoring keys are developed. Breaugh and Dossett recommended that WABs include only biodata items that are verifiable (to encourage honesty among applicants) and that are known, according to accepted psychological theories, to underlie turnover. Rational selection of items would improve face validity of WABs, making them acceptable to applicants.

Following these criteria, Breaugh and Dossett (1989) designed a WAB to predict turnover among bank tellers. They chose tenure on the previous job as a predictor, a choice that agrees with the consistency principle. They also selected several items based on past research: employee referrals (a recruitment source) and relevance of prior work experience to index the realism of the applicants' job expectations, which enhance job survival (Wanous, 1980). Finally, they added educational attainment, presuming that educated applicants are prone to quit because they have better job opportunities elsewhere (Cotton & Tuttle, 1986). Altogether, these biodata items moderately predicted turnover ($R = .44$). The Breaugh-Dossett method is a practical (because it avoids the large sample requirements of empirical scoring keys) and defensible (because it uses theory-based item selection) way to design WABs and may overcome resistance from employers.

Relatedly, Bernardin (1987) used a WAB using several items that were validated. Several items were desire for full- or part-time work, referral by an employee of the company, having relatives working for the company, and intention to continue in school. Using a small sample of customer service representatives ($n = 43$) and a composite measure based on unit weights, Bernardin found that this composite significantly predicted turnover ($r = .28$), showing that WABs can be useful even when objectionable items are not present.

Biographical Data

Although space does not allow us to spend a lot of time on this method, we briefly mention the biographical data (biodata) questionnaire and its potential for reducing employee turnover. More useful and practical treatments are available on this topic (e.g., Gatewood & Feild, 1998), so the interested reader should consult them.

A meta-analytic review of validity studies found an average validity coefficient of .21 when a biodata questionnaire was used to predict employee turnover (Schmitt et al., 1984); another review found an average validity coefficient of .26 with employee tenure (Hunter & Hunter, 1984). A recent conversation with a Circuit City executive found that the company reported its use of biodata as being highly successful in reducing turnover.

Biodata questionnaires are much different from WABs because they are broader and longer than WABs. Biodata questionnaires may contain 100 or more items, whereas WABs may have only 10 to 15 items. Biodata questionnaires can cover a variety of topics, such as educational experiences, hobbies, family relations, use of leisure time, personal health, and early work experiences. WABs, on the other hand, focuse on limited, factual, verifiable information (Gatewood & Feild, 1998).

The use of biodata questionnaires is based on the following assumptions (from Gatewood & Feild, 1998, pp. 451-452):

1. The best predictor of a job applicant's future behavior is his or her past behavior (previously, this was called the consistency principle and underlies the basic idea behind WABs).
2. If we can measure applicants' past behavior and life experiences systematically, we can indirectly measure their motivational characteristics.
3. People are less defensive in describing their past behaviors and experiences than they are in discussing their motivations for those behaviors.

Legality of Biodata Questionnaires

In general, legality concerns are valid when considering the use of biodata for selection: Biodata questionnaires or items can be used for selection if it can be shown that (a) they are job related and (b) they do not unfairly discriminate against protected groups of job applicants. Unfair discrimination might be established if it can be shown that a biodata item, total score, or a dimension affects a protected group disproportionately. Thus, it always is advisable to check for validity and fairness (Gatewood & Feild, 1998, pp. 465-466).

The Selection Interview

If designed appropriately and used correctly, the selection interview is an excellent tool for selecting employees with a large majority of employers using on-site interviews (Gatewood & Feild, 1998). Moreover, two recent meta-analyses examined interviews as predictors of turnover. Briefly, one meta-analysis (McDaniel, Whetzel, Schmidt, & Maurer, 1994) found that interviews modestly predict job tenure. The sample-size-weighted average correlation corrected for measurement error was .13. Because this effect size was obtained from myriad structured and unstructured interviews, even stronger effect sizes might be derived from a meta-analysis of only structured interviews—the preferred approach. Indeed, Schmidt and Rader (1999) later documented that an empirically developed structured telephone interview can forecast tenure accurately. The sample-size-weighted average correlation corrected for unreliability and range restriction was an impressive .39.

The interview process is extremely complex and should be taken seriously as a selection tool. This means doing everything possible to maximize the effectiveness of interviews (for a complete discussion on using the interview, see the chapter on the selection interview in Gatewood & Feild, 1998). One important way employers improve the selection interview is to train interviewers in more ways than simply improving their interpersonal skills and/or their abilities to evaluate applicants (Gatewood & Feild, 1998). The researchers (p. 495) indicate a number of errors that interviewers commit that could be reduced via appropriate training programs:

- Talking excessively
- Asking inconsistent questions among the different applicants
- Asking questions either unrelated or slightly related to performance on the job
- Being unable to put the interviewee at ease
- Being overconfident concerning his or her ability to judge applicants
- Stereotyping applicants and using personal biases when evaluating them
- Being influenced by nonverbal behaviors
- Rating many applicants the same (e.g., either superior, committing the leniency error; average, committing the central tendency error; or harshly, committing the strictness error)
- Allowing one or two good or bad characteristics to influence the evaluation (committing either a positive halo or negative halo effect)
- Allowing the quality of previous applicants to influence the ratings of the present applicant (contrast effect error)
- Making a quick evaluation of the applicant in the first few minutes (committing the first impression error)
- Evaluating the applicant favorably because he or she is similar to the interviewer in some way (committing the similar-to-me error)

The second major way to produce a more valid interview process is to use a structured interview. The structured interview is usually contrasted to the unstructured interview, which is usually useless in validly selecting employees. Using a structured interview refers to the interviewer's use of predetermined, job-relevant questions, scoring formats, and decision rules. A list of common topics are asked of all applicants, thus making the comparison of applicants directly possible. Probing questions, which are not predetermined, may be asked if the interviewer is to obtain enough information on the topic, depending on the nature of the conversation between the interviewer and interviewee (Gatewood & Feild, 1998).

Gatewood and Feild (1989) mention a computerized twist to the interview, whereby up to 100 questions are asked. Using a multiple-choice format, the questions are presented to the applicants one at a time. Applicants are not allowed to scroll through the interview, and they must respond to each one by pressing the appropriate key. Upon completion of the interview, the interviewer is provided a printout, whose results may be used as a part of the personal interview. Also, a scoring program could be developed to indicate superior/deficient areas or contradictions. We believe this use of technology may become more prevalent as more companies use online screening of applicants.

Personality Predictors

Unlike WABs, traditional research reports low predictive validity for personality measures and interest inventories (Griffeth & Hom, 1988b; Mobley, 1982; Mowday, Porter, & Stone, 1978; Muchinsky & Tuttle, 1979; Porter & Steers, 1973). Generally speaking, early studies showed that personality tests provided modest or insignificant predictions of turnover. For example, Griffeth and Hom (1988b) calculated that the widely varying correlations reported in published reports averaged only .18. Such ubiquitous findings motivated Muchinsky and Tuttle (1979) to conclude that personality has a "very marginal impact on turnover" (p. 48).

Modern personality research suggests that pessimistic conclusions about personality predictions of quits may be premature. One reason for this optimism is that conventional narrative reviews underestimated predictive validity (and overestimated inconsistency in predictors) because they did not take into account statistical artifacts, such as unreliability, range restriction, and sampling error (Hunter & Schmidt, 1990). Recent meta-analyses conclude that personality tests do reliably predict turnover (Barrick & Mount 1991; Schmidt et al., 1984). Schmidt and his colleagues (1984) estimated a sample-weighted mean validity coefficient of .12 between personality tests and job retention. This validity (corrected only for sampling error) does not exceed Griffeth and Hom's (1988b) .18 estimate, but early reviewers misinterpreted the utility of modest predictive validities (Premack & Wanous, 1985). After all, a predictor's true usefulness depends not only on its predictive validity but also on selection ratio (proportion of applicants hired to those applying) and base rate (proportion of employees who quit) (Arvey & Faley, 1988). To illustrate, Premack and Wanous (1985) showed that a .12 correlation between realistic job preview (RJP) and job survival (which scarcely differs from existing personality validities) translates into a 6% improvement in job survival attributed to RJPs. RJPs have more impact when job survival is low (e.g., 20% survive) than when it is high (e.g., 80% survive). As Premack and Wanous (1985) wrote, "This is analogous to saying a selection test will have more impact when the base rate of success is low than when it is high" (p. 716). Thus, base rate determines the usefulness of any predictor, including personality tests.

Early critics condemned personality inventories as susceptible to falsification by job applicants, who present themselves in a favorable light to obtain employment (Bernardin, 1987). However, this claim has been disputed by more recent work finding that job applicants do not usually inflate descriptions of themselves any *more* than do incumbents (Hough, Eaton, Dunnette, Kamp, & McCloy, 1990). Tett, Jackson, and Rothstein's (1991) meta-analysis found that personality scales do *not* predict the performance of recruits less validly than that of current employees. This finding contradicts the conventional wisdom that recruits distort self-descriptions to obtain employment, thereby invalidating personality scales. Relatedly, Hough et al. (1990) found that a measure of social desirability (or the deliberate self-inflation of personal qualities) hardly moderated the predictive validity of personality inventories. That is, the criterion-related validity of personality tests was slightly lower for employees given to inflated self-descriptions than for employees who describe themselves honestly.

Historically, personality measures were often adopted arbitrarily without much thought being given to their theoretical correspondence to turnover or job behaviors (Tett et al., 1991; Weiss & Adler, 1984). Yet Tett et al.'s meta-analysis revealed stronger predictive validities (.19) when personality scales are chosen for their clear conceptual linkages to performance criteria than when empirically chosen without any rationale for their performance linkages

(.12). Trait measures selected based on a job analysis that identified a job's personality requirements yielded a mean predictive validity of .37. Relatedly, Barrick and Mount's (1991) meta-analysis uncovered higher validity co-efficients when personality tests matched occupational requirements. For example, extroversion positively related to sales effectiveness but negatively to professional performance (where work often is done alone). In a recent study, Barrick and Mount (1996) found that these personality dimensions can exhibit even higher predictive validity for long-haul truck drivers. Specifically, conscientious and emotionally stable truckers were less likely to leave. The uncorrected correlation between those two personality traits and turnover (measured 6 months after personality testing) was about −.20. These encouraging findings suggest that individuals with high turnover propensities can be identified prior to organizational entry.

Traditional reviews collapse predictive validities across different personality dimensions; the possibility that some dimensions predict turnover more accurately than do others is overlooked. Present-day meta-analyses estimating predictive validities for the "Big Five" personality dimensions disclose different validities (Barrick & Mount, 1991; Tett et al., 1991). For example, Barrick and Mount (1991) discovered that conscientiousness (for which the average correlation was .12, after correcting for sampling error, range restriction, and measurement error), agreeableness (corrected correlation = .09), and openness to experience (corrected correlation = .11) best predicted job retention across various occupations. Extroversion (correlation = −.03) and emotional stability (correlation = .02) barely predicted tenure, but that does not mean they are irrelevant for all jobs, such as sales (see previous discussion). A Big Five Personality Scale with good reliability (courtesy of Lewis Goldberg, http://ipip.ori.org/) is presented in Table 5.3 and could be used for selection if your job analyses find any of the dimensions to be relevant to the job (Goldberg, 1999).

Contemporary research has established that personality scales, given recent methodological and theoretical advancements, can predict turnover. Barrick and Mount (1991) validated conscientiousness, openness to experience, and agreeableness as robust predictors. Employers can increase the validity of personality tests by identifying the personality requirements of a given job through job analysis and then by choosing or developing valid measures of relevant personality traits (Tett et al., 1991). Employers should safeguard themselves against applicants who distort their self-descriptions by including social desirability scales, though research shows that falsification of

Table 5.3 Items Measuring the Big Five Personality Characteristics

Instructions

On the following page(s), there are phrases describing people's behaviors. Please use the rating scale below to describe how accurately each statement describes you. Describe yourself as you generally are now, not as you wish to be in the future. Describe yourself as you honestly see yourself, in relation to other people you know of the same sex as you are, and roughly your same age. Please read each statement carefully and then fill in the box that corresponds to the number on the scale.

Response Options

1 = Very Inaccurate
2 = Moderately Inaccurate
3 = Neither Inaccurate nor Accurate
4 = Moderately Accurate
5 = Very Accurate

	1	2	3	4	5
NEUROTICISM (α = .86)					
1. Often feel blue	☐	☐	☐	☐	☐
2. Dislike myself	☐	☐	☐	☐	☐
3. Am often down in the dumps	☐	☐	☐	☐	☐
4. Have frequent mood swings	☐	☐	☐	☐	☐
5. Panic easily	☐	☐	☐	☐	☐
6. Seldom feel blue (R)	☐	☐	☐	☐	☐
7. Feel comfortable with myself (R)	☐	☐	☐	☐	☐
8. Rarely get irritated (R)	☐	☐	☐	☐	☐
9. Am not easily bothered by things (R)	☐	☐	☐	☐	☐
10. Am very pleased with myself (R)	☐	☐	☐	☐	☐
EXTROVERSION (α = .86)					
11. Feel comfortable around people	☐	☐	☐	☐	☐
12. Make friends easily	☐	☐	☐	☐	☐
13. Am skilled in handling social situations	☐	☐	☐	☐	☐
14. Am the life of the party	☐	☐	☐	☐	☐
15. Know how to captivate people	☐	☐	☐	☐	☐
16. Have little to say (R)	☐	☐	☐	☐	☐
17. Keep in the background (R)	☐	☐	☐	☐	☐
18. Would describe my experiences as somewhat dull (R)	☐	☐	☐	☐	☐
19. Don't like to draw attention to myself (R)	☐	☐	☐	☐	☐
20. Don't talk a lot (R)	☐	☐	☐	☐	☐

	1	2	3	4	5

OPENNESS TO EXPERIENCE (α = .82)

21. Believe in the importance of art ☐ ☐ ☐ ☐ ☐
22. Have a vivid imagination ☐ ☐ ☐ ☐ ☐
23. Tend to vote for liberal political candidates ☐ ☐ ☐ ☐ ☐
24. Carry the conversation to a higher level ☐ ☐ ☐ ☐ ☐
25. Enjoy hearing new ideas ☐ ☐ ☐ ☐ ☐
26. Am not interested in abstract ideas (R) ☐ ☐ ☐ ☐ ☐
27. Do not like art (R) ☐ ☐ ☐ ☐ ☐
28. Avoid philosophical discussions (R) ☐ ☐ ☐ ☐ ☐
29. Do not enjoy going to art museums (R) ☐ ☐ ☐ ☐ ☐
30. Tend to vote for conservative political candidates (R) ☐ ☐ ☐ ☐ ☐

AGREEABLENESS (α = .77)

31. Have a good word for everyone ☐ ☐ ☐ ☐ ☐
32. Believe that others have good intentions ☐ ☐ ☐ ☐ ☐
33. Respect others ☐ ☐ ☐ ☐ ☐
34. Accept people as they are ☐ ☐ ☐ ☐ ☐
35. Make people feel at ease ☐ ☐ ☐ ☐ ☐
36. Have a sharp tongue (R) ☐ ☐ ☐ ☐ ☐
37. Cut others to pieces (R) ☐ ☐ ☐ ☐ ☐
38. Suspect hidden motives in others (R) ☐ ☐ ☐ ☐ ☐
39. Get back at others (R) ☐ ☐ ☐ ☐ ☐
40. Insult people (R) ☐ ☐ ☐ ☐ ☐

CONSCIENTIOUSNESS (α =.81)

41. Am always prepared ☐ ☐ ☐ ☐ ☐
42. Pay attention to details ☐ ☐ ☐ ☐ ☐
43. Get chores done right away ☐ ☐ ☐ ☐ ☐
44. Carry out my plans ☐ ☐ ☐ ☐ ☐
45. Make plans and stick to them ☐ ☐ ☐ ☐ ☐
46. Waste my time (R) ☐ ☐ ☐ ☐ ☐
47. Find it difficult to get down to work (R) ☐ ☐ ☐ ☐ ☐
48. Do just enough work to get by (R) ☐ ☐ ☐ ☐ ☐
49. Don't see things through (R) ☐ ☐ ☐ ☐ ☐
50. Shirk my duties (R) ☐ ☐ ☐ ☐ ☐

NOTE: Items marked with an "R" should be reversed scored (i.e., subtract rating from 6) before summing (Goldberg, 1999).

personality scales is not pervasive and does not automatically threaten predictive validity (Hough et al., 1990). Social desirability scales may identify dishonest job candidates (motivating a closer scrutiny of other hiring criteria) and may be used to adjust statistically personality scores for intentional falsifications (Bannister, Kinicki, DeNisi, & Hom, 1987). Alternatively, employers might develop forced-choice personality inventories to control for social desirability bias (Bernardin, 1987).

Affective Disposition

Contemporary research suggests that "negative affectivity" might influence job stability, because it is a dispositional source of job satisfaction (Staw et al., 1986). People with negative affectivity evaluate themselves, others, and situations unfavorably and thus experiences negative emotional states (Brief, Burke, George, Robinson, & Webster, 1988; George, 1990). Prone to cynicism, negative affective people process work experiences negatively and thus feel more job dissatisfaction (Staw et al., 1986). Staw and colleagues showed that negative affectivity measures taken during adolescence reliably forecast job attitudes in adulthood—predicting satisfaction as long as 50 years later: The adolescents who had viewed life negatively eventually judged their adult work unfavorably. Other research extends these findings, showing that negative affectivity encourages absenteeism and intentions to quit (George, 1989, 1990).

Nevertheless, Judge (1992, 1993) identified many conceptual and methodological pitfalls in studies on dispositional sources of job satisfaction. Specifically, many negative affectivity measures confound affect intensity and affect frequency and presume a false dichotomy between negative and positive affectivity. Moreover, negative affectivity research demonstrates how subjective well-being rather than affective traits shape morale (Judge & Locke, 1993). Dispositional studies fail to distinguish between a general disposition to be happy (affective disposition) and how happy an individual currently is with his or her life (affective state) (Judge, 1992; Judge & Hulin, 1993).

More recently, the independence of positive affectivity and negative affectivity, and consequently its measurement, have been called into question. Russell and Carroll (1999), in a critical examination of that literature and the measurement of positive affectivity and negative affectivity, found that when the actual predictions of a bipolar model are considered and error is taken into account, bipolarity resulted in a parsimonious fit to existing data, rejecting the independence of what were once conceived to be opposites.

Judge (1993) introduced an alternative index of affective disposition adapted from Weitz (1952). Weitz's "gripe index" assesses satisfaction with 44 items common in everyday life, such as modern art and telephone service. This index may assess the dispositional trait of affective orientation better than do existing negative affectivity indexes, which reflect experienced affect. After adapting Weitz's scale (deleting irrelevant items and modernizing the wording), Judge (1992, 1993; Judge & Locke, 1993) showed that this measure discriminably differed from subjective measures of well-being (which included negative and positive affectivity scales). Judge and Locke found that this dispositional index influenced job satisfaction and work avoidance indirectly through subjective well-being.

Recently, Judge (1993) demonstrated that the Weitz scale moderates the translation of job dissatisfaction into exits. Judge argued that employees positively disposed toward life are more likely to quit a dissatisfying job than are the negatively predisposed employees. Relative to other things in their lives, happy individuals feel more dissatisfied with a bad job than do unhappy individuals, for whom job dissatisfaction is no more meaningful or exceptional than other dissatisfying events in their lives. Judge found correlations higher between job satisfaction and voluntary quits for medical clinic personnel with positive orientations than for negatively disposed employees.

In a recent study of mood and withdrawal behavior, Pelled and Xin (1999) examined the impact of positive affectivity and negative affectivity in a longitudinal study of employees in an electronic firm. They found that positive affectivity reduced absenteeism, whereas negative affectivity increased both absenteeism and turnover. They also found that job satisfaction moderated the relation between positive affectivity and absenteeism. These results indicate that *both* job attitudes—like job satisfaction—and mood need to be monitored when attempts are made to predict and manage withdrawal behavior. The implications for managers who are interested in increasing employee attachment to the organization are to monitor employees' moods and job satisfaction levels regularly. Steps to ameliorate negative attitudes and moods might include redesigning features of the work environment that cause the negative affect and providing counseling programs.

Employers might use measures of affective traits (or states) for employee selection and placement. For example, negatively oriented newcomers could be assigned to work groups that have positive affective tones (i.e., shared norms of positive affectivity) to curb their downcast affect (George, 1990). In turn, mood elevation may reduce work avoidance. Measures of dispositional affect might identify those employees who would most benefit from morale-boosting interventions, although recent work finds that affective dispositions do not constrain the impact of job enrichment (Arvey, Bouchard, Segal, & Abraham, 1989; Judge, 1992). Beneficial treatments may be most likely to raise the morale of positively affective employees who currently dislike their jobs and to retain them, because they are prone to quit dissatisfying work (Judge, 1992, 1993). Judge and Locke (1993) recommend training employees to overcome dysfunctional thinking about their jobs and lives in general to increase their subjective well-being and job satisfaction (ultimately reducing job avoidance; Judge, 1992). Despite the claims of many dispositional researchers (Arvey et al., 1989; Staw, Bell, & Clausen, 1986), affective states and dispositions are not immutable, as Neck (1992) demonstrated.

Person-Environment Fit

Research on the fit between person and environment also suggests that personality fit can forecast quits (Chatman, 1991). Following interactional psychology (Schneider, 1985), O'Reilly, Chatman, and Caldwell (1991) reasoned that shared and deeply held values of the members of an organization embody the organizational culture and that employees' adherence to those cultural values fosters job commitment (O'Reilly & Chatman, 1986). To assess the fit between a person and a company, O'Reilly et al. (1991) introduced the Organizational Culture Profile (OCP), which compares people and organizations according to values (enduring preferences for a specific mode of conduct or end-state of existence; Rokeach, 1973) that are relevant and commensurate descriptors of both individuals and companies.

The Organizational Culture Profile identifies value profiles for the individual and the firm and uses a template-matching procedure to assess the similarity of their profiles (Caldwell & O'Reilly, 1990; O'Reilly et al., 1991). To generate a personal profile, an employee uses a Q-sort procedure to classify 54 value statements (drawn from extensive writings about corporate culture) into nine categories, ranging from the most to the least descriptive of her ideal company, and allocates a specified number of statements into each category. Specifically, a respondent sorts fewer items into the extreme categories and more items into the middle categories, following this distribution for items: 2-4-6-9-12-9-6-4-2. To profile the firm, senior managers sort value statements, according to which they describe the firm following the same distribution pattern. The correlation between individual and firm profiles yields a person-company fit score. The Organizational Culture Profile is a methodological breakthrough over customary personality tests because it assesses the relative salience and configuration of variables (values) within entities (persons or firms) rather than the relative standing of individuals across variables (Caldwell & O'Reilly, 1990). O'Reilly et al. (1991) and Chatman (1991) further validated the Organizational Culture Profile, showing that person-culture fit among new accountants predicted job attitudes and retention.

Employers can use the OCP to select new hires who would fit the company culture and remain loyal to the company. Employers can also use the OCP company profile as a form of realistic preview, allowing job applicants to better self-select themselves for preferred organizational cultures.

Person-Job Fit

Using a different operationalization of person-job fit, Bernardin (1987) designed a forced-choice personality inventory to screen out job applicants ill-suited for work as customer service representatives of a newspaper. A forced-choice inventory controls falsification by having respondents choose a descriptor from a pair of descriptors matched on social desirability, only one of which is a valid choice. However, Bernardin matched descriptors on the basis of discomfort. Bernardin interviewed employees and superiors to identify discomforting work events and wrote statements about those events. He also wrote statements about discomforting situations that were irrelevant to the job. Judges then rated the discomfort levels of both relevant and irrelevant statements. The final inventory comprised pairs of relevant and irrelevant statements matched for discomfort. Respondents would choose a statement from each pair depicting an event most distressing to them. For example, a job applicant would circle two of the following situations that would most discomfort her (a valid or scored item is indicated with a *v*):

1. Your schedule for work or school changes from day to day. (v)
2. You are inside watching television all day. (v)
3. You buy a new television and it goes on sale next week.
4. You have a project the boss needs for a 3:00 p.m. meeting and you can't get it finished.

Using a concurrent validation design, employees completed the personality inventory. A positive relation was found between those selecting valid discomforting descriptions and terminations ($r = .31$). In short, this personality scale identifies job applicants who fit the job poorly because they would be distressed by stressful events that are part of the job and would thus more readily quit.

Bernardin (1987) noted that the newspaper used WABs and the discomfort scale in a multiple-hurdle selection system. He reported that the turnover rate was significantly lower in the 6 months following the implementation of the new system than in the previous four 6-month periods (24% vs. 59%, 68%, 49%, and 73%, respectively). This study shows the utility of this person-job fit model to reduce turnover.

More recently, and driven by a need for a method to represent person-job fit (Villanova, Bernardin, Johnson, & Dahmus, 1994), Bernardin (1987) developed the Job Compatibility Questionnaire to be used in developing personnel selection instruments and intervention strategies. (The Job Compatibility Questionnaire is a proprietary measure, so it is not reproduced in this book. If one is interested in using it would be best to contact the creator, John Bernardin, directly.[1]) The underlying assumption of the Job Compatibility Questionnaire is that the greater the compatibility between a job applicant's preferences for job characteristics and the actual characteristics of the job, the more likely the applicant will be effective and stay in the job. The goal of the Job Compatibility Questionnaire methodology is to derive perceptions of job characteristics from job incumbents and to develop a selection instrument capable of assessing the extent to which job applicants' preferences are compatible with job attributes. The selection instrument derived from the Job Compatibility Questionnaire is designed to predict and ultimately increase employee effectiveness (Bernardin & Russell, 1998).

The 400-item Job Compatibility Questionnaire measures a variety of job factors shown by previous research to be related to one or more effectiveness criteria (e.g., turnover, absenteeism, job performance). Items from the Job Compatibility Questionnaire comprise the following job factors: task requirements, physical environment, customer characteristics, coworker characteristics, leader characteristics, compensation preferences, task variety, job autonomy, physical demands, and work schedule.

Steps in Using the Job Compatibility Questionnaire

Development of Forced-Choice Tetrad of Job Characteristics (Job Compatibility Questionnaire)

The Job Compatibility Questionnaire is first administered to job incumbents (minus items that do not apply to the job) who are asked to make two ratings: (a) how desirable the item is for jobs in general and (b) how descriptive it is for "your present job only." A sample list of items follows:

- Having customers who are polite and friendly
- Having my performance judged by how I did against a specific goal or standard
- Having to wear a uniform
- Having a job with no health benefits
- Getting harassed by a total stranger
- Having an opportunity to be creative at work

Next, forced-choice tetrads of job characteristics were formed from the items based on their desirability and descriptive mean ratings, such that all four items per tetrad had relatively equal mean desirability ratings but unequal descriptiveness ratings, with two items of the tetrads having a mean descriptive rating of 3.5 or higher, and the remaining two items having a mean descriptiveness of 2.5 or lower. The high descriptiveness items for each tetrad were considered to be valid items, whereas the low descriptiveness items were considered invalid job descriptions.

Validation of the Job Compatibility Questionnaire

Briefly, the Job Compatibility Questionnaire is validated using a standard predictive model by first administering it at Time 1 to job applicants, most of whom are then hired based on the organization's usual method of hiring applicants. Then, 6 months to 1 year later, criterion data such as performance or turnover are collected at Time 2. The test is then correlated with the criterion. The results indicate the degree to which the test predicts the criterion and whether it can be used for selection. Usually, these results are cross-validated using a second sample.

To accomplish this, job applicants are asked to select the two job characteristics of each of the four tetrads that either were desirable or undesirable to them. The total number of valid items selected represents the applicant's "compatibility" score. What follows are examples of undesirable and desirable tetrads (the v indicates a valid item; Villanova, Bernardin, Johnson, & Dahmus, 1994):

1. Sample Undesirable Tetrad
   a. Frequently having to interact with senior citizens (v)
   b. Being forced to keep my composure around people under trying circumstances (v)
   c. Frequently having to deal with unintelligent people
   d. Frequently being bored at the work I have to do

2. Sample Desirable Tetrad
   a. Learning about computers
   b. Having my pay directly tied to my performance (v)
   c. Learning about machinery
   d. Having a flexible work schedule (v)

In studies of low-wage jobs—such as customer service representatives, security guards, telephone interviewers, theater personnel, and counter personnel—the Job Compatibility Questionnaire did well at predicting employee turnover, with correlations in the .30s. It is important to note that no evidence of adverse impact has been found (Bernardin & Russell, 1998). In conclusion, the Job Compatibility Questionnaire methodology represents an innovative way to increase employee retention.

Summary of Suggestions on Employee Selection

As with all selection, organizations should base their methods of employee selection on a thorough job analysis. The following points summarize the suggestions in this chapter concerning job analysis:

1. Develop a WAB.
2. Use an existing biodata questionnaire.
3. Use WABs and biodata questionnaires in conjunction with other selection methods; they have been found to be particularly useful for selecting people in sales, clerical, and secretarial positions.
4. Use a structured selection interview.
5. Use personality measures like the "Big Five" when the job analysis reveals certain personality traits may be important (e.g., extroversion, conscientiousness).
6. Try selection methods that improve person-environment or person-job fit.

Note

1. Dr. H. John Bernardin can be contacted at the College of Business, Florida Atlantic University, 777 Glades Road, Boca Raton, Florida 33431-0991.

Using Employee Surveys to Predict Turnover and Diagnose Turnover Causes

onsultants, researchers, and human resources professionals often rely on surveys of the current workforce—or job incumbents—to predict who will quit a company as well as what induces them to quit. Why carry out surveys? We believe surveys—if they ask the right questions—can help predict the future incidence of voluntary quits. Such predictions can help your company forecast (and manage) staffing levels and alert your company about potential turnover problems. In addition, incumbent surveys diagnose causes of voluntary turnover more accurately than do informal impressions of supervisors of why people quit or exit interviews by human resources managers. For example, turnover scholars have long known that managers' perceptions of why employees quit often do not match employees' actual reasons for leaving (see Chapter 9). Moreover, some firms rely on exit interviews. Yet, exiting employees are often reluctant to state their true motives for fear of "burning their bridges." If your firm misdiagnoses the reasons why employees leave, your firm may introduce inappropriate or ineffective interventions to curb turnover (addressing the wrong causes). Given surveys' potential benefits, in the following sections, we highlight survey questions that can help predict turnover and diagnose its causes, how to interpret survey results, and the survey administration process.

Survey Questions: Measuring Turnover Predictors and Causes

Over the decades, turnover researchers have identified many factors that forecast or cause voluntary resignations (Brayfield & Crockett, 1955; Carsten & Spector, 1987; Cotton & Tuttle, 1986; Griffeth et al., 2000; Hom & Griffeth, 1995; Mathieu & Zajac, 1990; Mobley, 1982; Muchinsky & Tuttle, 1979; Price, 1977; Steel & Ovalle, 1984; Tett & Meyer, 1993; Vroom, 1964). Generally, scholars use survey methodology to uncover these factors and to estimate how strongly they affect turnover. We next review the turnover literature to pinpoint leading turnover causes and to discuss a theoretical framework that pulls together these diverse findings on turnover determinants (Hom & Griffeth, 1995; Lee & Mitchell, 1994).

Nonetheless, we caution that these empirical generalizations may not apply—or apply to the same degree—to your turnover problems. We thus suggest the use of customizing survey questions and statistical analyses of survey data to identify the relevant turnover causes for your company. Still, existing research and theory can provide broad guidance on which turnover causes to consider for survey assessment. To illustrate, job dissatisfaction may drive job turnover in most settings and occupations, but working conditions that are dissatisfying likely would vary across different circumstances. Rather than standard scales, survey questions often must be customized to target those idiosyncratic workplace features.

Diagnostic Model of Turnover Causes

After reviewing the turnover literature, Hom and Griffeth (1995) developed a general framework to summarize the numerous turnover causes documented by research studies over the years. Exhibit 6.1 shows an abbreviated

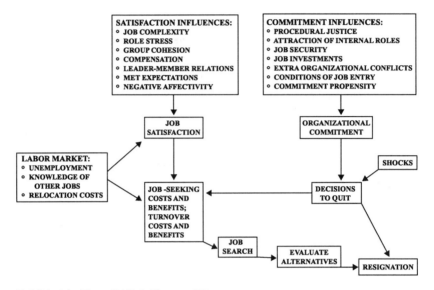

Exhibit 6.1. Hom-Griffeth Theory of Turnover

version. In their view, employees who become dissatisfied with their jobs or lose their organizational commitment form decisions to leave. Some employees leave soon after making this decision, whereas others undertake a job search if they believe that quitting is not costly to them and that the prospects for employment elsewhere are good. Job seekers then solicit alternative jobs, and, if they obtain alternatives that are superior to their present job, they will quit.

Our framework also identifies various causal antecedents of job satisfaction and organizational commitment. (For clarity's sake, the diagram assigns each determinant with a particular attitude, but these influences likely shape both attitudes.) Specifically, Hom and Griffeth (1995) contend that repetitive and meaningless work (job complexity; see Chapter 2), role stress (conflicting, vague, or excessive work role requirements), conflicts with coworkers, inadequate compensation, poor working relationships with superiors (weak leader-member relations), unmet expectations (initial expectations not fulfilled at work), and negative affectivity (personality disposition to view the job and oneself negatively) create job dissatisfaction. Similarly, inequitable distributions of rewards and benefits (unfair procedural justice), job insecurity, and conflicts between work and nonwork roles (inability to participate in family or other outside pursuits due to work demands and scheduling) undermine feelings of commitment to the organization. By comparison, expectations of securing better positions inside the firm (attractive internal roles), job investments (accumulated pensions and seniority benefits), commitment-enhancing conditions of the original decision to join the firm (a free, irrevocable, and public job choice), and a personal inclination to commit to the firm all strengthen company commitment.

Recently, a more comprehensive theory (which subsumes portions of our model) suggests that traditional thinking overlooks nonattitudinal causes—that many people quit even when they are not dissatisfied (Lee & Mitchell, 1994). Campion (1991) similarly faulted traditional attitudinal theories for their inability to account for turnover due to "unavoidable" reasons (e.g., childbirth) that organizations cannot "control." To address this oversight, this unfolding model advances the notion of *shocks,* jarring events that stimulate thoughts of quitting. Shocks are personal (e.g., pregnancy, acceptance into graduate school), organizational (e.g., hospital changes its nursing philosophy), or external (e.g., unsolicited job offer or inquiry) events that can trigger exits (Lee, Mitchell, Holtom, McDaniel, & Hill, 1999; Lee, Mitchell, Wise, & Fireman, 1996). Shocks are not necessarily unexpected or negative (e.g., quitting to bear and raise children). Given this latest development, we revise the Hom and Griffeth model to include shocks as another determinant of withdrawal cognitions (or quit decisions).

Decisions To Quit

Accumulated evidence concludes that the single best predictor of turnover is an employee's decision to quit the job (Griffeth et al., 2000; Hom & Griffeth, 1995; Steel & Ovalle, 1984; Tett & Meyer, 1993). Exhibit 6.2 reports two sample questions validated by Hom and Griffeth (1991) for assessing quit decisions. Using data from Hom and Kinicki's (2000) survey of retail store personnel, Exhibit 6.3 displays a frequency distribution plotting the percentage of employees answering the first intention question differently. This plot shows that 6.2% of this workforce planned to quit their job within the coming year, and another 16.7% were uncertain about their plans.

To illustrate predictive efficacy of measured quit decisions, we plotted actual turnover rates for employees answering this intention question differently. After the survey, Hom and Kinicki (2000) tracked retail store employees

Instructions: Describe your plans about staying with or leaving this organization. For each question, circle a number corresponding to your response.

- I intend to leave this organization within a year:
  1. Definitely not
  2. Probably not
  3. Uncertain
  4. Probably yes
  5. Definitely yes

- What are the chances that you will leave this organization within a year?
  1. No chance
  2. 25% chance
  3. 50% chance
  4. 75% chance
  5. 100% chance

Exhibit 6.2. Decisions To Quit

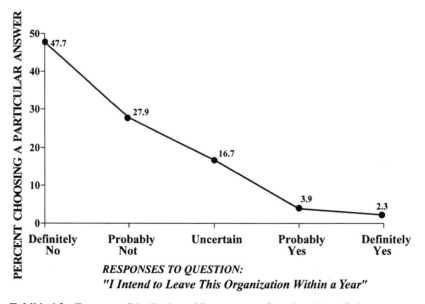

Exhibit 6.3. Frequency Distribution of Responses to Question About Quit
Intentions

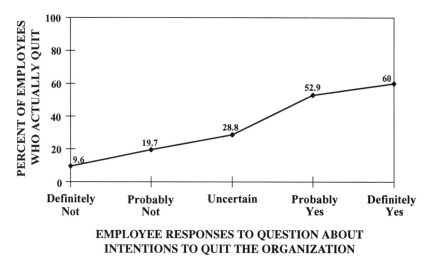

**EMPLOYEE RESPONSES TO QUESTION ABOUT
INTENTIONS TO QUIT THE ORGANIZATION**

Exhibit 6.4. Prediction of Actual Turnover by Intentions To Quit

for 6 months to determine who would actually resign. Exhibit 6.4 shows how quit intentions can predict turnover. Specifically, 60% of the retail store employees who answered a "Definitely Yes" to this question resigned 6 months later. In contrast, 9.6% of those answering "Definitely Not" to that question left. It is interesting that another 28.8% who were unsure about quitting actually did quit.

Thus, your survey should include measures of turnover decisions to ascertain future turnover rates in your company. You can use quit intentions as a surrogate for turnover (given its strong prediction of actual turnover) and perform statistical analyses on survey responses to ascertain which factors differentiate between intended stayers and leavers in your workforce. Such statistical analyses can identify which factors "predict" and motivate intentions to quit (and, by extension, future turnover). After all, it is not feasible for surveys administered by your human resources staff to predict actual turnover. Your surveys ordinarily would not ask employees to identify themselves on the questionnaire. Otherwise, they would hesitate to answer candidly if they knew their answers were not anonymous (invalidating the survey). Because you cannot match employees' surveys to personnel records about their future turnover actions, you are not able to predict actual quits from survey responses. Therefore, we recommend using measured quit intentions as a proxy for actual turnover and using your survey to predict quit intentions. As turnover research shows, employees who express strong intentions to leave eventually do leave.

In what follows, we describe how statistical comparisons based on employee answers to questions help identify relevant turnover causes in your organization. Our illustration uses a question from Exhibit 6.2 that assesses employees' plan to quit within a year. However, your intention questions might specify different time periods depending on your firm's needs. For example, a manufacturing firm might be concerned about maintaining the current staffing level for the next 2 years to meet projected demands for its products during that time; thus, this firm would survey employees' plans to leave during the next 2 years. Or your firm might be interested in whether new employees stay employed for the first 3 years of employment so that the firm can recoup its expensive investment in new employees (e.g., training costs); thus, this firm would query newcomers, asking them whether they intend to quit within the next 3 years. We note that stated intentions are less effective in predicting turnover that transpire in the distant future because people often change their minds about staying or leaving over a long time period (Griffeth et al., 2000; Mobley, Griffeth, Hand, & Meglino, 1979).

Job Satisfaction

Your surveys should assess employees' feelings of job satisfaction, a key turnover determinant. Your surveys can measure overall level of job satisfaction or satisfaction with particular facets of the job (e.g., pay, coworkers). We recommend measuring facet satisfaction to diagnose which specific features of the work environment produce dissatisfaction (for an example of a facet satisfaction scale, see Spector, 1997). After diagnosing the sources of discontent, you can implement certain remedies to remove those dissatisfying job aspects. Moreover, assessing facet satisfaction is an economical way to assess the satisfaction influences described in the Hom and Griffeth (1995) model (e.g., job complexity, compensation).

First, you should carry out a preliminary investigation into the particular sources of dissatisfaction (and satisfaction) that pertain to your workplace, using focus groups or open-ended surveys with a representative sample of employees. Though somewhat biased, exit interviews with exiting employees also may disclose dissatisfying job features that produce turnover. These sources likely go beyond those enumerated in our theoretical framework, which was designed to represent a generic rather than exhaustive taxonomy of

Instructions: How satisfied or dissatisfied are you with various facets of your job? For example, if you feel satisfied with your "chances for recognition," then circle *4* or *5*. Circle a number for each job facet.

Job Facets	Very Dissatisfied	Dissatisfied	Neither Satisfied Nor Dissatisfied	Satisfied	Very Satisfied
1. Chances for recognition	1	2	3	4	5
2. Training programs	1	2	3	4	5
3. Health care benefits	1	2	3	4	5
4. Paperwork	1	2	3	4	5
5. Promotional opportunities	1	2	3	4	5

Exhibit 6.5. Job Satisfaction

turnover causes. For example, suppose you interview a group of employees, asking them to mention satisfying and dissatisfying aspects about their work. Suppose they suggest that they or their colleagues are unhappy with chances for recognition, training programs, health care benefits, promotional opportunities, and paperwork duties. You can write survey questions based on their comments. Exhibit 6.5 shows how you would list each job facet as a separate question, accompanied by a numerical rating scale to gauge satisfaction levels. This scale defines each satisfaction level numerically and verbally. Thus, the lowest satisfaction level is a 1 (*very dissatisfied*), and the highest satisfaction level is 5 (*very satisfied*).

After surveying employees, you could generate a chart to profile satisfaction levels for different job facets. That is, you would average numerical responses for each question, computing a mean satisfaction score for that job facet. More specifically, you would "score" each employee's response to the satisfaction scale, assigning a 1 if an employee reported that he or she was very dissatisfied, a 2 if he or she was dissatisfied, and so forth. After scoring employees' answers to a particular question, you would average their scored responses. This group average would represent the level of overall satisfaction with a particular job aspect. Exhibit 6.6 reports an abbreviated satisfaction profile from a survey of hospital nurses (Hom & Griffeth, 1991). This profile discloses that nurses were most unhappy with their parking accommodations

Exhibit 6.6. Nurses' Satisfaction With Job Aspects

(average rating is 2.5 out of a 5-point satisfaction scale) and paycheck (mean rating is 2.3).

   Although revealing, simply analyzing overall satisfaction levels for different job facets is insufficient. One also must compare satisfaction levels between employees intending to stay and those intending to leave. In other words, you should divide survey participants into two subgroups based on their answers to a question about quit intentions. Thus, one group would represent "intended leavers," who answered "Probably Yes" or "Definitely Yes" to this question about their plans to leave (see Exhibit 6.2), and another group would comprise "intended stayers"—those answering "Definitely Not" or "Probably Not." For each subgroup, you would compute mean satisfaction levels for the different job aspects. You would then compare the subgroups to determine whether their feelings about various job facets are different or alike.

   Again borrowing from Hom and Griffeth's (1991) work, Exhibit 6.7 illustrates how nurses planning to leave felt more dissatisfaction with certain job features than did those intending to stay. This group comparison is essential, for it detects the main turnover causes for your firm—identifying which attitudes differentiate between intended stayers and leavers. For instance, Exhibit 6.7 reveals that both intended stayers and leavers felt similarly dissatisfied with parking. Thus, parking dissatisfaction did not represent a potential turnover cause because it did not distinguish between prospective stayers and leavers. By contrast, pay dissatisfaction is far worse among intended leavers than among intended stayers, indicating that this attitude is a potential determinant of future turnover. Given this finding, raising pay (and pay satisfac-

Exhibit 6.7. Satisfaction With Job Aspects: Differences Between Intended Stayers and Leavers

tion) would promote nursing retention; improving parking accommodations would not. In summary, group comparisons—locating which attitudes differ between intended stayers and leavers—reveal the particular attitudes driving turnover. Simply identifying which job facets are most dissatisfying for the entire workforce is not enough (though intended leavers often express more dissatisfaction with such job facets than do intended stayers).

Nonetheless, we must go beyond eyeball inspection of group differences. One also must perform statistical tests (e.g., *t* tests) to determine precisely if apparent satisfaction differences are statistically significant. Statistical tests take into account not only the difference in group means but also group overlap—the extent to which responses from members in one group resemble responses from members in the other group. For instance, charts in Exhibit 6.8 depict frequency distributions for how intended stayers and leavers answered a question about satisfaction with a job feature. In both charts, frequency distributions for both groups overlap: Some stayers express less satisfaction than most leavers, while some leavers express more satisfaction than many stayers. Yet, the top chart features a significant group difference in satisfaction, and the bottom chart shows a nonsignificant difference. Though mean differences between groups are identical in both charts, frequency distributions overlap

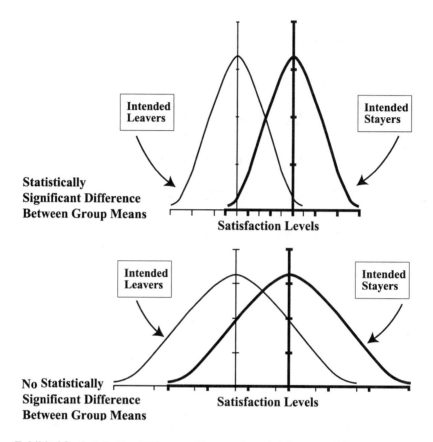

Exhibit 6.8. Satisfaction Differences Between Intended Stayers and Leavers

more in the bottom chart than in the top chart. More leavers express high job satisfaction—feeling like stayers—in the bottom chart than in the top chart. As a consequence, the group difference in the bottom chart is not statistically different.

Going back to our running example, *t* tests disclose that satisfaction with weekends worked, frequency of shift rotation, and pay statistically varied between nurses deciding to quit and those deciding to stay employed (see Exhibit 6.7). Unless the hospital improves these specific conditions, nurses unhappy with weekend work, shift rotation, or pay will likely quit. By comparison, intended stayers and leavers felt the same way about parking, number of evenings worked, and tuition assistance; these attitudes are *not* turnover causes. In conclusion, you should carry out statistical comparisons between group means to determine if those differences are real or illusory.

Organizational Commitment

Besides job satisfaction, your survey should assess organizational commitment—or employee identification with the organization's goals and values (Mathieu & Zajac, 1990; Mowday, Porter, & Steers, 1982). Many studies affirm that organizational commitment is an attitude distinct from job satisfaction and that it separately influences turnover (Hom & Griffeth, 1995; Tett & Meyer, 1993). That is, employees may dislike their particular job duties (feeling dissatisfaction) but still remain if they feel committed to the firm (Mowday et al., 1982).

Many definitions and measures of commitment exist, but we favor a conception advanced by Meyer and Allen and their associates (Meyer & Allen, 1997; Meyer, Allen, & Gellatly, 1990; Meyer, Allen, & Smith, 1993) known as *affective commitment*. They conceive this attitude as positive feelings of identification with, attachment to, and involvement in the organization. Drawing from recent psychometric work, Exhibit 6.9 displays questions for assessing this affective commitment (Ko, Price, & Mueller, 1997; Meyer et al., 1993). After employees answer these questions, you can compute an overall commitment score by summing their responses to each question. This score would range from 6 to 30, indicating whether she or he possesses very weak or very strong company commitment.

Although commitment predicts turnover in most occupations (Mathieu & Zajac, 1990; Tett & Meyer, 1993), you should check if commitment levels are indeed weaker for intended leavers than for intended stayers in your workforce (and thus if commitment is a relevant turnover cause). Again, we borrow data from the Hom and Griffeth (1991) study of nursing quits to illustrate this group comparison. That survey also assessed nurses' commitment to their hospital. We split the nursing sample into intended leavers and stayers (based on whether they planned to quit) and computed average commitment levels for these groups. Exhibit 6.10 shows that intended leavers felt less committed to the hospital than did intended stayers, and a statistical test corroborated that those dissimilar commitment levels are significantly different. Thus, this hospital must implement steps to promote greater identification with their mission and goals to reduce potential nursing exits.

Instructions: Please indicate your agreement or disagreement with the following statements about your feeling toward your organization. For example, if you agree with "I would be very happy to spend the rest of my career with this organization," then circle the number 4.

	Strongly Disagree	Disagree	Neither Agree Nor Disagree	Agree	Strongly Agree
1. I would be very happy to spend the rest of my career with this organization.	1	2	3	4	5
2. I really feel as if this organization's problems are my own.	1	2	3	4	5
3. I feel a strong sense of belonging to my organization.	1	2	3	4	5
4. I feel emotionally attached to this organization	1	2	3	4	5
5. This organization has a great deal of personal meaning for me.	1	2	3	4	5
6. I feel like part of the family at my organization.	1	2	3	4	5

Exhibit 6.9. Organizational Commitment

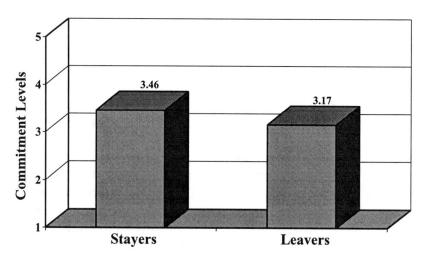

Exhibit 6.10. Differences in Organizational Commitment Between Intended Stayers and Leavers

Instructions: How will your employment improve during the next 12 months? Rate the chances that each aspect of your job will change for the better. For example, if you expect higher pay during the next 12 months, then circle the number 5 for "100% chance."

Job Improvements	No Chance	25% Chance	50% Chance	75% Chance	100% Chance
1. More bonuses	1	2	3	4	5
2. Better supervision	1	2	3	4	5
3. Better store location	1	2	3	4	5
4. Acquire more training	1	2	3	4	5
5. Better Coworkers	1	2	3	4	5

Exhibit 6.11. Job Attraction

Job Attraction

Many turnover theorists say that job attraction or employees' expectation of future improvements in their job or future attainment of other desirable positions inside the organization can deter turnover (Aquino et al., 1997; Carson, Carson, Griffeth, & Steel, 1993; Mobley, 1982a). Therefore, dissatisfied employees may not relinquish their job if they foresee improving workplace conditions or anticipate promotions or transfers to better jobs. Thus, your survey should capture job attraction, which may influence quit decisions.

To assess job attraction, we recommend carrying out focus group interviews or open-ended surveys with employees. Have them describe their expectations for how working conditions might improve in the coming months or years—what their future with the company might hold. Ask them how their job and career prospects might worsen. After identifying these expectations, your survey can include questions that query employee expectations about those job features. For a concrete illustration, we refer back to the retail store survey of Hom and Kinicki (2000). Preliminary interviews with employees uncovered a set of salient prospective job improvements, which then were represented as job-attraction questions in the survey (Hom & Kinicki, 2000). Exhibit 6.11 shows representative questions from that survey, which pair each potential job change with a 5-point probability scale.

As before, we recommend that you contrast job-attraction perceptions between intended stayers and leavers to identify which expected workplace improvements can deter potential exits. Thus, you would use employee

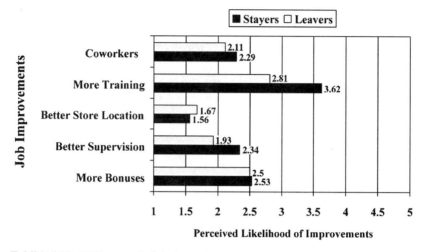

Exhibit 6.12. Differences in Job Attraction Between Intended Stayers and Leavers

answers to the intention question in Exhibit 6.2 to divide survey participants into intended stayers and leavers and compare their expectations for future change in various job aspects. For each group, you would average ratings for the questions about expected workplace improvements. Using the Hom and Kinicki (2000) retail store survey data, Exhibit 6.12 shows how job attraction varied between prospective stayers and leavers. Intended stayers and leavers shared similar outlooks about anticipated changes in coworker relationships, supervision, store locale, and bonuses. Therefore, these expectations would not affect turnover. According to statistical tests, however, the prospect for better training was a potential turnover deterrent. Intended leavers saw fewer opportunities for additional training than did intended stayers. Consequently, expected job training deters quits in this retail store workforce, and broadening training would enhance retention.

Perceived Job Alternatives

Turnover experts long have argued that job opportunities may induce even satisfied employees into surrendering their current job (March & Simon, 1958; Mobley, Griffeth, et al., 1979; Steel, 1996; Steel & Griffeth, 1989). Thus, it is vital that you understand and measure employee impressions of the job market. Nonetheless, there is considerable debate about how to define and operationalize those perceptions (Griffeth & Hom, 1988a; Steel, 1996). Many turnover scholars advocate assessing employee perceptions of overall job availability in their community or occupation (Price & Mueller, 1986; Steel, 1996), whereas others prescribe assessing workers' general impressions of the overall attractiveness of other work alternatives (Farrell & Rusbult, 1981; Youngblood, Mobley, & Meglino, 1983).

Both approaches have merit. However, measuring employees' perceptions of the attractiveness of specific alternative jobs and their chances of securing those jobs may yield the most practical information, helping employers to benchmark against labor supply competitors (Griffeth & Hom, 1988a; Hom & Griffeth, 1991). Traditional assessments are imprecise, simply collecting global impressions of generic alternatives. After all, leavers quit employment for specific jobs elsewhere (Hulin, Roznowski, & Hachiya, 1985). Therefore, assessing your workforce's impressions of particular employers will clarify how your firm stands relative to competitors who might lure away your workforce. We note that such competitors might reside outside your industry and geographic locale.

To illustrate, we designed a measure for nurses working in a Cleveland, Ohio, hospital (Hom & Griffeth, 1991). We first asked nursing recruiters and administrators from this hospital to name local employers who hire away their nurses. Exhibit 6.13 lists major hospitals in the Cleveland area and a format for gauging employee perceptions of those workplaces. For employment alternatives, we had nurses rate the desirability of a job there and their chances of getting a job there. According to the expectancy theory of motivation, individuals choose to pursue a job if they believe the job is attractive and they think they can obtain this job (Van Eerde & Thierry, 1996; Wanous, Keon, & Latack, 1983). Exhibit 6.13 also shows hypothetical ratings by a respondent. A job at Cleveland Clinic is evaluated as desirable and highly attainable, whereas St. Luke's hospital is considered both undesirable and unattainable. Expectancy theorists contend that job applicants avoid undesirable, attainable jobs or desirable, unattainable jobs. Rather, job seekers most strive for jobs that are attractive *and* achievable. Our hypothetical respondent would thus prefer a job at the Cleveland Clinic than one at St. Luke's.

After collecting both sets of ratings from each employee, you would multiply desirability and likelihood ratings for each alternative job. This product is known as the *motivational force,* reflecting strength of an employee's attraction to a job (Hom, 1980). Exhibit 6.14 shows the force scores for the Cleveland jobs based on the hypothetical respondent's ratings from Exhibit 6.13.

Other Nursing Jobs in Cleveland Area	DESIRABILITY OF OTHER JOBS					CHANCES OF OBTAINING OTHER JOBS				
	Indicate how desirable you think it would be to work in each job by circling a number for each job.					Rate your chances that you can obtain each job by circling a number for each job.				
	Very Undesirable	Undesirable	Neither	Desirable	Very Desirable	No Chance	25% Chance	50% Chance	75% Chance	100% Chance
CLEVELAND CLINIC	1	2	3	4	**(5)**	1	2	3	4	**(5)**
UNIVERSITY HOSPITAL	1	2	3	4	**(5)**	1	2	**(3)**	4	5
SINAI HOSPITAL	1	**(2)**	3	4	5	1	**(2)**	3	4	5
ST. LUKES	**(1)**	2	3	4	5	**(1)**	2	3	4	5
VETERANS ADMINISTRATION	1	**(2)**	3	4	5	1	2	3	4	**(5)**
KAISER	1	2	**(3)**	4	5	1	2	**(3)**	4	5
ST. VINCENT CHARITY	1	**(2)**	3	4	5	1	**(2)**	3	4	5
PARMA HOSPITAL	**(1)**	2	3	4	5	1	2	3	**(4)**	5
LAKEWOOD HOSPITAL	1	**(2)**	3	4	5	1	2	**(3)**	4	5
FAIRVIEW GENERAL	1	2	3	**(4)**	5	1	2	3	4	**(5)**
NURSING EMPLOYMENT AGENCY	1	2	**(3)**	4	5	1	**(2)**	3	4	5
NURSING HOME	1	2	3	4	**(5)**	1	2	3	**(4)**	5
DOCTOR'S OFFICE	1	**(2)**	3	4	5	1	2	**(3)**	4	5
NURSING POSITION NOT LISTED (Please Fill In and Rate):	1	2	**(3)**	4	5	1	2	3	**(4)**	5

Exhibit 6.13. Perceptions of Specific Employers

Thus, this hypothetical respondent would most pursue jobs at the Cleveland Clinic, Fairview General, and a Nursing Home: They are both attractive and attainable. By contrast, the respondent would less likely pursue hospital positions at St. Luke's, Sinai, St. Vincent Charity, and Parma; their motivational force scores are low. Furthermore, this respondent will shun employment at University Hospital and Veterans Administration. The former job is desirable (rating = 5) but difficult to attain (rating = 3), whereas the latter job is attainable (rating = 5) but undesirable (rating = 2).

Here too, we recommend comparing perceptions of alternatives between intended stayers and leavers to identify which employers may potentially lure your workforce away. Thus, if both groups regard a particular job as attractive, that job will not necessarily induce turnover. Only a job that is viewed more positively by intended leavers than by intended stayers can entice employees to quit. Using Hom and Griffeth's (1991) survey data, Exhibit 6.15 compares motivational force scores for Cleveland hospitals between nurses deciding to stay and those deciding to quit. After computing hospital force scores for all

MOTIVATIONAL FORCE SCORES
Compute a Motivational Force Score for Each Job by
Multiplying the Desirability Score by the Likelihood Score

Other Nursing Jobs in Cleveland Area	Rating of the Job's Desirability	Rating of the Chances of Attaining the Job	Motivational Force = Desirability of Job × Likelihood of Attaining Job
Cleveland Clinic	5	5	25
University Hospital	5	3	15
Sinai Hospital	2	2	4
St. Luke's	1	1	1
Veterans Administration	2	5	10
Kaiser	3	3	9
St. Vincent Charity	2	2	4
Parma Hospital	1	4	4
Lakewood Hospital	2	3	6
Fairview General	4	5	20
Nursing Employment Agency	3	2	6
Nursing Home	5	4	20
Doctor's Office	2	3	6
Nursing position not listed (Please fill in and rate):	3	4	12

Exhibit 6.14. Relative Attractiveness of Different Employers

nurses, we averaged force scores for each hospital for each group of nurses. *T* tests on group differences in hospital force scores indicate that prospective leavers considered a nursing employment agency, St. Vincent Charity, and University Hospital more favorably than did prospective stayers. Their motivational force scores for these jobs were statistically larger than those from intended stayers. In sum, these places of employment are potential future employers of nurses from the surveyed hospital. By comparison, intended leavers and stayers shared similar impressions of all other alternatives.

At this point, you might further investigate why your employees view some jobs as more desirable than others. According to expectancy theory,

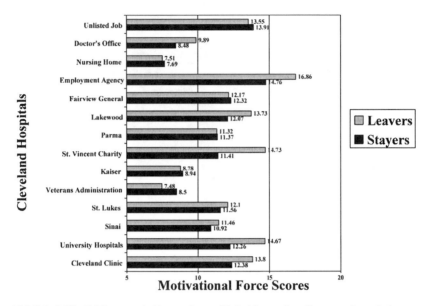

Exhibit 6.15. Differences in Perceptions of Job Alternatives Between Intended
Stayers and Leavers

employees or job applicants deem desirable those jobs that provide valued
rewards and benefits and undesirable those jobs that do not offer those rewards
(Van Eerde & Thierry, 1996; Wanous et al., 1983). Exhibit 6.16 shows how
you might identify the bases for job desirability. You would list a set of job
rewards and benefits that are desirable to your workforce in the left column
(extracted from prior interviews or open-ended surveys). Then, employees
would rate their chances of achieving those rewards (perceived "instrumentality" of a job for work outcomes) from other employers, using a 5-point probability scale. Using our running example from Hom and Griffeth's (1991)
work, nurses who believe that Cleveland Clinic furnishes good pay and fringe
benefits would circle the numbers 4 or 5, corresponding to a strong perceived
likelihood of obtaining those outcomes from that employer. However, they
also may believe that this hospital will not offer a good shift rotation policy
and would express this belief by circling the numbers 1 or 2 (indicating poor
chances of getting that outcome). Using this format, you can determine why
certain employers are perceived as desirable or undesirable by your workforce
and how you can ensure that positions in your company are more desirable
than those at your competitors.

What Are the Chances That You Can Obtain These Job Rewards from Other Jobs? Rate the Following Organizations in Terms of Your Chances of Getting These Outcomes by Using the Following Scale:

NO CHANCE	25% CHANCE	50% CHANCE	75% CHANCE	100% CHANCE
1	2	3	4	5

JOB REWARDS	Cleveland Clinic	University Hospital	Sinai Hospital	St. Lukes	Veterans Administration	Kaiser Hospital	St. Vincent Charity	Parma Hospital	Lakewood Hospital	Fairview General	Employment Agency	Nursing Home	Doctor's Office	Unlisted Nursing Job
GOOD PAY & FRINGE BENEFITS	12345	12345	12345	12345	12345	12345	12345	12345	12345	12345	12345	12345	12345	12345
LEARNING NEW SKILLS & PROCEDURES	12345	12345	12345	12345	12345	12345	12345	12345	12345	12345	12345	12345	12345	12345
WORKING IN A SPECIALTY OF YOUR CHOICE	12345	12345	12345	12345	12345	12345	12345	12345	12345	12345	12345	12345	12345	12345
HAVING A GOOD SHIFT ROTATION POLICY	12345	12345	12345	12345	12345	12345	12345	12345	12345	12345	12345	12345	12345	12345
FREEDOM TO DETERMINE OWN WORK METHODS	12345	12345	12345	12345	12345	12345	12345	12345	12345	12345	12345	12345	12345	12345

Exhibit 6.16. Perceived Instrumentality of Jobs for Work Rewards

Interrole Conflict

Turnover scholars are beginning to acknowledge that interrole conflict—the extent to which work demands, travel, and schedules interfere with participation in outside pursuits, such as family duties or schooling—can prompt employees to quit (Dalton, Hill, & Ramsay, 1997; Greenhaus et al., 1997; Hom & Kinicki, 2000; Netermeyer, Boles, & McMurrian, 1996). Indeed, experienced conflict between occupational and home lives may increasingly induce quits as working mothers, single parents, dual-income families, and families with elder-care duties increasingly populate the workforce (Frone, Yardley, & Markel, 1997; Netermeyer et al., 1996). On top of expanding family responsibilities, American workers are also working more hours (Hochschild, 1997; Lardner, 1999). Not surprisingly, a national survey reveals that nearly half the workforce (45%) has changed jobs to spend more time with their families ("Workers Switch Jobs," 2000). Moreover, interrole conflict is more common than previously imagined; a 1990 Los Angeles poll reported that 40% of fathers would quit to raise children if they could (Ganster & Thomas, 1995). Apart from work-family interference, even single, childless employees are frustrated by the invasion of work into their personal lives (such as recreation or community activities) (Babin & Boles, 1998).

Instructions: To what extent does your job get in your way of participating in the following activities? Please circle an answer for each activity.

Outside Activities	Never	Sometimes	Often	Always
1. Dating	1	2	3	4
2. Hobbies	1	2	3	4
3. Church events	1	2	3	4
4. Keeping in shape	1	2	3	4
5. Volunteer work	1	2	3	4
6. Education	1	2	3	4
7. Household chores	1	2	3	4
8. Other part-time work	1	2	3	4

Exhibit 6.17. Conflicts Between Work and Outside Activities

Given the significance of interrole conflict, your survey should assess the extent and nature of this conflict. First, carry out focus group interviews or open-ended surveys, asking a representative sample of employees to identify which kinds of outside roles they value (e.g., parenting, church duties). What roles are most salient to your workforce? Once these roles are identified, you can write questions for the survey to assess how much the job interferes with participating in these external pursuits (using a frequency scale). As illustration, Exhibit 6.17 reports sample questionnaire items from Hom and Kinicki's (2000) study of turnover among retail store personnel.

Here again, you should contrast interrole conflicts between intended stayers and leavers to determine which form of interrole conflict initiates turnover. By learning with which external roles the job interferes, your organization can craft an appropriate response. Thus, the remedy for addressing work-family conflict may be different from that for work-school conflict. Using Hom and Kinicki's survey data, we computed each group's average level of interrole conflict with each outside activity. Exhibit 6.18 shows how various interrole conflicts differed between intended stayers and leavers. Follow-up statistical tests revealed significant group differences for all forms of interrole conflicts, excepting household chores. Compared with intended stayers,

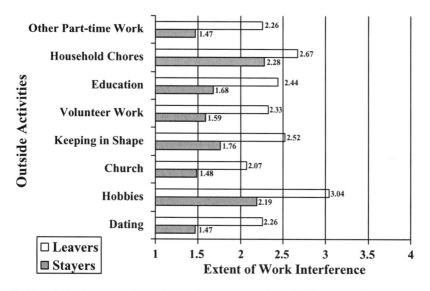

Exhibit 6.18. Differing Interrole Conflicts Between Intended Stayers and Leavers

intended leavers reported that their job duties interfered with various external activities. Should these conflicts continue, they are prone to switch to another job (or even leave the workforce) to meet those external demands (e.g., child rearing) or avocations (community service, schooling).

Costs of Quitting

Finally, we suggest that your survey measure employees' perceptions about the consequences of quitting the present job, notably turnover costs. Many turnover thinkers argue that employees—even if dissatisfied—will not exit a company if they must forfeit substantial personal investments (such as pension benefits or seniority rights) (Farrell & Rusbult, 1981; Hom & Griffeth, 1991; Mobley, 1977). Here, too, we recommend that you carry out focus group interviews or open-ended surveys with members of your working population to ascertain the salient costs and benefits of quitting. Once identified, these turnover consequences can be introduced into a survey format, such as that shown in Exhibit 6.19 (from the survey of Hom and Kinicki, 2000).

As before, you should compare perceptions of turnover consequences between intended stayers and leavers by computing their average ratings of

Instructions: What are the chances that each of the following events will occur if you quit your job? For example, if you believe there is little or no chance that quitting your job would reduce your stress, then circle "No chance." However, if you believe that it is very likely that quitting would reduce your stress, then circle "75% Chance" or "100% Chance."

Consequences Of Quitting	No Chance	25% Chance	50% Chance	75% Chance	100% Chance
1. Quitting my job reduces my mental and physical stress	1	2	3	4	5
2. Quitting my job increases time for my family or personal activities	1	2	3	4	5
3. Quitting my job leaves me unemployed for a long period of time	1	2	3	4	5
4. Quitting my job causes me to lose benefits I earned during my employment	1	2	3	4	5
5. Quitting my job prevents me from returning here for work	1	2	3	4	5

Exhibit 6.19. Costs and Benefits of Quitting

the chances of these turnover consequences occurring (if they should leave). Borrowing Hom and Kinicki's (2000) data, Exhibit 6.20 illustrates how perceptions of turnover's costs and benefits vary between stayers and leavers. As this comparison indicates, prospective leavers saw greater advantages for leaving than did prospective stayers (statistical tests confirmed that these mean differences are statistically significant). Leavers believed that abandoning their present employment would increase their personal and family time as well as lower their work stress. They also anticipated fewer costs associated with turnover. Unlike intended stayers, intended leavers did not believe that bad outcomes, such as losing fringe benefits and being prohibited from returning to the firm for work, would happen if they left. These results imply that a company might lower turnover by making quitting costly for employees. For example, a firm might introduce employment contracts invoking penalty clauses (written into the contracts) when premature quits occur (such as wage repayment; Lee & Maurer, 1997; Mobley et al., 1979), withhold a promised retention bonus if the employee quits before his or her "tour of duty" expires, tie more financial rewards to job seniority (e.g., longevity pay; Hom & Griffeth, 1995), or ban former employees from regaining employment.

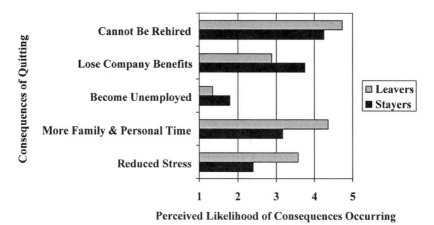

Exhibit 6.20. Differences in Perceived Consequences of Quitting Between Intended Stayers and Leavers

Shocks

Recent research by Lee et al. (1996, 1999) have shown how shocks can prompt employees to quit, even those who are satisfied with their job. Though the term *shocks* implies unpredictability, we believe that employers can assess their influence on employee turnover and forecast the extent of shock-induced resignations. Specifically, research on life stress events suggests a means to capture shocks (Bhagat, McQuaid, Lindholm, & Segovis, 1985). To illustrate, Bhagat et al. (1985) adapted Holmes and Rahe's (1967) Schedule of Recent Experiences to assess various positive and negative events at work and off work. Thus, employees would identify from a checklist of 83 events (e.g., "suffered a financial loss," "broke off a friendship," "trouble with in-laws") that they had recently experienced and rate its impact (positive or negative) on their lives. Bhagat et al. demonstrated that employees who experienced many negative job events intended to quit. We note that those who experienced many positive personal life events also planned to quit.

Refining this approach, Griffeth and Fink (1992) designed a comprehensive inventory that focused on work and nonwork events that have the most potential for instigating thoughts of quitting. Exhibit 6.21 reports sample questions from their "turnover events" inventory. In a pilot test, they asked retail store employees to complete this inventory, rating how often they experienced these (54) events during the past 6 months. Using another question of quit intentions, they split the sample into prospective leavers and stayers and

In The Last 6 Months, I Experienced	Did Not Occur	Seldom	Sometimes	Often	Very Often
1. Sexual harassment on the job	0	1	2	3	4
2. Health concerns, experienced child-birth, or cared for an elderly relative	0	1	2	3	4
3. An increase in workload, duties, or hours without corresponding increase in pay or benefits.	0	1	2	3	4
4. Better external employment opportunity	0	1	2	3	4
5. An "arbitrary" change in rules, policies, or standards	0	1	2	3	4
6. My benefits were inadequately or recently cut	0	1	2	3	4

SOURCE: © Copyright by Rodger Griffeth and Laurence Fink, 1992.

Exhibit 6.21. Experienced Shocks

calculated average event-frequency scores for these groups. Exhibit 6.22 (p. 144) shows how experienced shocks varied between groups. Stayers and leavers have similar but infrequent encounters with health concerns or sexual harassment. Yet, statistical tests suggest that leavers experienced compensation declines or inadequate pay for expanding workloads, being passed over for promotions, conflicts with superiors, public criticism and abuse from supervisors, arbitrary changes in policies and rules, and better employment prospects elsewhere more than did stayers. In this workforce, these particular shocks initiate thoughts of quitting.

Using this procedure, organizations can forecast shock-induced exits and take steps to reverse the effects of shocks (e.g., restore compensation cuts, have ready a system of counteroffers when employees receive unsolicited job offers) (Lee et al., 1996). Other shocks (e.g., pregnancy, geographic relocation to follow a spouse) are not so easily controlled by the company (often termed *unavoidable* turnover; Campion, 1991). Still, the ability to forecast unavoidable quits can help companies limit their disruptive effects. Employers can have more lead time to recruit and prepare replacements for upcoming job vacancies (Lee et al., 1996). In other works, corporations might adapt to such inevitable, shock-initiated turnover by focusing on recruitment rather than retention (Cappelli, 2000).

Using Surveys To Manage Dysfunctional Turnover

Thus far, our discussion has considered how surveys can help manage overall turnover. However, you can "fine-tune" this methodology for controlling dysfunctional turnover—that is, job exits among employees whose skills are difficult to replace or who are superior contributors. For example, you might survey only incumbents in critical jobs (e.g., knowledge workers for high-tech firms; Lee & Maurer, 1997) rather than the workforce at large. Then, you would contrast attitudes and beliefs between intended stayers and leavers from this occupational group to identify ways to reduce turnover for this crucial job category.

Similarly, you might use survey methodology to reduce turnover among high performers. You might identify key contributors from personnel records (or nominations from superiors) and survey them (presuming that you can assure confidentiality and explain why they were selected for this survey). Alternatively, you might survey the workforce at large (which better safeguards anonymity) and determine whether survey participants are high or low performers from additional questions on the survey. Because your survey is done anonymously (preventing individuals' surveys from being matched to their performance records), your survey might ask respondents to provide self-reported descriptions about work effectiveness. Perhaps, you might ask survey participants to describe how they are typically rated on the company's performance rating forms. After all, appraisal research indicates that self-ratings (especially when they are not used for administrative purposes) are related to supervisory ratings and objective performance indexes (Farh, Werbel, & Bedeian, 1988; Harris & Schaubroeck, 1988; Hoffman, Nathan, & Holden, 1991). You also might have participants report their salary growth or rate of promotion to gauge their value to the firm (cf. Trevor, Gerhart, & Boudreau, 1997).

For illustration, we report an analysis of data from our research on turnover among new nurses (Hom & Griffeth, 1991). Promising them confidentiality, we asked nurses to identify themselves on our surveys (they were surveyed several times during their first year of work). As a result, we could match individual nurses' survey answers to performance and turnover data from their personnel files. For the present analysis, we use supervisory evaluations of nurses' effectiveness during the probationary period (e.g., rated quality of work, initiative) and a question about quit decisions (taken from a survey given during the third week of work) to classify nurses into four groups: low-performing stayers; high-performing stayers; low-performing quitters;

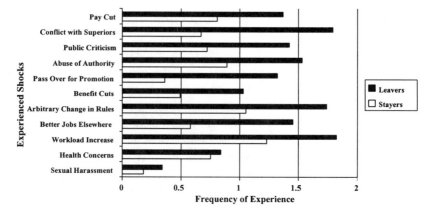

Exhibit 6.22. Differences in Experienced Shocks Between Prospective Stayers and Leavers

and high-performing quitters. Because performance ratings were skewed upward (due to leniency error), we used the median rating across different performance dimensions to identify high and low performers. Exhibit 6.23 shows the percentage distribution of these groups. That only a few (effective and ineffective) beginning nurses planned to quit may reflect the fact that quit intentions were measured during the third week of employment before they ordinarily would became disillusioned with the job (Kramer, 1974).

You then would compare the four groups on the various turnover causes (job satisfaction, commitment, interrole conflict, etc.) assessed in the survey. Continuing our running example, we consider how job satisfaction might affect dysfunctional turnover among new nurses. We also surveyed their satisfaction with various features of the job (cf. Exhibit 6.7). Now, we compare the job satisfaction of the four groups of nurses by computing each group's average satisfaction levels for different job facets. Exhibit 6.24 describes how their satisfaction with four job facets differs. An analysis of variance (ANOVA) confirms that these group differences are statistically significant. It is instructive to attend to the attitudes of high-performing quitters (they represent dysfunctional turnover) and how they differ from the other three groups. In Exhibit 6.24, high-performing leavers resemble low-performing leavers in unhappiness with work hours and colleagues; both groups are significantly more dissatisfied with those job features than are the two groups of stayers. If you were mainly interested in reducing overall quits, you might improve work hour scheduling and collegiality, because intended leavers—both superior and marginal performers—felt most unhappy with those work conditions.

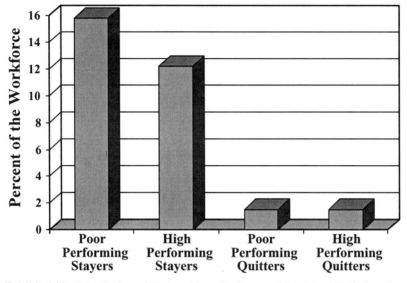

Exhibit 6.23. Distribution of High and Low Performers Who Intend To Quit and Who Intend To Stay

However, if you were more interested in preventing dysfunctional turnover, you would address concerns that are unique to one group: intended leavers who perform their job well. For example, Exhibit 6.24 (p. 151) also reveals that superior nurses who plan to quit felt more dissatisfied with promotional opportunities and chances to learn new skills than the other three groups. ANOVAs corroborate that these attitudes are significantly worse for high-performing quitters than the other groups. Consequently, this analysis suggests that the hospital can reduce dysfunctional turnover by increasing advancement prospects and learning opportunities for effective nurses.

Survey Administration

The next section highlights key features of the survey process that can improve the quality of survey data for turnover analysis. This discussion is not exhaustive. Thus, we refer you to Dunham and Smith (1979), Dillman (1978), and Schmidt and Klimoski (1991) for more extensive coverage of the survey process.

Survey Participation

Full participation of a (random) sample of your workforce best ensures that your survey results accurately represent your workforce's views and beliefs. To increase employee participation, we suggest that senior management express their support for the survey via company newsletter, announcements, letters attached to the survey, or e-mail (Dunham & Smith, 1979). They would describe the survey's purpose and why the survey would benefit both the corporation and respondents. Indeed, senior management might promise that they will respond to problems that the survey identifies. Such expressed willingness to listen will entice greater participation, as employees believe that the survey provides a direct channel for them to voice their complaints to top management. Besides promising to act on problems the survey reveals, you should guarantee participants timely feedback about survey findings (Schmidt & Klimoski, 1991). Promised feedback boosts participation as well as fulfills an ethical obligation to respondents.

Moreover, your employees should complete surveys on company time. Using work hours (rather than lunch or personal time) for survey completion conveys to employees that your company considers their input seriously enough that it will pay them to express their opinions. Furthermore, you might provide refreshments during survey sessions if you recruit employees to a particular facility for the survey. Thus, they would view survey participation as less arduous a task. Finally, we suggest that you avoid excessively lengthy questionnaires, though trying to address turnover causes thoroughly (as this chapter suggests) will expand survey length. Unfortunately, lengthy surveys lower survey response rates (Schmidt & Klimoski, 1991). Our suggestions for enhancing participation should not abrogate employees' right to refuse to participate. They must have genuine freedom to decline participation. Violation of this ethical principle will invalidate your results, because surveys done under coercion are surely distorted.

Confidentiality

You must assure confidentiality to employees to promote survey participation and validity. Obviously, employees will not provide honest answers if they suspect that management or the survey administrator can identify their survey responses. Thus, you would not ask employees to provide names or social security numbers. Requesting demographic background information poses a dilemma. Your company might have a genuine interest in comparing turnover rates and causes among different demographic subgroups. Besides, demographic indexes can provide a check on sampling representativeness (see subsequent discussion). Yet, demographic questions may threaten participant anonymity, lessening response rates or valid responses. Unfortunately, this problem has no easy resolution, and your firm must decide whether the desired demographic data is worth the risks to the veracity of survey answers. (Of course, employees may refuse to describe their demographic traits and should have the right to decline to answer any questions.)

Along these lines, your survey may solicit information about respondents' work unit or department. Such information does not necessarily compromise employees' anonymity (except if they belong to small units). However, results based on aggregating survey data by work units might be used to evaluate the performance of managers of those units (Schmidt & Klimoski, 1991). Organizations often are interested in comparing survey results across different facilities to identify "problem" facilities and therefore "ineffective" managers. Admittedly, many corporations increasingly rely on surveys to provide 360° feedback and appraisal of managers. Thus, companies might have the "right" to aggregate survey data by work units to evaluate their managers. Even so, this practice carries certain pitfalls. Managers might take steps to compromise the validity of survey data, especially if they themselves administer the surveys. For example, they might plead with subordinates for positive evaluations on the survey or promise them rewards for higher evaluations, much as college teachers are known to do when students are judging teaching effectiveness. Thus, your company should consider this issue carefully, deciding whether the benefits of work unit aggregation are worth the threats to survey validity (and alienating managers).

Needless to say, confidentiality guarantees for employees and their superiors must be real—and believed. Dunham and Smith (1979) outline certain steps to safeguard confidentiality during survey sessions. For one, they suggest that you administer to groups numbering at least 25 participants in a room. Sizable groups encourage a feeling of anonymity that might be lost in smaller groups. They also prescribe that questionnaires be placed on seats of chairs before participants enter the room or that they be picked up randomly by participants as they enter. Letting respondents determine their own seating would lessen their anxiety over secretly coded questionnaires. What is more, they suggest that the survey administrator leave the room after presenting instructions and answering questions. The administrator would neither monitor the room nor collect completed surveys. Rather, respondents would simply drop off completed surveys in a large box near the exit. Furthermore, the administrator should solicit two volunteers from participants in attendance. They would be given packing material and a preaddressed mailing label and would mail completed surveys to a central office. In this way, local management at the facility cannot intercept or see the completed surveys.

Sample Representativeness

To reduce costs, you might survey a random sample from your workforce population rather than the entire population (Dunham & Smith, 1979). According to Schmidt and Klimoski (1991), a population is the total group about whom you are interested in gaining information (e.g., average satisfaction level), whereas the sample is the set of respondents from this population from whom you would actually collect information. From measurements taken from the sample, you would estimate the population's characteristics. Thus, you would collect survey data from a sample of your workforce to estimate the average satisfaction level in your entire workforce.

To ensure that your survey results generalize to the population, random sampling is essential for choosing survey participants. To obtain a random sample, you must compile a complete list of all employees in your population (Schmidt & Klimoski, 1991). Then, you would select individuals in such a way that each person has the same chance to be selected. For example, you can draw names of people from an urn that includes all individual names or use a random numbers table (Winkler & Hays, 1975). Furthermore, we note that the larger the sample, the more accurate your survey results (Schmidt & Klimoski, 1991). Dunham and Smith (1979) present a table that identifies required sample sizes for representative sampling of populations of varying size.

When doing random selection, the cover letter accompanying the survey or announcement should convey to employees why they were chosen (because of scientific sampling) so that they will not feel that they are being singled out for some nefarious purpose (cf. Dillman, 1978). Because they represent a chosen few (whose opinions are sought by the firm), these potential respondents actually may feel privileged for being selected and thus participate (Dunham & Smith, 1979). Furthermore, managers should have sufficient lead time about the survey session so that they can schedule replacements for participating respondents from their department to minimize disruptions to day-to-day operations of their department.

Besides simple random sampling, you might use stratified random sampling. For this procedure, you would divide your population into subgroups (strata, such as departments or stores) and then randomly select individuals from each group. Stratified random sampling ensures that your sample is representative of critical subgroups. For example, you might be investigating why minority employees quit. Simple random sampling may not necessarily yield exact representative samples of minorities. Instead, you would estimate the proportion of minorities in your workforce (say, 10%). After obtaining a list of all minority workers, you would randomly select minorities so that the total number of those selected corresponded to their proportion in your employee population. (Of course, you might oversample minorities so that you have sufficient numbers for statistical comparisons with nonminorities.)

However, random sampling is insufficient to guarantee representative samples. Chosen participants also must respond to your survey. For those failing to participate, Schmidt and Klimoski (1991) suggest replacing the original randomly selected respondents with others randomly selected. Even so, those who ultimately participate may not be fully representative of the population. Perhaps, participants are more satisfied employees and thus comply with your request for survey participation. Thus, the final survey results might overstate the level of job satisfaction for the workforce.

When the response rate among your originally chosen respondents is not high (e.g., above 80%), you should check the relative representativeness of your sample (Schmidt & Klimoski, 1991). For this purpose, your survey would collect demographic information about respondents that are useful for comparing the achieved sample and the population. Your survey would ask about respondents' demographic traits (e.g., gender), including those that are well-established predictors of turnover (e.g., job tenure and age; Cotton & Tuttle, 1986; Griffeth et al., 2000; Hom & Griffeth, 1995). These same attributes also should be available on personnel files for your entire population so that you can compare demographic similarity between your sample and population to assess sampling representativeness. When these comparisons reveal a nonrepresentativeness on key variables, you should interpret your data with appropriate reservations. Thus, your sample might include employees who have greater seniority than the population, implying that their stated quit intentions are lower than those in the population (senior employees are less likely to quit; Griffeth et al., 2000). We caution that there are trade-offs between the capacity to test for sampling representativeness and confidentiality. Questions covering too much demographic detail may undermine survey confidentiality, increasing refusals to participate (or to answer such sensitive questions) or socially desirable responses.

In closing, we suggest random sampling as a cost-effective means to survey employees. Yet, a complete canvass—or attempt to survey the entire workforce—also has its merits. Though costlier, a complete canvass gives all employees the opportunity to voice their opinions. Despite its scientific merits, random sampling, however, limits this option to a select few, which may alienate others not selected for the survey (Dunham & Smith, 1979). What is more, those randomly chosen may not believe that they were "arbitrarily" chosen and may feel that their survey responses are not strictly confidential (Dunham & Smith, 1979). Moreover, the canvass method is more appropriate than random sampling for large decentralized companies (e.g., Sears) that comprise small units of employees working in widely dispersed stores, offices, or plants (Dunham & Smith, 1979). In these settings, the additional expense of a canvass may well be justified (Dunham & Smith, 1979).

Doing Predictive Study With Consulting Firms

To predict actual turnover from survey predictors, you might hire reputable external consultants or researchers who can administer a survey in which employees identify themselves. To induce employees to participate and answer questions honestly, your senior management and the consulting firm must assure respondents of absolute confidentiality and offer real safeguards for protecting their anonymity. To illustrate, Performaworks (www.performaworks.com)— an Internet-based consulting firm—surveys employees for client organizations via the Internet. This consulting firm requires service agreements with client companies that preserve the anonymity of respondents (who receive unique passwords), never sharing raw information on how individuals responded with their employers. More than this, Performaworks employs state-of-the-art encryption to ensure that survey data leaving employees' browsers are encrypted for transfer through the Internet.

To illustrate, Performaworks developed a special index to predict actual turnover (instead of quit intentions) for a client. Employees completed a survey administered by Performaworks via the Internet, asking them to report their impressions that the firm furnishes career opportunities, feelings of confidence about their long-term future with the firm, and expected duration of employment with the firm. An earlier analysis comparing current and former employees suggests that these questions have high potential for predicting turnover. Performaworks combined the three questions into a "retention index" and computed a score for each participant. Because Performaworks knew respondents' identities, its consultants could compare how each employee scored on this index with his or her actual employment status 6 months later. The client firm later furnished turnover data on survey participants. Exhibit 6.25 shows what this predictive study uncovered. Higher scores on this retention index predicted lower quit rates. For employees scoring 6 or lower on this index, their quit rate was 26.6%. For those scoring 10 or higher on the index, the quit rate was only 6%.

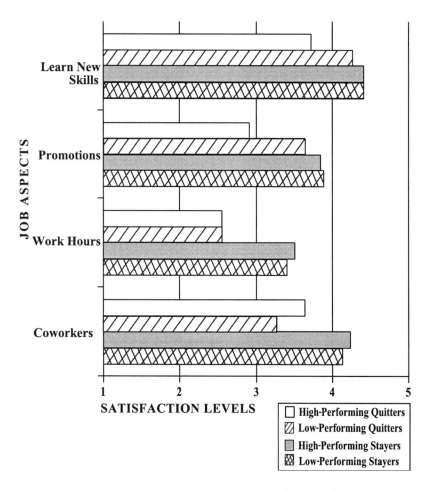

Exhibit 6.24. Satisfaction Differences Among High and Low Performers Intending To Quit and To Stay

Beyond predicting resignations, external consultants—who can persuade employees to complete honestly a survey that identifies them—can perform a similar analysis to forecast dysfunctional turnover. Knowing who filled out the survey, they can match employees' surveys to performance and turnover data from personnel records. By so doing, consultants can compare what attitudes and experiences distinguish high-performing leavers from stayers and low-performing leavers (cf. Exhibit 6.24). This comparison thus uncovers what factors induce high performers to exit and thereby suggests ways to decrease such dysfunctional turnover.

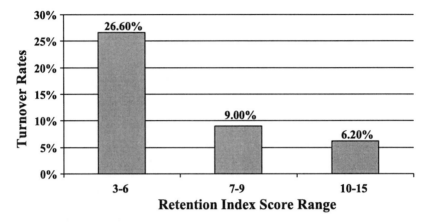

Exhibit 6.25. Predictive Study: Performaworks Retention Index

Summary of Suggestions for Survey Assessments of Turnover Causes

We believe survey methodology is the best approach for identifying potential relevant turnover causes, and we thus summarize with the following suggestions:

1. Use focus group interviews and pilot surveys to develop custom questions to assess the following turnover causes: job satisfaction, interrole conflict, job attraction, perceived alternatives, and turnover costs and benefits.
2. Use existing scales to assess organizational commitment (Meyer & Allen, 1997), shocks (Bhagat et al., 1985; Griffeth & Fink, 1992), and quit intentions (Hom & Griffeth, 1991).
3. Ensure representative sampling and respondent anonymity in your survey of the workforce.
4. Split your survey participants into intended stayers and intended leavers using questions about decisions to quit.
5. Compute the average scores on turnover causes (satisfaction, interrole conflict, job attraction, perceived alternatives, turnover costs and benefits, commitment, and shocks) for each group.
6. Employ statistical tests to verify apparent group differences on turnover causes.

Compensation and Rewards

Jim Jackson knocked lightly on his boss's open door. Bill looked up from a report he was writing.

"Hi, Jim. What's up?"

"I was wondering if . . . do you have a couple of minutes to talk about something?" asked Jim.

"Sure, Jim come on in," Bill responded, putting down his pen.

"I know you're busy, Bill, so I'll get right to the point. I just received a job offer for about 15% more money than I'm making here, for the same work. Although I like it here OK, I'm considering taking the offer. I just thought I would discuss it with you first," Jim said, nervously.

"WOW!" said Bill. "That's a pretty good raise. I didn't know you were looking for a new job, Jim."

"I wasn't. That's what's so strange about this. I went to that conference last month, as you know, and presented our new ideas, and afterward, one of the participants came up to me. Well, we started talking, he was clearly interested in the projects, and asked me for a résumé. I sent him one, a week or so after I returned, and then yesterday he called with the offer," explained Jim.

"I see," said Bill, thinking about the pay structure in the organization. Jim was one of his top performers in the group, and if he gave Jim a raise, he knew Jim would be worth it in the long run. He was clever and creative and always able to come up with the best solution to any problem. But the problem was, what about the others in the department? He had members who'd been with the company longer than Jim. Bill decided to apprise Jim of this. "The problem is this, Jim. If I gave you a raise, it would be very costly to the company, and I need to maintain internal equity around here. You do understand, don't you?"

"Sure, Bill, and you'll have my formal resignation letter on your desk by 5:00 p.m. today. I assume the normal 2-week notice is satisfactory?"

"Yes. I couldn't really expect much more. I'm really sorry we couldn't work this out to everyone's satisfaction," said Bill.

"Me, too, Bill. Well, I'd better let you get back to work." With that, Jim got up and left the office.

In this situation, it is apparent that Bill's decision not to present Jim with a counteroffer resulted in his voluntary turnover. It demonstrates one of the many issues managers have to deal with—the attempt to maintain internal equity, an issue we deal with later in this chapter. However, it opens other questions, as well. Is the company's pay structure externally equitable; that is, is the company's pay system in line with the structure of their competition? Have they fallen behind the competition? To answer these questions, the company needs to do a salary survey, a topic we also examine later.

Compensation professionals and turnover scholars uniformly believe that competitive pay and benefits are essential for attracting and retaining personnel. In a labor market in which the 4.2% joblessness rate sits at a 30-year low (Aversa, 1999), employers are creatively experimenting with various pay and reward programs to discourage employees from quitting (Gross, 1998; Wilson, 2000). This chapter thus focuses on more promising pay strategies for curbing turnover. Yet, we caution that most pay practices lack solid empirical support, although case studies and anecdotal reports attest to their presumed efficacy for curbing quits. Rather, scholarly research rarely has examined the effectiveness of particular compensation practices (mostly focusing on overall compensation levels) and has lagged behind current trends in compensation administration (Harrison, Virick, & William, 1996; Hom & Griffeth, 1995; Miller et al., 1999; Mitchell, 1983; Shaw, Delery, Jenkins, & Gupta, 1998; Williams & Livingstone, 1994). Nonetheless, we recognize that companies must follow the competition and offer prevailing inducements—whether or not they are proven remedies. Otherwise, they would be disadvantaged relative to their competitors in the "war for talent" (Miller et al., 1999). As one author put it, "The market demands it, and the market rules" (Capelli, 2000, p. 106).

New Forms of Base Pay

Career Ladders

Employers are revamping traditional methods for setting base pay for jobs. Among the most promising pay-setting approaches for retention are career ladders, skill- or knowledge-based pay, market pricing, and broad-banding (Lawler, 1990; Milkovich & Newman, 1999; Schuster & Zingheim, 1992). Career ladders represent a series of defined steps within a career field (e.g., engineering, human resources). Each step is a promotion entailing greater responsibilities, pay, and career advancement. High-tech firms have long popularized dual career ladders for engineers and scientists to deter them from leaving their profession (and company) for more "prestigious" and rewarding managerial jobs (Gomez-Mejia & Balkin, 1992). At Microsoft, career tracks for software design and test engineers encourage them to stay in technical fields by offering recognition and pay comparable to what general managers earn (Cusumano, 1995). The typical career path within a functional specialty is to move from new hire to mentor, team lead, and then manager of a functional area for an entire product (such as Excel development manager). Exhibit 7.1 illustrates a typical career path for Microsoft developers that culminates in Level 15, a position held by only five or six Microsoft developers and that requires Bill Gates's approval (Cusumano, 1995).

As practiced at Microsoft, compensation experts prescribe that career paths should base promotions on successful job performance (such as meeting specific requirements for the next career step) rather than job tenure (Gomez-Mejia & Balkin, 1992; Schuster & Zingheim, 1992). Otherwise, career tracks become "dump grounds" for technical professionals who cannot—or do not—become managers.

Skill-Based or Knowledge-Based Pay

Skill-based pay rewards employees for the depth, breadth, or type of skills they obtain and apply to their work (Schuster & Zingheim, 1992). Skill-

---

Level 10
New Hires
Duration: 6 - 18 Months

Level 11
Write Production Code without Much Supervision
Automatic Promotion from Level 10
Duration: 2 1/2 Years

Level 12
Significant Impact of Project
Level 11 Developers Can Write Zero-Defect Codes
and Can Do Basically Anything on Project
More Intensive Promotion Review

Level 13
Significant Impact on Business Unit
Intensive Promotion Review for Level 13
by Senior Management

Level 14
Significant Impact on Division
Manager Describes Level 11 Developer's Contributions
to Division to Senior Management

Level 15
Significant Impact Across Company
Promotion Requires Approval of CEO Bill Gates

Exhibit 7.1. Microsoft Career Track for Software Developers
SOURCE: From Cusumano's *Microsoft Secrets* (1995).

based pay differs from conventional job-based pay by basing wages on what incumbents know rather than on what they do (Milkovich & Newman, 1999). Under these plans, employees receive pay raises for increasing depth of knowledge in a professional or technical job (Leblanc, 1991) or expanding breadth of knowledge of multiple jobs corresponding to several stages in a continuous-process technology or manufacturing assembly (Ledford & Bergel, 1991; Ledford, Tyler, & Dixey, 1991). To illustrate, Exhibit 7.2 reports a maturity curve from a Phoenix public accounting firm. This pay plan ties salaries to staff accountants' years in the accounting profession, using occupational tenure as a crude proxy for professional maturity.

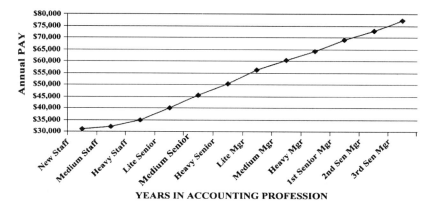

Exhibit 7.2. Maturity Curve (Public Accounting Firm)

Proponents claim that knowledge-based pay structures furnish both intrinsic and extrinsic rewards to employees. These plans encourage employees to learn new skills or jobs, increasing variety and challenge at work. Skill-based pay plans also offer more rapid pay increases (based on fairer criteria, such as employee demonstration of skill mastery) than do conventional job-based pay plans, although limited training opportunities may slow pay progress (Gomez-Mejia & Balkin, 1992). In support, Leblanc (1991) reports that Northern Telecom's skilled-based pay plan decreased job exits.

Market Pricing

Many companies are relying exclusively on external market forces to set salaries, deemphasizing concern with the fairness of internal pay differentials among jobs (Milkovich & Newman, 1999). "Companies can't afford to be concerned with internal equity," an Aon Corp. consultant contends (Conlin, Coy, Palmer, & Saveri, 1999, pp. 40-41). However, traditional pay structures strive to ensure both external and internal equity. Besides paying competitively, conventional approaches try to pay incumbents in more skilled or demanding jobs higher wages than those in less skilled or less responsible jobs. Global competitive and economics pressures nevertheless are pushing companies away from these twin goals and toward market wage-setting—or "market pricing," which bases pay on information drawn from salary surveys. More than this, market pricing frees corporations from the costly bureaucratic apparatus required to maintain internally equitable pay structures (e.g., elaborate job evaluation plans and detailed job descriptions) (Lawler, 1990). In addition, some companies (or consulting firms) carry out special surveys that focus on "hot" skills and "high-tech" skills to better track escalating wages in this more turbulent job market (Greene, 1998). By closely monitoring market rates, companies can erect higher-paid pay structures for "hot-talent" occupations (separate from the main structure) or establish "premium" ranges for these job clusters within the main wage structure (Greene, 1998). By keeping abreast of the competition, market pricing helps firms more readily ward off overtures from outside companies for their essential talent.

Although emphasizing external equity aids retention, neglecting internal pay equity also can hurt retention. Pay inequity can arise if employees earn less pay than others in more "marketable" jobs in which the demand outstrips the supply, although their skills or education are comparable (Hom & Griffeth, 1995). Similarly, pay inequity may occur if new incumbents in hot-talent occupations earn nearly as much as experienced incumbents in the same job because entry-level wages are rising faster than merit-pay budgets (Clark, 1999; Conlin et al., 1999). For example, research long has shown how pay compression induces more accomplished professors whose pay is not appreciably higher than that of new faculty to switch to other academic jobs (Gomez-Mejia & Balkin, 1987b; Schwab, 1991). Similarly, companies offering generous pay and perks to attract hot-talent employees, such as computer specialists and information technology (IT) professionals, can create pay compression for existing employees (Greene, 1998). Thus, 35% of firms in a recent survey reported that their special hot-talent pay packages created higher tension in the workforce (Bohl, 1999).

Besides this, setting base pay solely on external market rates is a more difficult undertaking than often imagined. Several implementation problems plague salary surveys, the prime tool for assessing market wage rates (Milkovich & Newman, 1999). For example, biased sampling of companies (other firms may not participate in wage surveys) and inappropriate salary data about jobs that imprecisely match the firm's job titles (listed in the survey) may distort survey findings. Even if a representative sample of firms from the company's relevant labor market participates, employees may not consider these firms among those for whom they would consider working. In a turnover study, we discovered that many nurses in a Cleveland, Ohio, hospital considered working in doctors' offices. Yet, Cleveland hospitals often surveyed other hospitals to gauge market pay for nurses, overlooking this alternative workplace for nurses.

Broad-Banding

Besides market pricing, many businesses are abandoning rigid job descriptions and simplifying pay structures by collapsing many pay grades into fewer grades having wider salary ranges (Milkovich & Newman, 1999). Such "broad-banding" encourages incumbents to focus on meeting business requirements rather than narrow job descriptions and rewards incumbents for lateral transfers, not just upward mobility (Bridges, 1994). Broad-banding might improve retention in several ways. Consider Marriott International, which classified its 14,500 managers into four broad salary bands (Bernstein, 1998). These managers thus received more opportunities to attain higher pay raises as well as to broaden their experience in varied functional areas without a formal grade increase. Given wider salary limits, broad-banding further allows companies to offer competitive wages to hot-talent positions without having to worry whether such offers would contradict internal pay differentials (Gross, 1998).

Variable Pay

Increasingly popular, variable pay—or pay other than base pay that varies with individual, team, or organizational performance—can discourage quits among high performers (or dysfunctional turnover), improve productivity, and avoid locking in higher fixed labor costs (Parus, 1999; Schuster & Zingheim, 1992). Corporations are increasingly disenchanted with merit pay, which simply adds to fixed payroll costs and hardly increases performance (cf. Heneman, 1990). Coupled with delayed delivery, the average 4.4% merit pay hikes given by most companies may not effectively induce strong work motivation (Parus, 1999). Such modest raises inadequately reward high performers who might leave owing to frustrations over insufficient rewards for their greater contributions.

Exhibit 7.3 shows new approaches for rewarding performance that might curb turnover, and Exhibit 7.4 reports special lures for retaining hot talent (Bohl, 1999). Companies whose core business is IT rely on these approaches more readily than do firms in which IT is not a core business (Zingheim & Schuster, 1999). Their "agile" reward systems include market pricing (periodic adjustments to match rising pay for marketable skills), competency-based pay (lump sum awards for new skill acquisition), variable pay based on divisional success and project completion, and long-term incentives (such as

- Cash profit-sharing
  - Earn bonus based on firm profitability
- Division or plant-wide incentives (gain-sharing)
  - Bonus based on achieving division performance goals
- Merit bonus
  - Pay increase is not permanent
  - Must re-earn bonus next year
- Spot bonus
  - Small cash award for exceptional performance
  - Nomination by anyone
  - Timely reinforcer
- Key contributor award
  - Sizable cash awards given by formal committee
  - Special recognition for achievement
- Stock options
  - Grant opportunity to buy a number of shares of stock in the future at the current stock price.

Exhibit 7.3. New Variable Pay

stock options and bonuses tied to long-term divisional performance) to retain the scarce talent needed for their business. Supporting variable pay, several studies have established that profit-sharing and individual incentives reduce overall quits (Blakemore, Low, & Ormiston, 1987; Miller et al., 1999; Wilson & Peel, 1991). Ironically, a Microsoft human resources manager once remarked to us about their special challenge of retaining employees who became wealthy through stock options.

It is important that turnover research has demonstrated that tying incentives to job performance can lower dysfunctional turnover (Harrison et al., 1996; Williams & Livingstone, 1994). In general, superior performers have greater corporate loyalty than do marginal performers (Hom & Griffeth, 1995; Williams & Livingstone, 1994). Nonetheless, basing financial rewards on productivity binds high performers to the organization even more because they earn proportionately greater rewards for their higher contributions (Williams & Livingstone, 1994). Indeed, our review of turnover studies published in the 1990s affirms this practice (Griffeth et al., 2000). As Exhibit 7.5 attests,

- Financial rewards
  - High starting salaries
  - Frequent market adjustments to base pay
  - Retention and hiring bonuses
  - Stock options or grants
  - Competency/skill pay
  - Incentive pay plans
  - Defined contribution (401K) plans
  - Health care coverage
- Noncash incentives
  - Career development opportunities
  - Education/training
  - Tuition reimbursement
  - Flexible hours
  - Telecommuting
  - Extended vacations

Exhibit 7.4. Strategies for Attracting and Retaining "Hot Talent" Workers
SOURCE: From Bohl (1999).

exceptional contributors are less likely to quit than are marginal contributors when employers tie rewards to performance (i.e., a negative correlation between performance and turnover). Yet, when performance-contingent rewards are absent, superior performers show a greater tendency to leave than low performers (a positive performance-turnover correlation).

All the same, a handful of investigations have established which type of variable pay prevents superior performers from resigning (Harrison et al., 1996; Trevor et al., 1997; Wilson & Peel, 1991). Specifically, one study reports that 100% sales commissions can enhance retention among effective sales representatives and drive out ineffective ones (Harrison et al., 1996). Another investigation finds that rapid salary growth (and accelerated promotions) can promote retention among high performers (Trevor et al., 1997).

Retaining Highly Visible Performers

Retaining high performers is a greater challenge when their accomplishments are visible or objectively verifiable to the external community. Successful professional athletes, chief executives of major corporations, academic superstars, and prominent scientists can easily find alternative employment because of their visible achievements (Jackofsky, 1984). Given media coverage (newspapers, business press, etc.), their superior qualifications are readily accessible to other employers and headhunters who might pursue their services. For instance, well-published scholars quit for other academic posts more than do less accomplished scholars because their scholarly output (e.g., number and quality of publications) is externally visible to other universities, which enhances their ability to move elsewhere (Schwab, 1991).

Superior performers who are not externally visible also can readily obtain alternative work if they can "objectively" document their achievements (e.g., industrial scientists and engineers, managers, sales personnel). After all, objectively verifiable accomplishments have more credibility with prospective employers than do less trustworthy résumés or references. To illustrate, Trevor et al. (1997) found that managers who accumulate many promotions during their tenure in a company can readily secure other jobs (although promotions also decrease quit propensity). Fast-track managers can document their superior credentials with verifiable evidence about promotion progress, increasing their employability. In summary, organizations must proactively implement variable pay programs to retain talented individuals—especially those working in occupations in which achievements are externally visible or objectively verifiable.

Employers might have ready a system of "counteroffers" to match pay packages offered by raiding firms to their high performers (Jarman, 1999). After all, employees are increasingly courted by other companies, given the prevalence of job opportunities (Cappelli, 2000). Yet, this tactic might be too late to dissuade key contributors from leaving if they have felt betrayed by their employer for inadequately rewarding or recognizing their contributions during their tenure. Moreover, a company policy of counteroffers might motivate other employees to solicit outside offers simply to obtain a pay raise. In other words, counteroffers cannot substitute for a key contributor program. Rather than rely solely on counteroffers, organizations should proactively reward and recognize high performers, "immunizing" them from temptation from other firms.

Deferred Compensation

Companies increasingly introduce retention bonuses or golden handcuffs to retain personnel, especially during mergers, downsizing, or reorganizations

(Poe, 1998). Thus, a nationwide survey by Coopers & Lybrand reveals that the number of companies dispensing retention bonuses increased to 43% in 1997 from 14% in 1995 (Poe, 1998). Such bonuses amount to 10% of the annual salaries of nonmanagement personnel and 50% of the annual paycheck of managers (Poe, 1998). Rewarding job tenure with monetary incentives is consistent with turnover thinking and research, which conclude that employees stay in a firm if they anticipate losing valued benefits or perks should they quit (Hom & Griffeth, 1995). Indeed, 70% of the firms in the Coopers & Lybrand survey reported that retention bonuses effectively hold personnel during transition periods (Poe, 1998). Poe (1998) further advises that firms should target valued functional areas and key employees for these bonuses (rather than disseminate them universally), pay them in installments, and impose contractual obligations on beneficiaries to stay for a specified time period.

Despite the popularity of the method, buying employees' loyalty has some drawbacks (apart from driving up pay) (Cappelli, 2000). Specifically, other raiding firms can easily lure away employees with large signing bonuses—"golden hellos"—which more than compensate leavers for forfeiting golden handcuffs. Ironically, deferred compensation programs may increase quits. Cappelli (2000) describes a semiconductor industry study that found that engineers often cashed in their profits to start a business when large profit-sharing bonuses were given or stock prices rose. Finally, deferred compensation—if used as the prime retention strategy—may be viewed as bribes that induce "continuance" commitment, wherein employees stay—not because they "want" to but because they "need to" (Meyer & Allen, 1997). Commitment research finds that such mercenaries—who are bound to a company for purely financial reasons—are neither exceptional performers nor good organizational citizens (Meyer & Allen, 1997). Indeed, such employees are easier to "poach" by other employers ("Career Evolution," 2000). To illustrate, Tang, Kim, and Tang (2000) documented that mental health professionals who strongly value money quit more often even if their jobs are intrinsically satisfying. Accordingly, companies should use golden handcuffs judiciously but must continue these programs because other companies offer them (Cappelli, 2000).

Fringe Benefits

Turnover and labor-economic studies have documented that traditional fringe benefits, such as pension and medical coverage, can lower quits

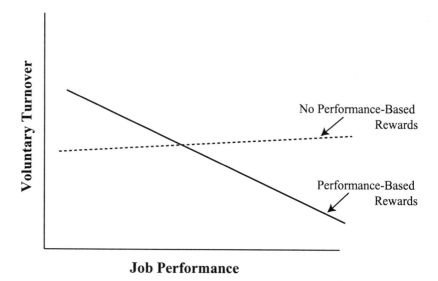

Job Performance

Exhibit 7.5. How Variable Pay Deters Dysfunctional Quits

(Bennett, Blum, Long, & Roman, 1993; Ippolito, 1991; Miller et al., 1999; Mitchell, 1983; Shaw et al., 1998). Conventional benefits may not necessarily bond all employees to an organization, because a growing segment of the workforce prefers nontraditional benefits. Given expanding work hours (Americans work 260 more hours per year than they did a decade ago; Conlin et al., 1999) and the growing numbers of married women with young children, dual-earner families, single-parent families, and families with elder-care duties in the workforce (Frone, Russell, & Cooper, 1992), employees increasingly face conflict between work and family roles (Kossek & Ozeki, 1998; Thomas & Ganster, 1995). Thus, a Boston University Center on Work and Family survey of 7,776 employees from 37 companies discloses that 42% feel that their work negatively affects their home life (Hammonds, 1996), and the Families and Work Institute estimates that the average mother and father spends 22 hours less every week with their children than parents did in 1969 ("Career Evolution," 2000).

Similarly, turnover research increasingly implicates such "interrole" conflict as inducing stressed employees to quit for other jobs (including leaving the workforce) that better accommodate family or personal pursuits (e.g., that involve less business travel or permit part-time work) (Dalton et al., 1997; Hom & Kinicki, 2000; Royalty, 1998). To illustrate, an examination of former managers and partners from the six largest accounting firms reveals that 60%

- Flexible scheduling
  - Flextime (79%)
  - Part-time work (66%)
  - Job sharing (40%)
  - Telecommuting (35%)
  - Compressed work schedules (29%)

- Child care help
  - Dependent care spending accounts (97%)
  - Resource and referral services (48%)
  - Sick or emergency child care program (15%)
  - On-site or near-site child care centers (11%)

- Elder care programs (40%)
  - Resource and referral services (32%)
  - Long-term care insurance (14%)

- Family and medical leave
  - More than mandated 12 weeks (12%)

- Convenience benefits
  - On-site personal service (automated teller machine; 62%)
  - Banking (39%)
  - Travel services (36%)
  - Dry cleaners (29%)

Exhibit 7.6. Benefits for Better Managing Conflict Between Work and Nonwork Roles

SOURCE: From 1997 Hewitt survey of 1,020 firms (Langdon, 1999).

of male and 82% of female leavers cite inability to "balance the rewards associated with this profession with its personal costs" for why they left (Dalton et al., 1997, p. 38).

Thus, companies are offering nontraditional benefits that help employees better manage conflicts between work and home (or personal) demands. Exhibit 7.6 shows results from a Hewitt survey of 1,020 domestic firms, detailing the frequency of these alternative benefits (Langdon, 1999). For example, PriceWaterhouseCoopers designed a "4 nights at home" program so that employees will be on the road for a maximum of three nights and at home for four nights (Gross, 1998). Still, empirical research verifying the effectiveness of family-family benefits remains sparse (Hom & Griffeth, 1995; Thomas & Ganster, 1995). Some investigations have shown that maternity leave and child care services or information reduces quits (Glover & Crooker, 1995; Hom & Griffeth, 1995). Case studies and employer surveys further suggest that alternative work schedules and telecommuting aid job retention (Hom & Griffeth, 1995). For example, 68% of employers surveyed by Catalyst believe that part-time work and job-sharing reduce exits among women (Hom & Griffeth, 1995).

More than this, employers rely on benefits, such as part-time hours and job sharing, to dissuade older workers from retiring. After all, Hanisch, Hulin and Roznowski (1998) regard voluntary retirement as a form of job turnover that derives from similar causes (e.g., job dissatisfaction). The retention of older employees assumes greater urgency, as experts predict an impending shortfall of workers that could last through the first half of the 21st century (Himmelberg, 1999). Given a looming labor shortage, employers might encourage older employees to postpone retirement with alternative work arrangements, such as contract work and part-time assignments. Thus, Deloitte Consulting launched a Senior Leaders Program to allow high-talent executives over age 50 to redesign jobs rather than lose them to early retirement (Reingold & Brady, 1999). Such bridge jobs help the organization retain its senior partners' valuable business experience and smooth their transition into retirement.

Low-Paid, Unskilled Workers

Employers of low-paid, unskilled workers, such McDonald's and Marriott, have pioneered various *soft* perks to attract and retain them (Grimsley, 1999; Yang, Palmer, Browder, & Cuneo, 1996). These firms confront astronomical quit rates, such as 100% annual turnover as fast-food restaurant workers readily leave for $1 more per hour elsewhere (La Lopa, 1999; Yang et al., 1996). In response, McDonald's offers 50% food discounts for workers' families, and Marriott supports a hotline in more than 100 languages to social workers who help with child care and transportation problems (Milkovich & Newman, 1999; Yang et al., 1996). Impressively, ConAgra Refrigerated Foods added on-site child care, prenatal care, and a 100-unit housing project to reduce its annual 100% quit rates among Hispanic and Asian immigrants working in rural meatpacking plants. To offset homesickness, company-sponsored housing allows workers to bring their families to

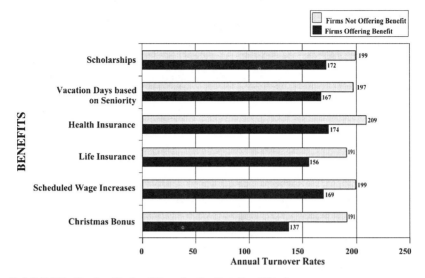

Exhibit 7.7. Purdue Study of Benefits for Fast-Food Workers

rural towns where housing is scarce and costly. Reflecting a new managerial philosophy, managers are thus behaving as social workers who address the sundry personal and family problems of low-wage workers. As the human resources vice president of the Las Vegas-based Mirage Resorts put it, "I see my job as the daddy" (Grimsley, 1999).

These employers have emphasized benefits and services as a prime retention strategy, believing that low-wage, low-skilled workers value these inducements more than (modest) pay increases. After all, minimum wage earners could not afford to buy these services on their own even if they received more pay (Milkovich & Newman, 1999). Moreover, employers believe that wage increases would confer no competitive advantage to them because other competitors would quickly match the pay hike (Milkovich & Newman, 1999). Therefore, an employer raising pay would be "stuck" with higher labor costs (as would its competitors) without gaining greater corporate loyalty.

Here, too, confirmation that these exotic perks build job loyalty is sparse. A Purdue University study of 209 fast-food chain restaurants (employing mostly part-time help) in Indiana identified the array of benefits that decrease turnover rates, which range between 133% and 238% annually (La Lopa, Felli, & Kavanaugh, 1999). As Exhibit 7.7 reveals, fast-food restaurants giving Christmas bonuses, scheduled wage increases, life insurance and health insurance, scholarships, and seniority-based vacation days had fewer quits than restaurants that did not. Additional analyses further discovered that pension plans, social benefits, and free uniforms also reduce attrition. The authors claim that these benefits are not as costly as excessive turnover. Thus, a restaurant employing 50 workers who quit at a yearly rate of 150% incurs an overall turnover cost of $37,500 if hiring and training each replacement costs $500. Indeed, "Some of the cheapest benefits were indicative of some of the lowest turnover rates. For example, life insurance benefits are one of the cheapest benefits to offer restaurant employees" (La Lopa, 1999).

Optional Benefits

Small companies often cannot afford fringe benefits for their workforce. Without absorbing any costs, smaller firms can offer "optional" benefits to employees who would buy benefits themselves (e.g., auto and life insurance) (Tannenbaum, 1999). Through their employer, employees could purchase benefits at a discount and pay for them through convenient payroll deduction (avoiding cash-flow problems of paying for a big auto insurance bill, for example).

To make optional benefits feasible, Ceridian Corp., a Minneapolis information-services company that processes payrolls of 23,000 small companies, teamed with RewardsPlus of America Corp., a Baltimore benefits company that ordinarily works with large businesses (Tannenbaum, 1999). Ceridian's clients are pooled together and treated as one giant company. RewardsPlus expects 60% of Ceridian's small-business clients to sign up within 3 years and 30% of their employees to buy at least one optional benefit. An enrolled Ceridian client (a printing company with 15 workers) contends that "Any time you can add benefits, you can retain employees a bit better and there's less turnover" (Tannenbaum, 1999, p. B3).

The Maquila Workforce

Services and benefits are critical retention strategies for another low-wage, low-skilled workforce: Mexican production workers in American-owned assembly plants south of the U.S. border. Over the years, U.S. companies ship components to their "maquiladora" plants for assembly and reexport assembled products duty-free (Teagarden, Butler, & Von Glinow, 1992). Capitalizing on the low Mexican wages ($6 hourly compensation, including benefits, compared with $16.70 in the United States; Koretz, 1994), the maquila industry has mushroomed into 3,200 plants that employ nearly 1 million Mexican workers (Dougherty & Holthouse, 1998; Krooth, 1995).

The tremendous growth of the maquila industry—accelerated by the passage of the North American Free Trade Agreement and a 30% decline in labor costs due to a devaluated peso (Baker, Lee, & Coy, 1991; Dougherty & Holthouse, 1998; Hecht & Morici, 1993)—has driven up demand for Mexican labor. Given ample maquila work, Mexican workers can find employment easily if they quit, and they quit at rates that routinely exceed 100% annually (Bannister & Peña, 1993; Picou & Peluchon, 1995). To deter quits, maquila employers bestow numerous services and perquisites, such as transportation, on-site health clinics, food coupons, and attendance and performance bonuses (Catanzarite & Strober, 1993; Teagarden et al., 1992). As one maquila manager put it, "Benefits are a way of staying competitive. As it gets harder to get workers, we have to raise benefits" (Catanzarite & Strober, 1993, p. 143). Like domestic employers of low-cost, unskilled American workers, maquila employers primarily rely on many noncash lures to attract and retain personnel.

All the same, the presumed efficacy of the array of maquila perks and services rests primarily on anecdotal evidence (Farquharson, 1991; Stinson, 1989). A preliminary examination involving 115 plants in Nogales, Juarez, and Reynosa (Mexico) reveals that most benefits do not improve retention (Miller et al., 1999). Still, maquila plants offering more generous profit-sharing and savings plans (higher company matching percentage) had lower turnover rates compared with plants that did not. Miller et al. nonetheless concluded that maquilas should not abandon their existing compensation programs. Because they are so easily imitated, most benefits do not confer any special competitive advantage to employers (Milkovich & Newman, 1999). Still, without such lures, maquila owners would surely be advantaged in terms of workforce attraction and retention. Rather, Miller et al.'s findings imply that maquila managers might expand and enrich the few inducements that do work (e.g., profit-sharing) and retain other customary benefits.

When studying *individual* worker reactions to benefits, West (2000) uncovered stronger support for maquila perks. Surveying workers from a single plant in Mexicali (Mexico), she assessed their level of satisfaction with different benefits using a 5-point scale, ranging from 1 (*highly dissatisfied*) to 5 (*highly satisfied*), and compared how those intending to stay differed in attitudes from those intending to quit (another question on the survey; cf. Chapter 6). Exhibit 7.8 summarizes her survey findings, identifying those benefits that

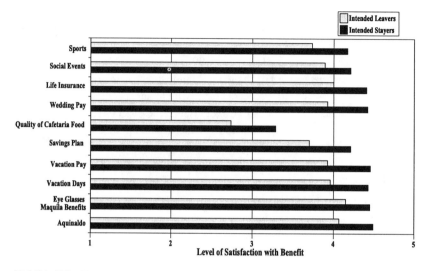

Exhibit 7.8. How Prospective Stayers and Leavers Differ in Satisfaction With
Maquila Benefits

have the potential to curb quits—because prospective leavers and stayers felt
differently about these benefits. In particular, prospective leavers were more
dissatisfied with company-sponsored social events, life insurance, quality of
cafeteria food, savings plan, vacation pay and days (Mexican law requires
25% extra pay during vacations and 6 to 14 days of vacation depending on service), and "aquinaldo" (a mandated December bonus worth at least 15 days'
wages) (cf. Miller et al., 1999). West's (2000) investigation suggests that this
Mexicali owner could increase worker retention by enriching those particular
benefits.

Fair Reward Allocation

Besides fair pay amounts (known as *distributive justice*), employers
should ensure *procedural justice*—that their procedures for distributing pay
and benefits are fair. Employees are loyal if they get the rewards they deserve
and those rewards are given in a fair manner. Company policies and procedures that justly administer rewards give employees a stake in the system by
showing that the organization values and respects them (affirming their self-
worth and according them positive status within the workplace community)

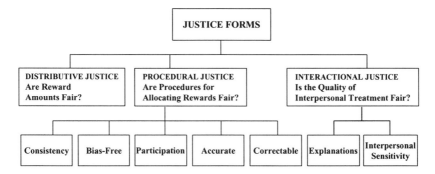

Exhibit 7.9. Forms of Justice

and assuring them they will receive fair outcomes throughout their career in the firm (Folger & Cropanzano, 1998). Time and again, many scholars have reported that unjust practices can undermine organizational loyalty (Aquino et al., 1997; Folger & Cropanzano, 1998). Indeed, Tyler (1990) contends that a managerial strategy based on procedural justice bonds employees to the company better than one based on distributive justice or favorable outcomes. Supporting this contention, Folger and Konovsky (1989) observed that fair distribution of pay raises commits employees to the firm even more than the actual size of the raise.

Social scientists have identified a set of principles for fair procedures (Folger & Cropanzano, 1998; Leventhal, 1980; Tyler, 1988). Exhibit 7.9 summarizes these principles, and Exhibit 7.10 illustrates their application for performance appraisal reviews (cf. Folger & Cropanzano, 1998; Folger & Konovsky, 1989; Taylor, Tracy, Renard, Harrison, & Carroll, 1995). Thus, a fair appraisal review enforces "consistency" by applying the same performance standards to all subordinates. A "bias-free" appraisal means that a supervisor's personal prejudice or favoritism does not distort his or her performance judgments. What is more, performance evaluations should be based on accurate information about employee performance. For example, employees would regard their appraisal as fair if supervisors frequently observe their behaviors and are knowledgeable about job requirements. Finally, just appraisals permit employee input, such as allowing subordinates to express views about their performance (self-appraisal) or to participate in setting performance goals.

Finally, a third dimension of organizational justice is *interactional* justice, or the superior's interpersonal treatment of employees (Folger &

- Consistency
  - Apply consistent performance standards to all subordinates at all times
    - Early notice of performance expectations
- Accurate appraisals
  - Evaluate employees on appropriate criteria
    - Relevant
    - Goal attainment
    - Work behaviors
  - Frequent supervisory observation and feedback
  - Document performance ratings
    - Performance diaries
  - Supervisory knowledge of job requirements
  - Solicit other raters' evaluations of the employee
    - Select competent raters
- Freedom from bias
  - Rater self-interests, prejudices, or favoritism do not bias ratings
- Participation
  - Solicit subordinate self-appraisals
    - Subordinate accomplishment log
  - Provide opportunity for subordinates to review or rebut performance evaluations
  - Subordinate participation in performance goal-setting and performance improvement plans
    - Train subordinates to participate in review session
- Truthful communications

Exhibit 7.10. Procedurally Fair Performance Appraisal

Cropanzano, 1998). Thus, companies may design equitable policies and procedures, but managers may not necessarily enact those procedures (Korsgaard, Roberson & Rymph, 1998). They may obey the "letter of the law but not its spirit" (Korsgaard et al., 1998). Managers show interactional justice through explanations and interpersonal sensitivity. That is, fair managers justify their reward decisions, giving convincing reasons in sincerity. They also express sensitivity for employees' feelings by being honest, courteous, and respectful of their rights.

- Justification
  - Provide adequate explanation for performance rating and merit pay decision
- Supportiveness
  - Showing helpful attitude during review session
- Constructive criticism
  - Specifies focus on behavior, not person
  - Avoids blaming employee as cause for poor performance
  - Considerate in tone and content
  - Avoids threats
  - Given in timely manner in appropriate setting

Exhibit 7.11. Interpersonally Fair Performance Appraisals
SOURCE: From Taylor, Tracy, Renard, Harrison, and Carroll (1995).

For greater illustration, Exhibit 7.11 summarizes attributes of "interpersonally fair" performance appraisals (Folger & Cropanzano, 1998). Specifically, fair superiors provide persuasive reasons for their merit-pay decisions. Even offering excuses (rather than justification) for why well-deserving subordinates receive meager raises can help defuse anger (e.g., blaming poor economic circumstances for the low pay-increase budget). Moreover, just supervisors show concern for subordinates during review sessions. Furthermore, they give constructive criticism when targeting areas needing improvement, with feedback focusing on subordinates' deficient behaviors rather than blaming them. Constructive feedback does not threaten subordinates and is given in a timely manner (soon after the poor performance is witnessed) in the privacy of an office rather than in public.

Fair Appraisal Training

Several studies have evaluated whether training programs that enhance fair performance reviews can improve retention (Korsgaard et al., 1998; Taylor et al., 1995). In particular, Taylor et al. (1995) proposed "Due-Process Performance Appraisal Review" for just performance reviews. Under the U.S. Constitution, due process of law guarantees citizens charged with legal violations (a) adequate notice (holding citizens responsible for obeying laws only when they have been published or communicated beforehand), (b) a fair hearing (all relevant evidence to the proposed violation is presented, and charged

- Adequate notice
  - Develop Standards
  - Communicate/clarify standards
  - Negotiate standards
  - Give feedback
- Fair hearing
  - Encourage two-way communication
  - How to use appraisal form
- Judgment based on evidence
  - Sample representative performance
  - Keep performance diary
  - Solicit performance data from employees

Exhibit 7.12. Training Program: "Due Process" Appraisal System

parties have the opportunity to provide commentary), and (c) judgment based on evidence (judicial decisions are free from external pressures, personal corruption, and other biases) (Folger, Konovsky, & Cropanzano, 1992). Taylor et al. (1995) designed a training program for supervisors based on these principles, incorporating features of distributive and interactional justice shown in Exhibit 7.12. In a field experiment, they trained managers to use these principles in performance reviews and compared them to untrained managers. This due process appraisal system improved employees' satisfaction with the appraisal system and strengthened their intentions to remain. Interestingly, trained managers expressed greater satisfaction with this system and gave lower performance ratings to their subordinates than the untrained managers.

In another intervention, Korsgaard et al. (1998) trained employees to be more assertive during appraisal interviews to increase supervisors' interactional justice. Presumably, superiors will hear and acknowledge subordinates' opinions of their performance if subordinates communicate assertively during performance reviews. That is, assertive subordinates can elicit interactionally fair behaviors, inducing supervisors to consider employee input and to justify their performance evaluations. To increase interactional fairness, Korsgaard et al. trained employees in a retailing firm on how to do self-appraisals (this firm let subordinates submit personal reviews of their accomplishments to superiors before appraisal interviews) and how to communicate assertively. More specifically, they instructed employees to (a) give information by stating their self-appraisal rating and the reasons for their view, (b) obtain information by asking superiors to provide justification for their ratings, and (c) use appropriate body language (e.g., maintain eye contact, sit up straight, lean forward, and take notes). Afterward, trainees watched two scripted role-plays, one showing assertive behaviors during a review discussion and the other displaying nonassertive behaviors. They then participated in an exercise to identify assertive and nonassertive behaviors.

Next, Korsgaard et al. (1998) compared the attitudes of trained employees with another group who did not receive assertiveness training, surveying them after their performance reviews. Compared to the untrained employees, those trained in assertive communication expressed a more positive attitude toward performance appraisals and greater trust in their managers. They also reported a slightly stronger commitment to the organization, though group differences were not statistically significant. Nonetheless, employees—whether trained or not in assertiveness—who encountered more interactionally fair behaviors from managers during performance review sessions felt much stronger organizational commitment.

In summary, managing how fairly rewards are distributed to the workforce is imperative for building organizational commitment. Indeed, equitable policies and procedures can alleviate—if not offset—felt disappointment when even well-deserving employees receive little or no rewards.

Salary Surveys

Organizations use salary surveys—either done by themselves or through a third party (e.g., consulting firm, trade association)—to monitor the pay and benefits of other firms to ensure that their pay package is sufficiently competitive to retain personnel. We suggest some additional questions for inclusion in conventional salary surveys.

Compensation Strategies

The compensation strategy field suggests new approaches for using pay practices and policies to reduce organizational quit rates (Gomez-Mejia &

Balkin, 1992). Milkovich and Newman (1999) assert that a strategic perspective on compensation focuses on the set of compensation policy decisions that help the organization acquire and sustain competitive advantage. Different compensation strategies comprise different types of pay practices. For example, Gomez-Mejia and Balkin (1992) distinguish between strategies that are *algorithmic* (which emphasize predetermined, standardized, repetitive procedures for processing pay decisions with minimal attention to mitigating circumstances and external factors) and *experiential* (flexible, adaptive policies that respond to changing circumstances, sudden environmental shifts, and idiosyncratic situations). Their research established that these pay strategies represent opposite ends of the same continuum. However, the pay strategies of most firms fall between these extremes and include features of both types.

Compensation studies have shown how pay strategies can enhance organizational performance, especially if strategies fit the overall business strategy (Gomez-Mejia & Balkin, 1992). This line of inquiry concludes that the best compensation strategy for a firm depends on its unique strategy and mission (Milkovich & Newman, 1999)—there is no ideal compensation strategy, although some authors contend that certain pay strategies are universally beneficial (Lawler, 1990).

Extending this work for turnover, Hom (1992) adopted a survey designed by Gomez-Mejia and Balkin (1992) to assess compensation strategy. Exhibit 7.13 shows a sample of the various pay policies and practices that represent the algorithmic or experiential compensation strategy. Directors of 24 mental health agencies in Arizona completed this survey, describing their pay strategies. Then, Hom (1992) compared pay strategies between agencies having high quit rates and those having low quit rates. Therefore, this comparison identified which pay strategies can reduce overall turnover rates. For example, this analysis determined that pay incentives and job-based pay were associated with lower quit rates, whereas pay secrecy increased quit rates. Given that there is no ideal compensation strategy that is universally effective, these findings may not generalize to other industries in which different pay strategies might deter job exits.

This initial extension of the pay strategy work seemed a promising refinement of wage surveys, which traditionally consider the quantity of different extrinsic rewards. Rather, surveying other features of pay administration— such as criteria for pay (e.g., using job evaluation vs. skill-based pay for setting base pay; basing raises on performance vs. tenure), design (relative mix of incentives, fixed pay, and benefits; setting pay policy above or below the market), and administration (centralized vs. decentralized decision making;

- Pay incentives
  - Emphasis on incentives
- Internal equity
  - Pay system emphasizes internal pay equity
- Participative design
  - Employees have say in pay policies
- Pay secrecy
  - Pay policies and practices are not openly disclosed
- Risk-sharing
  - Employee earnings vary with company success
- Market competitiveness
  - Pay and benefits exceed those of other firms
- Job-based pay
  - Pay reflects job duties and responsibilities rather than incumbent skills
- Bureaucratic pay policies
  - Pay structure is regimented with carefully defined procedures
- Executive perks
  - Special perks only for select few (e.g., executives)

Exhibit 7.13. Pay Practices Embodying Compensation Strategy

pay disclosure)—might yield valuable insight into what pay strategies are effective turnover deterrents (Gomez-Mejia & Balkin, 1992). To contrast pay strategies across high- and low-turnover firms, this "expanded" wage survey also must assess overall quit rates in other companies (and perhaps for different jobs) (see Chapter 6). Such "benchmarking" information about other firms' turnover rates also lets the company sponsoring the survey to ascertain whether its own resignation rate is excessive relative to industry competitors (Abelson & Baysinger, 1984) (see Chapter 1).

Identifying Relevant Competitors

As suggested previously, soliciting employees' perceptions might help identify major labor supply competitors (see Chapter 6). Otherwise, wage surveys might overlook important competitors for one's workforce. As Chapter 6

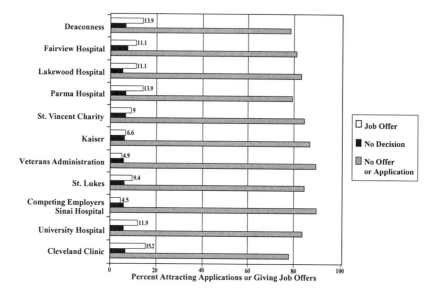

Exhibit 7.14. Percentage of Cleveland Nurses Applying to Competing Hospitals and Obtaining Job Offers

illustrates, an opinion survey can assess employees' attraction for other places of employment. To illustrate, we surveyed nurses in a Cleveland hospital, asking them to indicate whether they recently applied to various hospitals in the Cleveland area or received job offers from them (cf. Chapter 6). Exhibit 7.14 reports the survey results, showing the extent to which competing employers drew job applications from this hospital's workforce as well as which employers extended offers to this workforce. For example, 77.9% of the nurses did not submit job applications or obtain jobs from the Cleveland Clinic ("No Offer or Application"). Yet, 6.6% did apply for a position with this hospital but were still awaiting a decision ("No Decision") at the time of the survey, and 15.2% received a job offer from this hospital ("Job Offer").

Thus, a survey of the workforce may identify which companies represent significant competition who might raid or lure away employees. Our research suggests that the Cleveland hospital participating in our survey should clearly target the Cleveland Clinic, University Hospital, Deaconness, Fairview, Lakewood, and Parma hospitals for its wage and benefits surveys. Because these hospitals potentially can recruit a significant proportion of the present workforce, this hospital must closely monitor their compensation programs (and other enticements not ordinarily covered in salary surveys) and ensure that its own pay and benefits are competitive with respect to those particular competitors.

Multiple Wage Surveys a Year

Employers are coping with escalating wages for hot-talent workers by adjusting salaries more than once a year (Bohl, 1999; Greene, 1998). However, frequent market adjustments require firms to track changing pay rates throughout the year (via surveys or telephone interviews). Similarly, firms operating in tight labor markets may need to continually monitor the changing market pay in the community. For example, Norwest Bank carries out a local wage survey three times a year to be competitive in the Sioux Falls, South Dakota, area, where the unemployment rate is a mere 1.4% (Grimsley, 1999).

Summary of Suggestions

In closing, we suggest the following approaches to increase job retention:

1. Consider new ways of setting base pay, including career ladders, knowledge- or skill-based pay, market pricing, or broad-banding.
2. Monitor the compensation packages offered by competing firms, including nontraditional benefits and services.
3. When luring hot-talent employees with attractive pay and perks, keep an eye on how these inducements can undermine internal equity for existing employees in the same hot-talent occupations as well as "cooler" occupations.
4. Promote golden handcuffs or retention bonuses not as bribes but as symbols of the organization's respect and regard for beneficiaries.
5. Introduce a key contributor program before resorting to counteroffers to retain high performers.
6. Offer programs to help employees better manage conflict between work and home roles. After all, employees increasingly prefer a workplace where they can have both professional and personal lives.
7. Promote distributive, procedural, and interactional justice in pay and reward administration.
8. Although following the marketplace is essential, companies should not slavishly adopt popular financial inducements uncritically. After all, organizations can only achieve competitive advantage in the war for talent by designing unique difficult-to-imitate plans.

8

Reducing Turnover Among Special Groups

Minorities and Women

Tom sat across from his favorite employee, Sally Jones. Sally had been with the company for a little over a year now and had proven to be a very valuable asset to the company and to him. The only African American on his staff, she excelled at all aspects of her job. Tom was very pleased at himself because he had been instrumental in hiring her. He assumed she wanted to meet to discuss the Johnson account.

"So, Sally, what's on your mind," Tom said, curiously, smiling.

Sally cleared her throat nervously. "Well, Tom, this is difficult for me, but I've just accepted an offer from another company."

Tom straightened up in his chair; his face became ashen as he spoke.

"WHAT? WHY? I thought you really liked it here, Sally. This doesn't have to do with those, uh, remarks George made, does it? I straightened him out on this." About a month ago, George Henry had made some explicit sexual remarks to Sally, which she found offensive. After about a week of this, Sally had complained to Tom, and Tom had "counseled" George on the inappropriateness of such behavior, so he thought the matter was over.

"Well, uh, not re . . ., but . . ." Sally stammered. She didn't really want to make a big deal about this now because it hadn't stopped, but she'd decided to leave. The nature of the comments had acted as a major reason to begin looking for another job, but there were other reasons, as well. This whole line of conversation was very uncomfortable to her, so she decided to change the subject, hoping Tom wouldn't notice.

"In many ways, I do like to work here, Tom, but the new job is closer to my home, plus, I'll be able to telecommute 2 to 3 days per week, and the new company has an on-site child care facility, plus some of their other policies make them, uh, frankly, more family-friendly."

George closed his eyes for a second when he heard this. Just last week, he'd implored higher management to consider several new ideas of his to make the company more family-friendly. But management had "pooh-poohed" the ideas, saying these things were just another fad. Tom didn't believe this, showing that several other large companies had adopted such policies, enhancing their retention. He'd read where it also saved money and improved morale—sometimes even job performance. Now he was going to lose a top-notch employee because of their unwillingness to change with the times.

"I see," said Tom. "Are you sure there's nothing else we can do. You know, you're up for a promotion in a year or so, and I have no reservations about recommending you."

Sally smiled and said, "I appreciate that, Tom, and you've been very supportive of me. But I believe this is the best for me and my family."

At that, Tom could only nod. He agreed with her, in principle, which was why he'd made the recommendations in the first place. But that didn't make her leaving any easier.

Sally stood and started to leave. "I'll give the usual two weeks' notice, and you'll have my formal resignation by the end of the day. I better get back to work, now. Bye, Tom."

As is usually the case, employee turnover is complex, with multiple causes. The primary reason for Sally's leaving was the harassing coworker, but she felt very uncomfortable talking about this. So, even now with her impending exit, she decided to use the family friendliness of the new company as her primary reason. Tom may never know Sally was leaving because of sexual harassment and how close he and his company came to a

sexual harassment lawsuit. He believed his talking with the offending employee was enough but had not followed through to find out if the behavior
had stopped. As we show in this chapter, sexual harassment, family friendliness, and discrimination are potential causes for employee turnover, and there
are practices managers can engage in to lessen the chances of turnover.

Diversity is a hallmark of the modern American workforce (Cox, 1991).
It is well established that this demographic and cultural heterogeneity will
increase, as women and nonwhite men will constitute 85% of the net addition
to the labor force shortly after the turn of the century (Cox, Lobel, & McLeod,
1991; "Pay Equity Makes Good Business Sense," 1990). These demographic
trends and a shrinking labor supply are likely to cause stiff competition among
employers to attract and retain women and minorities (Fisher, 1992; "One
Company's Approach," 1991; "Promoting Women to Upper Management,"
1990). But just what is meant by diversity, and how and why should we
"value" it? For our purposes, *diversity* refers to the obvious differences like
race/ethnicity, sex, religion, age, and national origin. But we also broaden this
perspective to include physical ability, skills, attitudes, sexual orientation,
perspectives, and background (Joplin & Daus, 1997; Robinson & Dechant,
1997). *Valuing* diversity refers to the desire to include and use the varied
assets of workers, as potential employees, from the groups previously set out,
"rather than excluding or limiting contributions of any potential employee
because of any factor related to diversity (e.g., being male, Jewish, and/or
aged" (McMahan, Bell, & Virick, 1998, p. 199).

Why should we value diversity? The most often given, albeit general, reason for valuing diversity is to improve a company's competitive advantage.
Recently, McMahan et al. (1998) applied Wright and McMahan's (1992)
resource view to the way diversity can add to an organization's competitive
advantage. First, excluding employees because of irrelevant factors limits the
ability to hire workers who may possess skills not held by other workers. For
example, if the automobile manufacturer Chevrolet had a Spanish-speaking
employee involved in the naming of the *Nova,* they would have been able to
encourage the use of a different name. The Spanish phrase *no va,* when trans-
lated to English, means "it doesn't go" (Fernandez, 1993)—not a very effective way to distribute a car to Spanish-speaking markets.

In further support of the value of having different types of skills via a
diverse work group, Wartson, Kumar, and Michaelson (1993) found that
diverse groups were more effective in identifying problems and generating
solutions than homogeneous groups. Cox, Lobel and McLeod (1991) compared the cooperativeness of a diverse group of Asians, Hispanics, and Afri-

can Americans, representing people from a collectivist culture, with a group of white Americans, who represented an individualist culture. He found the diverse group exhibited more cooperative behaviors than did the nondiverse group. Taken together, these two studies support the idea that a diverse workforce would enhance a company's competitive advantage.

Second, for a resource to be a source of competitive advantage, it should be rare. McMahan et al. (1998) apply this to a diverse workforce, too, by noting that a truly diverse workforce is still very rare because a great deal of segregation still continues in most organizations, in which women work with women and men work with men, and women and minorities are concentrated in the lower-level occupations across most organizations.

A third way to sustain competitive advantage is by having a workforce that competitors cannot duplicate or imitate (McMahan et al., 1998). It is unlikely that competitors are going to know the extent to which an organization has a diverse workforce. Thus, they are unable to copy or duplicate that diversity, and the company will continue to have this competitive advantage over the competitor.

The inability to find substitutes for a resource is the fourth way to maintain competitive advantage, and it is called *nonsubstitutability.* The greater the nonsubstitutability of the workforce, the greater the competitive advantage because employees have learned from one another over time, and each one's assets were used when circumstances warranted. These diverse employees are likely to be motivated because nonjob or nonperformance factors (such as race or gender) would not affect their opportunities, rewards, or future (McMahan et al., 1998).

Despite the changing workforce composition, turnover researchers rarely have examined quits among minorities and women or why they quit (Nkomo, 1992). Many case studies and journalistic accounts report higher turnover among minorities and women (Gleckman, Smart, Dwyer, Segal, & Weber, 1991; Schwartz, 1989). National statistics indicate that African Americans quit 40% more often than whites do, and statistics gathered by Corning Glass and Monsanto show that women professionals resign at twice the rate shown by men (Cox & Blake, 1991; Fisher, 1992). However, that trend may be changing; recent meta-analyses of turnover research find that neither minorities nor women have a higher probability of quitting than whites or men (Griffeth, Hom, & Gaertner, 2000; Hom & Griffeth, 1995) According to exit surveys of minority and female leavers (James, 1988; Schwartz, 1989), that exodus arises from discrimination—real or imagined. In 1995, we described several sources of discrimination as potential causes of turnover (Hom &

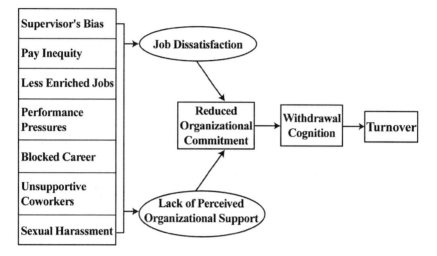

Exhibit 8.1. Potential Causes of Turnover Among Minorities and Women

Griffeth, 1995). Today, we believe these causes are more distal in the turnover process than we earlier thought. Figure 8.1 describes the role of discrimination sources in our new thinking. Briefly, the model shows that discrimination sources, of which we identify seven major categories, lead to job dissatisfaction and lowered perceived organizational support, both of which reduce organizational commitment. Depressed commitment leads to withdrawal cognitions and ultimately to turnover. Subsequently, we summarize these potential sources of discrimination.

Supervisor Bias

The popular press blame poor or indifferent treatment from supervisors for inducing minorities and women to quit. For example, Gleckman et al. (1991) reported that minorities who exit describe their supervision as arbitrary and unfair. Moreover, more than 75% of surveyed CEOs from Fortune 100 firms believed that stereotyping blocked career progress for women ("Title VII's Overseas Reach: Upward Mobility for Women," 1991). At least one research study found that supervisors frequently underrate the performance of minorities and women (Sackett, DuBois, & Noe, 1991), and another study found that managers underestimated the accomplishments of their black subordinates but positively evaluated the accomplishments of women over men (Tsui & O'Reilly, 1989).

Pay Inequity

Typically, women and minorities earn less pay because they mostly work in lower-paying occupations (Bovee, 1991; Gleekman et al., 1991; Hom, 1979; R. M. Kantor, 1977; Morrison & Von Glinow, 1990). Even when women and minorities are hired into management and into professions dominated by white males, they still earn less and express more pay dissatisfaction ("Black College Graduates," 1991; Morrison & Von Glinow, 1990). For example, one study of female vice presidents found that they earned 42% less than their male peers (Morrison & Von Glinow, 1990). Relatedly, another study revealed that salary negotiations yielded higher payoffs for men than women MBA graduates (Gerhart & Rynes, 1991). In an impressive comparison of male and female managers, Stroh, Brett, and Reilly (1992) found that female managers were paid less than male managers despite their similar education, family power, industry, employment patterns, and willingness to relocate.

Less Enriched Jobs

Minorities and women frequently possess jobs that are less intrinsically satisfying. In turn, this may weaken their job loyalty (Mathieu & Zajac, 1990). Many hold routine jobs that have little or no discretion (Hom, 1979; Morrison & Von Glinow, 1990). These circumstances apply even to female and minority professionals and managers who are often given less enriched, less challenging work (Cose, 1993; Kantor, 1977; Morrison & Von Glinow, 1990). Because they lack informal "empowering" alliances with mentors and peers, nonwhite or female managers may have less authority and autonomy than white male managers (Cleveland & Kerst, 1993; Kantor, 1977). Superiors also may give them fewer challenging assignments to solve urgent problems in the organization because they doubt the competence of minorities and women in nontraditional roles (Heilman, Rivero, & Brett, 1991; Kantor, 1977; "Title VII's Overseas Reach," 1991). Several studies describe how women have fewer developmental assignments involving start-ups, troubleshooting, or international experiences (Morrison & Von Glinow, 1990; "OFCCP Glass Ceiling Initiative," 1991). Depriving minorities and women of such opportunities makes them less visible to top management and less prepared for executive posts (Garland, 1991). Becoming discouraged or dissatisfied with the lack of challenge, women and minorities may leave.

Performance Pressures

In many organizations, new hires consisting of women and minorities represent "tokens," symbolic evidence of diversity. Tokens in traditional white male occupations feel that they must excel (Kantor, 1977; Thomas, 1993). Basically, tokenism itself creates unique pressures to perform because of publicity, representative symbolism, and "tokenism eclipse" (the token's personal attributes—for example, race or gender—obscure the token's achievements; R. M. Kantor, 1977). Tokens are highly visible due to their race or gender (Morrison & Van Glinow, 1990). They face more pressures to perform, conform, and to avoid mistakes, which are glaringly obvious (Kantor, 1977), because tokenism creates the impression—when there are only a few members of minorities or women in a firm—of their being representative of a category. Viewed more as symbols than as individuals, tokens strive to be exemplary models to prove that their group can succeed in jobs from which they historically have been excluded. Thus, tokens must overachieve to make their performance more noticeable than their auxiliary traits. The extra pressures to perform that are imposed on women and nonwhites in nontraditional careers may become overwhelming over time, prompting them to leave the company. Indeed, minorities or women who are preferentially selected due to affirmative action pressures may feel less competent and devalue their own accomplishments (Heilman et al., 1991). Therefore, minorities and women must excel to reverse their own beliefs and those of others that they were unqualified for admission to formerly exclusive positions (Gleckman et al., 1991).

Blocked Career

Scarce or blocked promotions initiate turnover, especially for minority and female departures. We previously noted that women and minorities primarily hold jobs in the secondary labor market with limited advancements (Cox, 1991; Hom, 1979; Kantor, 1977). Advancement comes slowly even among those assuming professional or managerial jobs and eventually is blocked by a "glass ceiling" (Fisher, 1992; Morrison & Von Glinow, 1990). Women trapped in white-collar "ghettos" (Gleckman et al., 1991; Konrad, 1990; Morrison & Von Glinow, 1990), Asians trapped in technical professions (Duleep & Sanders, 1992; Mandel & Farrell, 1992), and black executives in departments of community relations and public affairs—these all reflect occupancy in short-ladder occupations or what had been termed *pigeon-holing* (Cose, 1993).

Although not shown in our model (Exhibit 8.1), career stagnation for minorities and women also may prompt involuntary quits. A cycle of disadvantage stems from limited advancement opportunities, reconfirming the belief that they are only competent to work in dead-end jobs. Kantor (1977) observed that women assigned to dead-end tracks become less committed to the company, underestimate career aspirations, withdraw from extra responsibilities at work, and question their competence. As a result, they become undesirable candidates for promotion. If the alienation worsens, they eventually are fired.

Unsupportive Coworkers

The popular press reports widespread antagonism or indifference from white male coworkers (Morrison & Von Glinow, 1990), due to prejudice (Heilman, 1983; Jones, 1972; Stockdale, 1993) or dissimilar cultural values (Cox et al., 1991; O'Reilly, Caldwell, & Barnett, 1989; Tsui & O'Reilly, 1989). Well-publicized affirmative action programs may provoke a backlash from white males who resent incoming people of color or women, regarding them as unqualified or as threats to their own jobs (Brimelow & Spencer, 1993; Cox, 1991; Gates, 1993; Gleckman et al., 1991; Solomon, 1991).

Whatever its origin, rejection from Caucasian men hampers the careers of women and minorities and may drive them out of the company. Peers have widespread influences on each other and can facilitate careers, including the socialization of newcomers (Cleveland & Kerst, 1993; Feldman, 1988); provision of vital information about the job, including career advice (Lobel, 1993; Luthans, Rosenkrantz, & Hennessey, 1985); cooperation on joint projects; and political support from informal alliances and coalitions (Cleveland & Kerst, 1993; Kantor, 1977). Relatedly, supervisors solicit input from coworkers, including reports about collegiality (a critical basis for managerial promotions), for performance evaluations (Cleveland & Kerst, 1993; Kantor, 1977).

Sexual Harassment

Last, but certainly not least, is the potential role of sexual harassment on turnover. Briefly, sexual harassment is a form of sex discrimination that often motivates women to quit (Gutek & Koss, 1993; "How Employees Perceive Sexual Harassment," 1992). Our earlier review of this area indicates how widespread it was (Hom & Griffeth, 1995). It would appear from the abundance of writing on the subject in the late 1990s that it remains an issue. Clearly, sexual harassment may drive women from organizations in search of a less hostile work environment—a right to which everyone is entitled. And they may sue their employers in the process.

White Male Flight

Paradoxically, the entry of people of color and women into the workplace may induce exits among white men by dissolving group cohesion, because their presence engenders conflicts and miscommunications and threatens white male self-identity (Tsui, Egan, & O'Reilly, 1992). The shifting demographic composition of the referent group—the White Male Club—undermines the group as a basis for social identify and self-esteem. Thus, some white men ask themselves, "Do I belong here?" and decide to quit.

Tsui et al. (1992) found that growing female representation in 151 work units weakened the men's commitment to the organization and inclination to stay. Growing minority concentration in the units intensified white flight. These provocative findings question the conventional assumption behind the cultural diversity movement that heterogeneity inevitably enhances interpersonal relationships among group members.

Perceived or actual reverse discrimination may prompt some white men to desert companies that aggressively implement affirmative action. They may feel that affirmative action programs have become means to discriminate against them rather than ways to combat racial and sexual discrimination (Gates, 1993). In a 1984 poll, 1 white man in 10 believed that quotas had cost him promotions (Brimelow & Spencer, 1993). Similarly, a national poll taken by *Newsweek* magazine disclosed that 48% of white men feel that "white males should fight against affirmative-action programs"; only 36% rejected this belief (Cose, 1993). Such sentiments are fueled partly by employers who notify white male applicants that they were denied employment so that they could meet affirmative action goals (Cose, 1993; Solomon, 1991). Though face-saving, this rationale surely angers excluded white men, who feel that they unfairly lost jobs or promotions to unqualified minorities or women. Perceived or real reverse discrimination may diminish the loyalty of white men to organizations.

Strategies for Reducing Sexual Harassment

Sexual harassment is such a harmful behavior that we have a special section on programs that organizations can use to reduce the likelihood of it occurring.

There are a number of strategies to deal with sexual harassment, and today most organizations have enacted policies prohibiting it (Fitzgerald & Shullman, 1993; Gutek & Koss, 1993). Perhaps more effective than written policies are personal statements from executives, like that of a midwestern utility CEO who mailed a brochure and letter to all 7,000 employees publicizing his "zero tolerance for sexual harassment" (Segal, 1992). Another popular remedy has been sensitivity training for men, the main perpetrators of sexual harassment (Cleveland & Kerst, 1939). Many men may mistake friendliness in a woman for sexual overtures and may not see a problem if one exists (Deutschman, 1991; Stockdale, 1993).

At the very least, organizations should monitor sexual harassment using sound instrumentation, such as the Sexual Experience Questionnaire (Fitzgerald & Shullman, 1993). Briefly, this measure assesses sexual harassment with three subscales: gender harassment, unwanted sexual attention, and sexual coercion (Fitzgerald, Gelfand, & Drasow, 1995). An example of the first subscale is "Have you ever been in a situation where a supervisor or coworker habitually told suggestive stories or offensive jokes?" (Fitzgerald et al., 1995, p. 428).

Alternatively, organizations could potentially screen out job candidates who are likely to sexually harass others. For this selection, employers might consider Pryor, LaVite, and Stoller's (1993) Likelihood to Sexually Harass (LSH) scale. This measure has men imagine themselves in 10 situations in which they control rewards for attractive women and estimate their chances of using rewards to exploit women sexually. An example of an item from this scale follows:

> Imagine that you are the news director for a local television station. Due to some personnel changes you have to replace the anchor woman for the evening news. Your policy has always been to promote reporters from within your organization when an anchor woman vacancy occurs. There are several female reporters from which to choose. All are young, attractive and apparently qualified for the job. One reporter, Loretta W., is someone whom you find very sexy. You initially hired her, giving her a first break in the TV news business. How likely are you to do the following things in this situation?
>
> Assuming that you fear no reprisals in your job, would you offer Loretta the job in exchange for sexual favors?

Respondents would indicate the likelihood of their performing these behaviors on a 5-point scale, ranging from 1 (*not at all likely*) to 5 (*very likely*).

Survey research indicates that high-LSH men have adversarial sexual beliefs and express stronger rape intentions. In laboratory experiments, high-LSH men (acting as trainers) sexually touched a female trainee more often than did low-LSH men after both had observed an authority figure sexually harassing this trainee. It is important to mention one caveat with a scale like this: It is one thing to show that a measure performs well in a developmental research context, but it is entirely different when used as a selection tool. Obviously, this scale should undergo validation for employee selection, which must establish that social desirability bias will not jeopardize predictive validity.

Another thing employers can do is to change the workplace structurally by improving the balance of women to men in work groups, especially in male-dominated occupations. Research shows that when work groups have a few token women and women join nontraditional jobs, sexual harassment increases (Deutschman, 1991; Fitzgerald & Shullman, 1993; Lach & Gwartney-Gibbs, 1993). Promoting more women into management may lessen sexual harassment because women working for male bosses face more sexual harassment from their coworkers (Fitzgerald & Shullman, 1993). Grievance procedures for filing harassment claims—and safeguards against retaliation—may deter turnover (Gutek & Koss, 1993). After all, slow-responding complaint systems that provide few guarantees of confidentiality or protection from reprisal can motivate victims to leave (Deutschman, 1991; Gutek & Koss, 1993; "How Employees Perceive Sexual Harassment," 1992; Lach & Gwartney-Gibbs, 1993). Several companies have developed alternatives that assure confidentiality, such as an ombudsperson who counsels victims privately or allowing victims to file complaints with their superiors, the human resource department, or a panel of peers (Segal, 1992). DuPont has a private 24-hour hotline offering suggestions on personal safety and sexual harassment (Deutschman, 1991).

As companies strive to prevent sexual harassment, other sociodemographic trends outside the workplace may frustrate their efforts (Lobel, 1993). Growing female representation in organizations increases contact between men and women, creating more nonharassing and harassing sexual behavior. According to a Gallup poll, 57% of working Americans view workplace dating as acceptable (Lobel, 1993). To prevent sexual harassment without prohibiting office romances, employers might introduce policies restricting certain forms of sexual behaviors (Lobel, 1993; Segal, 1992). In particular, they might prohibit superiors from dating subordinates and have in place policies embodying women's definitions of inappropriate kinds of sexuality in the workplace. A "reasonable woman" standard should set company norms, because it is women who most often interpret certain acts as sexual harassment (Segal, 1992; Stockdale, 1993).

Cultural Diversity Management

Responding to changing workforce demographics, many corporations have tried to improve their management of cultural diversity. Cox (1991) developed a taxonomy of cultural diversity management and cataloged practices that advance cultural diversity goals. Briefly, Cox proposed five goals that facilitate cultural diversity:

1. Pluralism is a prime diversity objective—the valuing of cultural differences to the extent of permitting minority culture to shape company culture. To further pluralism, Cox recommended specific training (such as managing and valuing

training in cultural diversity), the orientation of new members (help for minority and female workers to adjust to their new jobs), and language training (e.g., English instruction for immigrants). Beyond training, Cox argued that top management support is essential in fostering pluralism. Toward this end, he prescribed representation of minorities and women on key committees; the inclusion of diversity goals in mission statements; and the formation of advisory groups—comprising minorities and women—for senior management to provide advice on improving diversity.

2. Structural integration—the broad representation of minorities and women at all organizational levels and functions—should be a second diversity goal. Cox proposed educational efforts to develop the skills of minorities. Aetna Life Insurance Company is a leader in this regard, providing in-house basic education programs and exchanging jobs for customized education by community agencies and private schools. Cox also highlighted special career development programs, such as McDonald's "Black Career Development Program," which provides career enhancement advice and fast-track career paths for minorities. Other examples can be seen in affirmative action for top-level jobs ("Moving Past Affirmative Action," 1990), such as Pepsico's "Black Managers Association," which serves "as a supplemental source of nominees for promotion to management jobs, and the practice of hiring qualified minorities directly into managerial and professional jobs" (Cox, 1991, p. 43). Other practices that further structural integration are the inclusion of diversity management in managerial appraisals and rewards and flexible work arrangements and schedules (to reduce conflicts between work and family that burden women). For example, Xerox strove for a 35% female representation in 300 top executive jobs in one division by 1995 and held managers accountable for that goal ("Moving Past Affirmative Action," 1990). Baxter International and Monsanto tied managers' raises to affirmative action goals (Fisher, 1992; Konrad, 1990).

3. The third goal for cultural-diversity programs should be integration in informal networks (Cox, 1991). Mentoring programs, company-sponsored social events, and support groups for minorities can facilitate their involvement in networks. Security Pacific's "Black Officers Support System" recruits and retains blacks (Morrison & Von Glinow, 1990); Honeywell and Pacific Bell team young women and minorities with executives who coach them on career strategies and corporate politics (Fisher, 1992; Konrad, 1990). Sustaining such prescriptions, surveys describe effective diversity programs as embodying networking, mentorships, and requirements that management be accountable for achieving diversity results ("Managing Diversity: Successes and Failures," 1991).

4. The fourth goal toward effective diversity management is combating cultural biases and prejudice. The goal encompasses seminars on equal opportunity that include sexual harassment workshops, training on civil rights legislation,

and workshops on sexism and racism. Cox also suggested establishing focus groups (small groups confronting attitudes and feelings about differences within the group), such as Digital's "Valuing Differences" groups, who attempt to achieve four major objectives: (a) stripping away stereotypes, (b) examining assumptions about out-groups, (c) building important relationships with people regarded as different, and (d) raising levels of personal empowerment ("Moving Past Affirmative Action," 1990). Another technique, called bias-reduction training, is a program designed to change attitudes. For example, Northern Telecom has a 16-hour program to identify and modify negative attitudes toward people of different cultural backgrounds. Internal research that examines the career progress of minority and female employees may lessen bigotry in the workforce. Companies have instituted a tracking system for minority and female managers to ensure that they acquire developmental experience for upward mobility ("OFCCP's Glass Ceiling Initiative," 1991; "One Company's Approach," 1991). A task force organized by Equitable Finance addresses women's problems identified by its surveys.

5. Finally, effective diversity management should reduce conflict between different groups (Solomon, 1991). Organizations can do this through special communications. For example, by being open with employees about specific features of new initiatives targeting minorities, Xerox diffused backlash from whites. Similarly, U.S. West (now Qwest) reported how promotion rates were seven times higher for white men than for white women and 16 times higher than for nonwhite women. In summary, Cox (1991) proposed a family of promising techniques for promoting cultural diversity that may help minorities and women stay on the job. However, because most supportive evidence comes from testimonials ("Managing Diversity: Successes and Failures," 1991; "One Company's Approach," 1991), and given the growing significance of cultural diversity, there is a strong need for empirical research to determine their effectiveness for reducing turnover (Morrison & Von Glinow, 1990).

Managing Work-Family Conflict

As we have documented previously (Hom & Griffeth, 1995), one of the greatest problems, particularly for women, is balancing family and work. It is so demanding, in fact, that several surveys have shown that many women leave the workforce to devote more time to the family. For example, the Department of Labor found that, of all women leaving paid employment in 1986, 33% did so to devote more time to the family; of all men who left, 1% gave that reason (Mattis, 1990). Also, a Yankelovich Clancy Shulman survey disclosed that a third of working mothers want to quit to become full-time homemakers (Spiers, 1992). A more recent Yankelovich survey found that nearly half the workforce (45%) has changed jobs to spend more time with their families. This is surprising in light of the fact that this is nearly as many as the 47% of workers who told the pollsters they have changed jobs to make more money. Commenting on the new survey findings, Richard Eyre, an authority on family values, said: "People still desire material things, but they view time and relationships as scarce and realize that possessions alone are not enough to provide the level of personal satisfaction they desire" ("Workers Switch Jobs," 2000).

Work-family conflict is not likely to lessen as time demands from work and family increase with the fast pace of modern life. Compared to employees who do not experience work-family conflict, those who do are three times more likely to think about quitting (43% vs. 14%; Johnson, 1995). In the section to follow, we examine several promising approaches cataloged by Zedeck and Mosier (1990) for reducing work-family conflict: maternity and parental leave, child- and dependent-care services, alternative work schedules, and telecommuting. The Families and Work Institute used these strategies to devise an overall company index of family-friendliness (Bernstein, Weber, & Driscoll, 1991). We have modified this index to include telecommuting (see Exhibit 8.2). The object is to use the index to evaluate a company's policies toward family-friendliness so companies can use it as a report card to assess how well they are doing with family-friendly policies. The higher the companies score, the more family-friendly it is and the lower turnover is likely to be from these causes.

Family Leave

Exit interviews and surveys reveal that many women leave the workplace—temporarily or permanently—to bear or raise children (Gerson, 1985; Huey & Hartley, 1988). Without doubt, maternity or parental leave would reduce exits (Cook, 1989; Johnson, 1990). In particular, the 1993 Family and Medical Leave Act may sustain loyalty by guaranteeing women and men 12 weeks of unpaid leave for childbirth or family sickness. This law ensures that the same—or a similar—job is available on return and that medical coverage continues during the leave. Although they ease conflicts between work and family, these federal provisions are limited. The law excludes firms employing fewer than 50 workers, and, unlike many European laws, it does not mandate

Policy	Score
Flexible schedule	105
Family leave	40
Financial assistance	80
Corporate giving and community service	60
Dependent care services	155
Management change	90
Work-family stress management	80
Telecommuting	125
Total possible score	735

Exhibit 8.2. Revised Index of Corporate Family-Friendliness
SOURCE: Adapted from The Families and Work Institute's Index of Family-Friendliness (Bernstein, Weber, & Driscoll, 1991).

paid leave. Some companies offer more ample benefits than the law requires, especially informally (Bernstein, 1991). Forty percent of working women have partial or full paid maternity leave, given as a disability or sickness benefit. New parents at AT&T can receive up to 1 year's unpaid leave (Galen, 1993; Zedeck & Mosier, 1990).

Despite their promise, there is little evidence that family leave policies truly reduce exits, a prime reason for their adoption (Bernstein et al., 1991; Galen, 1993). Because other family-responsive measures were adopted concurrently, the studies mentioned previously merely suggest that accommodation for pregnancy decreases turnover (Trenk, 1990). Aetna Life & Casualty introduced a family leave policy because, prior to 1988, 23% of the women returning to work after childbirth quit later (Trenk, 1990). This leave—allowing new mothers up to 6 months off without pay—and part-time work cut turnover by more than 50%, resulting in an 88% to 91% retention rate for leave-takers over the past 5 years. Aetna calculated that this reduction in turnover represents more than $1 million in annual savings (Johnson, 1995). More recently, Glass and Riley (1998), in a large study of 324 randomly selected pregnant women, found that length of leave available for childbirth and the ability to avoid mandatory overtime on return significantly decreased job attrition after controlling for the effects of wages, partner's income, and number of existing children.

Child and Dependent Care Services

Many businesses provide day care services, usually in the form of information and referral programs or flexible spending accounts (Goff, Mount, & Jamison, 1990; O'Reilly, 1992; Zedeck & Mosier, 1990). Most employees with children want on-site or nearby child care, which is also the costliest day care service (Kossek, 1990; Zedeck & Mosier, 1990, Yalow, 1990). Secret, Sprang, and Bradford (1998), in a survey of staff members in a survey research center, found that the presence of infants at the work site increased employees' job satisfaction and job productivity and had no effect on their completion of deadlines. Moreover, the overwhelming majority of employees (92%) felt proud to be associated with an organization that recognizes this need of parents. Although Goff et al. (1990) found that on-site child care did not decrease work-family conflicts, the Campbell Soup Company believed that on-site child care at its headquarters lowered exits (Yalow, 1990). More convincingly, Milkovich and Gomez (1976) observed that mothers enrolling their children in company-sponsored day care resigned less often than did mothers who did not. Youngblood and Chambers-Cook (1984) and Secret et al. (1998) found that the availability of day care decreased employees' intentions to withdraw, while Glass and Riley (1998) found that social support from supervisors and coworkers reduced actual turnover among childbearing women. Relatedly, Aryee, Luk, and Stone (1998) found work-family support from supervisors to be positively related to stay intentions in a large Hong Kong sample ($N = 228$) of employed parents in a human service authority.

One of the authors of this book (Cohen, Griffeth, & Barksdale, 1994) examined the effects (at a large hospital in northern Virginia) of an employer-sponsored on-site child care center in a quasi-experimental, longitudinal field study. The study started at the opening of the center and examined the effects on three distinct groups of employees after 1 year. The hospital provided the researchers with the three lists of employees: a group who was going to use the child care center, a group who had children but who were not using the center, and a group who had no children. These latter two groups were randomly selected from a longer list of employees. Job satisfaction, organizational commitment, job and work involvement, and perceived organizational support were measured at the opening of the center and 1 year later. Moreover, we measured absenteeism, performance (as rated by supervisors), and voluntary turnover for the year after both surveys. The results showed that, although the employees without children were significantly more committed to the organization and more involved in their jobs, they and the employees using the child care center had lower absenteeism than the employees with children who did not use the child care center. Moreover, the employees using the center had higher performance ratings and lower turnover than the employees with no children (4% vs. 16%, respectively). In conclusion, parents using on-site child care are more likely to remain and be higher-performing members of the workforce.

Alternative Work Schedules

Alternative work schedules help employees balance home and work duties but experimental tests find that flextime does not affect quits (Dalton & Mesch, 1990; Ralston & Flanagan, 1985). Compressed work schedules—longer hours but for fewer days—may build loyalty by giving the employees more days to handle personal duties (Pierce & Dunham, 1992). Compressed work weeks—with recuperative days off—can compensate for the disruptive effects of shift rotation, a leading cause of turnover (Choi, Jameson, Brekke, Podratz, & Mundahl, 1986; Newby, 1980; Zedeck, Jackson, & Summers, 1983). Pierce and Dunham (1992) observed that police officers on shorter work weeks felt higher morale and greater able to manage outside demands. These results hold for employees in other countries, as well. Aryee et al. (1998) found, in their large ($N = 228$) sample of employed parents in Hong Kong, that satisfaction with work schedule flexibility was negatively related to turnover intentions.

Part-time work and job-sharing—two employees sharing a full-time position—may deter resignations (Galen, 1993; Shellenbarger, 1992; Zedeck & Mosier, 1990). Hospitals have long experimented with part-time and temporary work to retain nurses and attract inactive nurses back into nursing (Bogdanich, 1991; Huey & Hartley, 1988; Laird, 1983; Newby, 1980; Wandelt, Pierce, & Widdowson, 1981). Many mothers in other occupations credit part-time hours and job-sharing for their return to work (Johnson, 1990; Mattis, 1990). Woman lawyers and certified public accountants increasingly can work part-time and take extended paths to partnership (Ehrlich, 1989). However, it is suggested that such "mommy tracks" may derail women's careers (Schwartz, 1989). Nevertheless, many employers believe that part-time work and job-sharing improve the retention of women employees. One company offers valued employees job-sharing in an effort to retain them (Shellenbarger, 1992).

Telecommuting

We first defined telecommuting as working at home and electronically transferring the results to the office (Hom & Griffeth, 1995). However, we now believe a more inclusive definition is offered by Feldman and Gainey (1997) as "the use of telecommunications technology (e.g., personal computers, fax machines, cellular phones, dial-up access, etc.) to give employees the ability to accomplish their work physically away from company premises" (p. 370). Over the years, telecommuting has received a large amount of popular support in the business press, even though the empirical research and conceptual understanding have not kept pace with the anecdotal evidence (Feldman & Gainey, 1997). Moreover, by 1997, a majority of U.S. companies (51%) had some kind of telecommuting program in place, with an estimate of between 7 million to 11 million telecommuters (Allen, Renn, & Griffeth, 1999).

Telecommuting may help reduce work-family conflict by enabling parents to be more available during the day and not to waste huge amounts of time commuting (Zedeck & Mosier, 1990). For example, it is not uncommon for parents to spend 2 to 4 hours per day commuting to work, which obviously detracts from their family-related activities, increases work-family conflict, and gives the appearance that the family is less important to Americans. However, this is a misperception because, as was pointed out previously, nearly as many employees reported changing their jobs to spend more time with their families (45%) as did those who changed jobs to receive more money (47%) ("Workers Switch Jobs," 2000).

Telecommuting has been suggested as one of a number of low-cost strategies for reducing turnover caused by work-family conflict (Alexander, 1998). For example, some corporations, like Travelers Insurance and Metropolitan Life Insurance, have reported that absenteeism and turnover have decreased as a result of telecommuting. Relatedly, a recent study found that employees who telecommute can save their employers $10,000 each in reduced absenteeism and turnover costs ("Telecommuting Can Save Employees $10,000 per Worker," 2000). An early study found that female office employees disclosed that telecommuting let them care for children and strengthened their company commitment (Olson & Primps, 1984). However, they perceived that they earned lower pay and benefits and faced more conflict over the simultaneous demands of work and family. Male professionals, on the other hand, reported less work and commuting stress and enjoyed more leisure opportunities. In a recent study comparing telecommuting and regular salespeople, Igbaria and Guimaraes (1999) found that telecommuters reported less role conflict and ambiguity and tended to be happier with their supervisors and more committed to their organizations. But they also reported lower satisfaction with their peers and with promotions. Unfortunately, most of this research has been qualitative or weak empirically and not guided by theoretical explanations. More recently, several researchers have started to propose theoretical frameworks in the hope of stimulating more rigorous research on the subject and to better understand it.

Feldman and Gainey (1997), drawing from the literatures on contingent employment, job design, and social isolation, developed a framework for understanding how different telecommuting arrangements can lead to different patterns of employee attitudes and behaviors. In this framework, Feldman and Gainey propose seven major sets of relationships in need of exploration to fully understand telecommuting. They propose that job attributes (such as job autonomy and task interdependence) and telecommuting arrangements (such as hours, schedule, and location) influence each other and are mediators between individual differences (demographic status and personality dimensions) and work outcomes, such as performance, absenteeism, and turnover. For researchers, they include several suggestions for further study, such as more rigorous, controlled research; sampling across the different telecommuting arrangements; quantitative assessments of outcomes (in contrast to qualitative statements like "saved floor space" or "lowered absenteeism"); examination of other outcomes, such as organizational citizenship behaviors; and effective measurement of key variables. For managers, they include some avenues to consider, like acknowledging that telecommuting involves some type of job redesign whether it involves the division of labor, integration of work group projects, the type of supervision required, task interdependence, or the management of external stakeholders. They also recognize that the use of satellite offices may be a viable intermediate step toward telecommuting and note that several companies, such as Pacific Bell, Panasonic, and Georgia Power, have effectively used such centers to organize telecommuters. Moreover, they acknowledge that there may be wide variances in how individual employees respond to telecommuting. They realistically point out to managers that demographic group membership and personality styles may enhance or even suppress the proposed benefits of telecommuting. Consistent with the need for empirical research, Feldman and Gainey advance a number of testable propositions of the various linkages in their model. With organizations like GE Plastics, Apple Computer, the federal government, and the Phoenix, Arizona, municipal government, where telecommuting has grown, the benefits of telecommuting are significant. However, to truly benefit from this innovation, we need better theoretical frameworks and more rigorous research (Feldman & Gainey, 1997).

Another attempt to understand telecommuting comes from a recent article by Allen et al. (1999), who also propose an individual-level model of telecommuting, shown graphically in Exhibit 8.3. As that exhibit depicts, autonomy, perceived organizational support, and role ambiguity serve as mediators between telecommuting dimensions and work outcomes. They build on some of Feldman and Gainey's ideas of telecommuting dimensions but suggest that a percentage of work time continuum would better describe the dimensions as opposed to either-or propositions. They also advance a number of testable propositions. Clearly, attempts to understand telecommuting are being proposed. Hopefully, rigorous empirical research will follow.

Summary and Conclusions

Here, we set out a number of suggestions that the savvy manager can use to reduce turnover of minorities and women:

- Evaluate employees fairly.

- Pay equitably.

- Examine jobs for simplicity, boredom, and lack of challenge, using the procedures described in Chapter 2.

- Treat minorities and women as individuals, not as symbols of their race or gender.

- Expand opportunities for upward mobility and career prospects; don't pigeonhole minorities and women (e.g., Asians in technical professions, African Americans in community relations, public affairs, EEO departments).

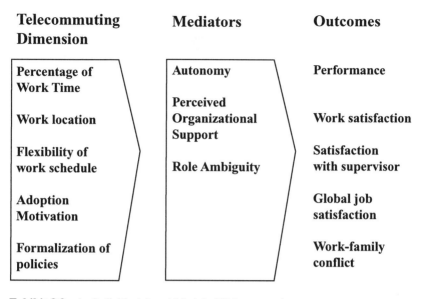

Telecommuting Dimension	Mediators	Outcomes
Percentage of Work Time	Autonomy	Performance
Work location	Perceived Organizational Support	Work satisfaction
Flexibility of work schedule	Role Ambiguity	Satisfaction with supervisor
Adoption Motivation		Global job satisfaction
Formalization of policies		Work-family conflict

Exhibit 8.3. An Individual-Level Model of Telecommuting

- Monitor departments for sexual harassment.
- Explore cultural diversity management programs.
- Help alleviate work-family conflicts by implementing family leave policies, child and dependent care services, alternative work schedules, and telecommuting.

In summary, many companies are implementing family-assistance programs to help employees balance their personal lives with their work. Several family-supportive policies and practices, such as family leave, child care support, flexible working arrangements, and telecommuting, do appear to enhance retention. As we previously noted (Hom & Griffeth, 1995), evaluations of these efforts have primarily examined the overall impact of a host of family-responsive measures, which appear considerable. Despite the impressive results, there is still need for more rigorous experimental (or quasi-experimental) tests of how effectively family-responsive measures deter resignations. To date, most evidence rests mainly on testimonials of successful cases (which may not be representative) (Goff et al., 1990; Kossek & Grace, 1990). The few existing empirical evaluations are plagued by a lack of control groups and statistical controls for extraneous confounds (Miller, 1984). Firms usually install several family benefits simultaneously, making it difficult to isolate the efficacy of a particular benefit (cf. Trenk, 1990). In the light of rising demands for family benefits, more inquiry is still urgently warranted to ascertain which approaches prolong employment (Kossek & Grace, 1990).

Managing Exiting Employees

Norm sat across the desk from Tracy, who was just ending her last day with Acme Accounting. Tracy had been with the company only about 8 months, and she was an outstanding employee in his department. Norm didn't know where to begin, so he looked at some papers on his desk while Tracy sat quietly. After about 30 seconds, when the silence became unbearable to Norm, he looked up and smiled.

"Any chance I can talk you into staying?"

Tracy smiled politely. "I don't think so, Norm. I've really enjoyed working here, with you and the others. I just think it's time to move on. Greener pastures, you know."

Norm smiled again, hoping she'd tell him why she was leaving, but realized it probably wasn't going to happen. Tracy was the third good employee this month who had decided to quit. He was beginning to doubt his management skills.

"Was there something *I* could have done differently that would have made work more enjoyable?"

Tracy's smile vanished as she looked down at her lap. Looking up again, she said, "I don't think so, Norm. By and large, I really liked everything here. This opportunity just came up closer to home, and so I decided to look into it, and when Ron and I evaluated everything, I decided to take the offer."

Ron was Tracy's husband. Norm wondered what his role in all this was. From conversations with Tracy's friends here, Norm knew that "closer to home" really meant about 5 miles. Not a big difference, he thought.

"Well, I wish you the best of luck," Norm said as he leaned across the desk to shake Tracy's hand. "Remember, you can have your old job back, if you want. It'll only take a phone call to me, and I can have you back in the system overnight."

"Thanks, Norm, I'll be sure to let you know if that happens," she said as she stood up to leave. What a jerk, she thought. He doesn't have a clue as to why all his good employees were leaving, she thought as she headed for the door. She wanted to tell him the actual reasons for her leaving, but she needed the letter of recommendation to get the job. She had the job now, so why didn't she tell him? She didn't know why she didn't tell him now, but it really wasn't her responsibility to tell him, especially now that she was leaving, either. Eventually, he'd probably learn the real reasons why she and the others had quit.

Norm sat back in his chair and watched her leave. Another good employee gone. He'd have to talk to HR about how the recruiting efforts were going. It shouldn't be that hard to hire another new accountant.

Several things are apparent from this exit interview. First, does Norm really know how to conduct an exit interview? Apparently not. He seemed uncomfortable with the whole process. Second, did he really learn anything from Tracy? No. What he knew about her leaving was from her coworkers, and that really was not very much. Was it likely that Tracy was ever going to tell him the real reasons for her quitting? Not likely. Why not? Tracy needed a positive letter of recommendation from this company to get her next job, and she did not want to jeopardize that. But she had the job now; why didn't she tell him? We'll probably never know the answer to this question, but one reason could be that she did not want to leave on a confrontational note. Many people avoid confrontation or situations that they perceive will be unpleasant. Also, she probably did not want to "burn her bridges behind her." This is a common practice of many employees. Did Tracy appear to respect Norm? Not really. It was obvious to her that Norm did not know why she was leaving. One last question needs to be asked regarding this case: Should Norm have been conducting the exit interview? We do not believe so, because Tracy may have been leaving because of Norm's policies or practices,. Later in this chapter, we suggest others who should have conducted the interview. Research shows that when reasons given for quitting in exit interviews are compared to reasons given in attitude surveys, employees usually give nonjob-related factors as their reasons for quitting in an exit interview (Fottler, Crawford, Quintana, & White, 1995), as Tracy did. To arrive at actual reasons for quitting, we recommend the use of a different, less reactive method than the exit interview.

Background

During the last days of an employee's tenure, a number of organizations initiate interviews between the parting employee and one of their managers. Such a discussion between a representative of an organization and a person whose employment with the organization has been ended is referred to as the *exit interview* (Giacalone & Duhon, 1991).

It is widely believed that exit interviews can help to determine why employees quit working for their organization (e.g., Hinrichs, 1975), as a manager of a large insurance company in Montreal notes:

> [The exit interview] is a tool to help us look at our company policies. For instance, if everyone's leaving because of salary, we will investigate salary trends. The exit interview is a check for us to see how we're doing. (Brotheron, 1996, p. 45)

Exit interviews also serve other purposes. First, they might be used as a final attempt to salvage the quitting employee (Lefkowitz & Katz, 1969), as Norm tried very lamely to do in our case. Second, they can be a public relations tool for the organization (Lefkowitz & Katz, 1969) by ensuring that the parting employee leaves the company on a positive note. Norm's attempt at this was very weak, at best. For example, the exit interviewer could invite the parting employees to keep the door open by offering them the chance to continue attending company events in the future. Norm was not skillful enough to do this, but it is a possibility if the company wants to rehire the person. Third, the exit interview can serve as a final opportunity to inform parting employees about their remaining rights and obligations and understand their benefit packages (Brotheron, 1996; Kiechel, 1990), if they have any. It can be used to make them aware of their duty to protect the intellectual property of the organization (Cundiff, 1993; Kiechel, 1990) and to remember to return company property before they leave (Brotheron, 1996). Finally, the exit interview can protect organizations from lawsuits by providing information about incidents of sexual harassment and discrimination in the workplace (Brotheron, 1996; Giacalone, Knouse, & Ashworth, 1991; Giacalone, Stuckey, & Beard, 1996).

These multiple purposes make the exit interview potentially useful for most organizations. Particularly as a tool for gaining information about turnover reasons, the exit interview has gained widespread popularity in corporate America. Some even claim that the exit interview is the most common technique used in U.S. organizations to determine why employees quit working for their organizations (Hinrichs, 1975). According to a survey conducted by Robert Half International, 93% percent of the executives in large U.S. companies believe that the exit interview provides useful information (Brotheron, 1996).

Reasons for this widespread optimism are not hard to find. The popular idea supporting the use of exit interviews as a tool for information gathering is that many employees should feel free to speak honestly about their employer in their last days of organizational membership (Smith & Kerr, 1953). Yet, optimism or popular thought cannot substitute for rigorous research. Contrary to popular thought, rigorous research (however scarce it may be; Feldman & Klaas, 1999) provides grounds for a less enthusiastic conclusion regarding the exit interview as a tool for data collection: Exit interviews are a highly inaccurate source for gathering information (e.g., Hinrichs, 1975; Lefkowitz & Katz, 1969; Zarandona & Camuso, 1985). In this chapter, we briefly review the evidence showing the inaccuracies of the exit interview, attempt to explain why exit interviews are inaccurate, show ways to make them more accurate, and outline an alternative to the exit interview as a source for gathering information about why employees quit.

Inaccuracies and Other Problems With the Exit Interview

The major challenge in determining whether exit interviews are inaccurate is that it is difficult to find a suitable "criterion." That is, anyone who wants to determine whether a parting employee provides a true reason for leaving needs to know that true reason—which, of course, is impossible to know for the manager/scholar in most cases. Lacking such a criterion, researchers resort to two techniques for measuring the accuracy of exit interviews. First, the information given in an exit interview is compared with the information given in a questionnaire that is sent to the parting employees some time after they quit. Second, the information given in an exit interview is compared with the information given to independent consultants who guaranteed confidentiality to the parting employee.

Using such designs, it was found that the information given in exit interviews diverges quite a bit from the information given in follow-up questionnaires or from interviews conducted by independent consultants (Hinrichs, 1975; Lefkowitz & Katz, 1969; Zarandona & Camuso, 1985). Zarandona and Camuso, for example, found that employees indicated in exit interviews that they left because of salary and benefits (38%), career advancement (28%), position responsibilities (20%), work environment (9%), and supervision (4%). Yet, when responding to a mail questionnaire 18 months later, the same employees indicated rather different reasons for quitting. Two of the largest differences were that only 12% (rather than 38%) now claimed that they left because of salary and benefits and that 24% (rather than 4%) blamed their leaving on poor supervision. This divergence of results should be troublesome to each manager who attempts to base organizational change on the results of exit interviews. If that manager were to rely on the results of the exit interview, she would increase the pay of the employees. If another manager were to rely on the follow-up interview instead, he would take a closer look at the supervisors.

Similar patterns of findings were obtained in all studies that probed the accuracy of exit interviews (e.g., Hinrichs, 1975; Lefkowitz & Katz, 1969), as seen in other relevant findings obtained in this research:

- Employees are more likely to give a definite reason for quitting when they are asked 6 months after they quit rather than on their day of exit (Lefkowitz & Katz, 1969).
- Employees are more likely to blame negative features of the organization for their decision to leave when they are interviewed by independent consultants rather than by company management. (Hinrichs, 1975)

Thus, research indicates that exit interviews are not a trustworthy informational basis for the identification of factors that cause turnover in an organization. Yet, these findings do not reveal why exit interviews are inaccurate. These reasons are explored in the next section.

Reasons for the Inaccuracies in Exit Interviews

Responding to a query from Info World, several employees voiced their opinions regarding exit interviews. Three of those opinions are set out here:

> Respondent 1: A former coworker, in her exit interview, told the HR person exactly what she thought of her current boss. When this worker's new job fell through, it was too late to go back: She had already burned her bridges.

> Respondent 2: Never, ever tell the complete truth in an exit interview, just as you never tell the complete truth of why you left or are interested in leaving at a job interview. If you bad-mouth your former employer, you will most likely not get hired by the interviewer, despite their assertions to the contrary.

> Respondent 3: My HR director knew what was happening and thanked me for all I had to say. I still talk to my former fellow employees, and things have gotten a little better for them. (Steen, 1999, p. 85)

For many years, researchers and practitioners alike only used common sense to derive possible reasons for the inaccuracies of exit interviews (Giacalone et al., 1996). Only recently (e.g., Giacalone & Duhon, 1991) did these attempts become more systematic, involving deeper theoretical reasoning and empirical evidence. Now there exist two perspectives on the reason why exit interviews are inaccurate. These are described here.

The Rational Distortion Perspective. The rational distortion perspective regards the exit interviewee as a rational being who responds honestly only if a cost-benefit analysis reveals that speaking the truth promises a larger payoff than lying. This perspective is presented from two camps of researchers. The first camp regards the exit interview as a final opportunity for the parting employee to leave a favorable impression (e.g., to get a better recommendation; Giacalone & Duhon, 1991; Giacalone et al., 1991). The second camp regards the exit interview as a final opportunity for the parting employee to exercise voice and to bring about changes for the organization (Feldman & Klaas, 1999). Both angles to the rational distortion perspective are complementary in that the latter emphasizes benefits of telling the truth in an exit interview that are widely missing in the former. Combined, those two views outline the costs and benefits of lying or telling the truth in exit interviews.

The *costs of lying* in an exit interview are minimal because exit interviewees provide information that is unique to them—information that is difficult to verify (Giacalone et al., 1991). In other words, exit interviewees can get away with lies because the information that they provide is personal in nature (i.e., their personal reasons for quitting their jobs) and cannot be verified.

The *costs of telling the truth*—for the most part—also determine the benefits of lying (and vice versa). That is, lying is particularly beneficial if telling the truth is costly. Most of the literature that is concerned with exit interviews points out that telling the truth in exit interviews can be a quite risky strategy—particularly when the truth might hurt influential individuals who remain in the organization. Costs that are attached to telling the truth include the following:

- The risk of burning bridges with the former employer (Embrey, Mondy, & Noe, 1979; Hinrichs, 1975; Zarandona & Camuso, 1985)
- The risk of repercussions from the former employer, such as poor references (Embrey et al., 1979; Hinrichs, 1975; Lefkowitz & Katz, 1969)
- The risk of conflicts with individuals in the former organization (Embrey et al., 1979; Giacalone & Knouse, 1989)
- The intangible costs attached to sharing information about one's personal life (Giacalone & Knouse, 1989)
- The risk of incriminating or otherwise harming friends and coworkers who remain with the organization (Giacalone & Knouse, 1989)

Probably many of these reasons were present in Tracy's case. Of course, there are also potential direct *benefits of lying*. Some researchers acknowledge, for example, the existence of calculative characters who intentionally distort information in an exit interview as a means for revenge (e.g., Giacalone & Knouse, 1989). However, those direct benefits are rarely discussed in the exit interview literature.

Finally, there are *benefits of telling the truth*. Feldman and Klaas (1999) note that these benefits are mostly altruistic in nature. That is, telling the truth can be beneficial if it causes organizational change that helps friends and coworkers of the exit interviewee who remain in an organization. Feldman and Klaas also point out, however, that such a benefit can be expected only if the exit interviewee perceives that his or her comments are actually valued by the organization. Thus, organizational practices such as conducting exit interviews during the hurried last day of employment (Giacalone & Knouse, 1989) or using untrained exit interviewers (Hinrichs, 1975) can be very detrimental to the accuracy of an exit interview.

Empirical evidence, however scarce, confirms the proposed relation between costs/benefits and exit interview accuracy (Feldman & Klaas, 1999; Giacalone, Knouse, & Montagliani 1997; Giacalone et al., 1996). One very recent example is the study conducted by Feldman and Klaas (1999). They used a paper-and-pencil experiment and 227 graduate students (84% of whom had prior work experience) to test the impact of several characteristics of hypothetical exit interviews on the students' intentions to respond accurately. That is, the students were given written scenarios that described the circumstances surrounding their exit, the organization, and the exit interview. Then, they were asked whether they would respond honestly in that exit interview. The results indicated that the participants were more willing to speak the truth if they were told that the confidentiality of their responses would be maintained and if they knew that their responses would have no impact on the references given to their new employer. Both findings support the notion that the inaccuracies inherent in exit interviews can be reduced by limiting the potential costs for telling the truth for the exit interviewee (i.e., both confidentiality and a guaranteed independence between the reference given and the exit interview reduce the potential costs of telling the truth). Feldman and Klaas also found support for the notion that a perceived increase in the benefits of telling the truth increases the accuracy of the exit interview. That is, they found that interviewees are more likely to disclose their real reasons for quitting when they have evidence that the organization takes actions to fix problems identified in exit interviews.

The Difficulty-to-Recall Perspective. It is interesting that most scholars who are concerned with the inaccuracies of exit interviews assume that they are caused exclusively by some form of willful act on the part of the exit interviewee. An alternative position—that the exit interviewee simply does not recall why he or she decided to quit—is widely ignored in research and practice. One scholar (Leonard Greenhalgh from Dartmouth's Tucker School of Business) expressed this alternate view in an interview with *Fortune* magazine (Kiechel, 1990). Greenhalgh pointed out that there is a physical quit point (i.e., the day on which the employee actually leaves) and a psychological quit point (i.e., the day on which the employee decides to leave). These two quit points might be quite distant in time, as was found in research studying the turnover process (e.g., Hom & Griffeth, 1991). Greenhalgh then noted that employees may state quite accurately what they think is the reason why they quit at the physical quit time. This, however, does not necessarily reveal what they felt at the psychological quit time. Unfortunately we are not aware of any research that supports (or refutes) this possibility. As it stands, this perspective is a useful reminder that inaccuracies in exit interviews are not necessarily caused by willful distortion.

Other Problems With the Exit Interview. Although the inaccuracies of an exit interview are certainly the most discussed shortcoming of that practice, there are several other problems that deserve brief mentioning. First, organizations may not really know what to do with the information they receive in exit interviews (Brotheron, 1996). Instead, the information obtained is often just filed away and forgotten. The results of one study revealed that only slightly more than 50% of the organizations surveyed actually use the information obtained in their exit interview (Drost, O'Brien, & Marsh, 1987). It is no surprise, then, that some regard the exit interview as a symbolic but otherwise hollow gesture (e.g., Garretson & Teel, 1982). Second, it is not always easy to find and/or train qualified interviewers who can interrogate and record the employees' reasons for quitting without actually biasing the responses obtained from the exit interviewee (Lefkowitz & Katz, 1969). Indeed, some scholars (e.g., Giacalone & Duhon, 1991) require exit interviewers to possess skills that can barely be expected from trained psychiatrists (we discuss this problem in a later section). Here, we intend merely to clarify that the selection and/or creation of trained interviewers is a necessity when exit interviews are performed—one that costs some time and money. Third, sometimes the exit interview is just not a feasible way to end an employment relationship simply because it puts the interviewer and the interviewee in an awkward situation (Giacalone et al., 1996). Clearly, Norm felt very awkward in our opening case, possibly because he really had not received any training on how to conduct an exit interview. Imagine, for example, a situation in which an employee was terminated for stealing company property and is then asked to comment on the advantages and disadvantages of being employed at Company *X*. The potential for awkward situations like this one, of course, is not a shortcoming of every exit interview, but it is a reminder that not every employee is a suitable target for exit interviewing. There is little reason to expect truthful reporting from employees who were discharged or laid off.

In concluding our treatment of the exit interviews' shortcomings, we note that those shortcomings are numerous indeed. Whether an organization can overcome them depends heavily on the methods chosen to increase the accuracy of the exit interview. In the next section, we discuss the suggestions from the literature for a better exit interview.

Suggestions for Improving the Exit Interview

There are several suggestions from the literature to improve the accuracy of the exit interview. In discussing those suggestions set out subsequently, we need to stress, however, that they are preliminary and not based on much empirical evidence. We identified six areas in which scholars and practitioners offer suggestions for a more accurate or valid exit interview. These relate to the structure of the interview process, the training of interviewers, confidentiality, the protection of exit interviewees against repercussions, accuracy checks, and an interview process that ensures that the information provided in an exit interview is actually used.

Structured, Semistructured, or Unstructured Interviews. The term *structure* in interviews refers to the standardization of an interview in terms of questions asked, method of recording answers, method of summarizing responses, and so forth (Campion, Palmer, & Campion, 1997). Structured interviews are well-known in the context of employee selection and were found in numerous studies to be more accurate than unstructured interviews (Campion et al., 1997). Based on these findings, most experts on the selection interviews advise that the interview process should be standardized to get more accurate results. However, this suggestion does not seem to be as accepted in the context of exit interviews. Here, several authors suggest semistructured interviews, in which the interviewer is allowed to ask probing questions (e.g., Embrey et al., 1979; Fottler et al., 1995; Giacalone & Duhon, 1991) to elicit additional information when the interviewee seems reluctant to speak.

We argue that there are at least three serious problems with using probing questions in exit interviews. First, probing questions can easily guide the interviewee into a direction that is consciously or subconsciously intended by the interviewer (Dipboye, 1982). It might be, for example, that the interviewer "believes to know" what is wrong with the organization and tries to direct the interviewee toward an answer that is consistent with this belief. Thus, probing questions may have a biasing effect on the answers obtained. Second, the use of probing questions to elicit accurate answers from a participant is a highly complex task requiring skills exceeding those obtainable in a reasonable time period. This was probably the case with Norm, in our opening case. As such, we suggest that it is highly unlikely that an organization has access to a sufficient pool of exit interviewers who possess those skills. Third, the suggestion that semistructured interviews improve the quality of the exit interview is made without any empirical evidence.

Based on these real and potential problems of semistructured interviews, we suggest the use of structured exit interviews (e.g., Zarandona & Camuso, 1985). That means to provide the interviewer with a set of open-ended questions and a standardized tool for reporting answers (e.g., a tape recorder or an answering form). It also means to instruct the interviewer to avoid asking any follow-up questions unless they are necessary for clarifying questions asked or answers provided. Today, given the computer resources of all but the smallest organizations, an interactive program could be developed that could identify actual reasons for quitting and preserve the anonymity of the departing employee.

Train Interviewers. Although some scholars note that the exit interviewers have to be trained (e.g., Giacalone & Duhon, 1991; Lefkowitz & Katz, 1969), further recommendations in that literature are sketchy and not based on any empirical evidence. Consistent with our earlier suggestion, we propose that interviewers need to be trained to possess the skills needed to conduct structured interviews (e.g., Campion et al., 1997). These skills are easily obtained (Howard, Dailey, & Gulanick, 1979) and are analogous to skills required from other test administrators (Society for Industrial and Organizational Psychology, 1987). Thus, the interviewer has to learn to stick meticulously to the questions provided in an exit interview manual, to avoid probing and follow-up questions, and to take detailed notes.

Confidentiality. Probably the most frequently voiced suggestion regarding the exit interview is that it guarantee confidentiality and anonymity to the departing employee (e.g., Feldman & Klaas, 1999; Zarandona & Camuso, 1985). The main rationale for this suggestion is that confidentiality protects the exit interviewee against retaliation and other costs of telling the truth outlined previously (Fottler et al., 1995; Smith & Kerr, 1953; Zarandona & Camuso, 1985). This suggestion is one of the few that has received empirical support (Feldman & Klaas, 1999). One widely overlooked problem with confidentiality in exit interviews is, however, that such promises of confidentiality cannot always be kept. Stephen D. Bruce, a practitioner and business writer, says, "There are some things people may reveal that you can't ignore—an accusation of harassment, for example" (Brotheron, 1996, p. 50).

Thus, an actual promise of confidentiality should not be given to exit interviewees. Instead, an exit interviewer should state that confidentiality will be maintained, unless legal obligations (such as Title VII of the Civil Rights Act of 1964) prohibit such confidentiality.

Other Means for Protecting the Exit Interviewee Against Repercussions. Because absolute confidentiality and anonymity cannot always be guaranteed in exit interviews, other means for protecting the exit interviewee against repercussions are necessary. Several of those have been proposed.

First, many authors recommend that exit interviews should not be conducted by the direct supervisor but by a manager who had no previous contact with the departing employee (Giacalone & Duhon, 1991). The reasoning here is that a "neutral" person is more likely to obtain honest information from the parting employee than is a direct supervisor who may be the primary reason why the employee is quitting. Usually, such a neutral person will be a member of the HR department (Fottler et al., 1995; Zarandona & Camuso, 1985), but this does not have to be the case always. If the organization is willing to spend some money, an external consultant could take on that role (Fottler et al., 1995; Giacalone & Knouse, 1989; Hinrichs, 1975).

A second possibility is to limit the references given to mere statements of the dates of employment and the job title. This way, employees know that the exit interviews do not have an impact on their references because those references would not contain any substantive information anyway. Feldman and Klaas (1999) found in their empirical study that such a strategy in fact increases the willingness of the participants to tell the truth. Accordingly, the suggestion to limit references to employment dates and job title in order to increase the accuracy of exit interviews seems sound to us. Nevertheless, we add that this suggestion is unfortunate from a broader perspective because references can provide useful information for future employers (Muchinsky, 1979).

A final possibility is to convince employees that the reference process is independent from the exit interview by creating trust in that process over time. Kiechel (1990) suggested that this is easiest to achieve if information provided in exit interviews has not been used against exiting employees in the past. Although this approach is certainly necessary to secure employees' confidence in the exit interview process, it is not sufficient. Giacalone et al. (1996) add that employees are probably more likely to trust the exit interview process if a positive work climate prevails in the focal organization. Interestingly, parting employees may not have many negative things to say about their organization if a positive work climate exists. Thus, paradoxically, those organizations that do not really require honest feedback—because they already have a positive work climate—are the most likely to receive it because parting employees trust their exit interview process. And, of course, organizations with a negative work environment may be the least likely to receive honest feedback, but they are clearly in most need of it.

In summary, employers should attempt to increase the confidence of parting employees in the exit interview process over time. At a minimum, this requires that the information provided in exit interviews must not be used against parting employees. Repeated guarantees and measures to effectively communicate the fairness of the reference process are other means to improve the trust of the workforce in the exit interview process. These measures may not allow an organization to maintain a substantive reference process for the benefit of other employers. It is also advisable that exit interviews not be conducted by the direct supervisor of the parting employee.

Conduct Accuracy Checks. Psychometricians and other researchers appreciate the usefulness of and need for checking the accuracy of data through repeated administration of questionnaires, multiple questions, and other means. Several authors in the realm of exit interviews suggest that the results of exit interviews not be used without checking their accuracy first (Hinrichs, 1975; Zarandona & Camuso, 1985). Several methods for checking the accuracy of exit interviews were proposed. First, Zarandona and Camuso suggest asking colleagues and supervisors of the exiting employee to report their perceptions of why the employee is leaving. A second suggestion is to conduct a follow-up study on the exit interview (e.g., a mailed questionnaire or another interview) approximately 6 or more months after the employee departs (e.g., Fottler et al., 1995; Hinrichs, 1975; Lefkowitz & Katz, 1969). A follow-up study could be a good supplement to the exit interview for several reasons. First, feelings of revenge on the part of the parting employee may be forgotten by then. Second, fear of retaliation from the old employer may not exist anymore, and third, multiple methods (e.g., personal interview and written questionnaire or different interviewers) may provide multiple perspectives to the same problems and, thus, more useful and valid information (Giacalone et al., 1991).

Use the Information. The suggestion to actually use the information obtained in an exit interview is trivial indeed. Yet, as the study by Drost et al. (1987; see previous discussion) showed, only slightly more than 50% of the organizations seem to do so. To ensure that the information obtained in an exit interview is adequately used requires a goal-directed approach (Giacalone et al., 1991). In such an approach, processes have to be developed that ensure that the information provided is analyzed, summarized, and fed back to the organizational decision makers. Such an approach will not only facilitate that the information provided in an exit interview is utilized, but it also sends signals to the employees that the exit interview is more than just a meaningless gesture.

An Alternative Approach

Even though there is still relatively little substantive knowledge explaining why exit interviews are inaccurate, most experts believe that the evidence demonstrating their inaccuracy is rather convincing. Mainly as a result of the exit interview's inaccuracy, most academic researchers concerned with employee turnover use the exit interview only as a secondary data collection tool. Instead, turnover researchers rely on a predictive research design that is identical to the criterion validity design used to validate selection tools. That is, the attitudes of employees are measured by surveys obtained at Time 1. Whether particular attitudes cause employee turnover is then assessed by correlating the employee attitude data with turnover data obtained through exit interviews about 6 to 12 months later (Time 2). Alternatively, turnover researchers could compare quitters to stayers on each of the attitude scales using a *t* test. In this way, one could tell which attitudes statistically and reliably distinguished between the two groups.

Before we elaborate on the advantages of this approach, however, we have to point out two caveats, and we need to make an important clarification. One caveat is that this approach is analytically more demanding than the use of exit interviews because it requires specialized knowledge of research methods, such as questionnaire development, correlation and regression analysis, or *t* tests. On the other hand, such advanced knowledge should be expected from master's graduates in fields such as human resource management and industrial/organizational psychology (of course, this knowledge also can be obtained from consulting firms and the faculty of a nearby business school or psychology department). The second caveat is that it requires that the employees identify themselves in some way on the survey (name, work ID, etc.) so that actual quit-stay data collected at Time 2 can be matched to their survey responses. (Note: This is not a stringent requirement. The authors have conducted dozens of such studies with little or no problems because we assure the confidentiality of the survey, and we always have maintained confidentiality despite occasional management pressures to do otherwise. For this reason, we highly recommend the use of an external consultant because we believe that this person's credibility will be higher than that of a member of the organization. Moreover, an external consultant would not be as susceptible to management pressures to disclose individual data.)

The clarification is that the exit interview is not totally abandoned but becomes a secondary tool for obtaining information of who stays and who leaves and whether the employees quit for voluntary or involuntary reasons— an important distinction we described in an earlier chapter. Furthermore, the exit interview serves many additional purposes that justify its use (see the earlier pages of this chapter).

A Case for the Employee Survey

Although attitude surveys are analytically more demanding and thus potentially more expensive, we argue that the benefits of assessing employee attitudes through their use far outweigh their costs.

First and most important, it was found that the information obtained from employee surveys tends to be richer and more detailed than the information obtained in exit interviews. This was demonstrated in the opening case. It is true that Norm was not a skillful interviewer; however, even interviews conducted by professionals may not reveal the true reasons for the employee's departure. For example, Fottler et al. (1995) compared data obtained through both methods in a sample of nurses and found

- That there is less reluctance to raise and discuss work-related causes for turnover in employee surveys than in exit interviews
- That employees provide more recommendations for improvement in attitude surveys than in exit interviews
- That the responses obtained in employee surveys were more detailed overall than in exit interviews

Second, attitude surveys are administered to a broader and more representative sample of employees than are exit interviews. That is, exit interviews are only administered to employees who are about to exit the organization, whereas attitude surveys are administered to all employees (or a random sample of all employees).

Third, confidentiality can be guaranteed more convincingly in employee surveys than in exit interviews, especially from the external consultant. This is because employee surveys usually are administered to all employees at roughly the same time. In addition, the questionnaires usually are returned to the consultant in large stacks representing the responses of all (or most) employees in a given department. Consequently, the external consultant is unlikely to have the time or inclination to go to the trouble of reporting a particular individual's questionnaire. In addition, this could result in a legal problem for the consultant via a breach of contract implicitly implied by the employee's consent to participate in the study and/or invasion of the employee's privacy. In contrast, the exit interview (even an exit questionnaire) is much easier to trace back to a given employee because it is administered to one employee at a time, usually at the actual time of departure.

Fourth, employees are probably more motivated to point out those organizational problems that they actually regard as most pressing in employee surveys than in exit interviews. This is because the results of employee surveys could cause organizational changes, which could lead to actual improvements in the quality of work life for employees who respond to that survey. In contrast, personal benefit from organizational change is impossible for the departing employees who respond to an exit survey during their last days of employment. As Tracy thought in the opening case, it really was not her responsibility anymore to tell management why people were leaving. It was their responsibility to find out.

Exit Interviews for the Measurement of Turnover Types. Consistent with the data collection procedure, we suggest important information can and should be obtained from the exit interview—information regarding turnover types. Previously, we discussed avoidable and unavoidable turnover. Here, we discuss *voluntary* and *involuntary* turnover.

Some may think at first that the determination of whether a given turnover case is voluntary, involuntary, avoidable, unavoidable, functional, or dysfunctional is simple. Unfortunately, prior research demonstrates that this is not the case at all. Campion (1991) sent questionnaires to 325 former employees and 568 of their supervisors in a U.S. university to test the accuracy of turnover type classifications made by these two types of organizational members. It turned out that agreement between departed employees and their supervisors on whether employees left voluntarily or were fired was modest ($r = .59$). The respective agreement of whether the employee's turnover was avoidable or not was even smaller ($r = .41$).

Thus, it is still important to pay close attention to an exit interview's accuracy and to design it using the strategies from the literature that were discussed in this chapter. For illustration, we include a good example of a proposed exit interview process in Exhibit 9.1. The exit interview process described in Exhibit 9.1 is based on Giacalone and Knouse's (1989) three-step process and the suggestions we discussed earlier in this chapter. In Exhibit 9.2, we illustrate a sample exit interview form that is designed to probe whether an employee truly left voluntarily, whether the turnover was avoidable from the perspective of the organization, and whether the parting employee is aware of any illegal occurrences in the organization. Exhibit 9.3 describes a questionnaire that could be administered to supervisors to supplement and to check the accuracy of the information given in an exit interview. This form is designed to probe whether an employee's turnover was functional, voluntary, and avoidable. In interpreting these suggestions, it is very important to note that they are in fact little more than illustrations of one possible exit interview procedure. Unfortunately, research on the exit interviews is still too sketchy to allow more reliable suggestions.

(text continued on p. 223)

First Step: Preparation

Conduct an initial meeting with the departing employee and inform him or her that an exit interview will be conducted in which your organization would like to receive some valuable information from the employee. During that meeting:

- Schedule that exit interview
- Encourage the departing employee to prepare for that exit interview by thinking about reasons why he or she quit
- Ask the departing employee which interviewe he or she would prefer
- Discuss topics that serve additional purposes of the exit interviews, such as intellectual property rights, and benefits

Second Step: Conduct the Exit Interview

Ask the interviewee to evaluate the former position, working conditions, reasons for leaving, type of turnover, and suggestions for organizational change using a standardized format, with mainly open-ended questions (see Exhibit 9.2). Avoid probing questions. Supplement the interview with a supervisor survey (see Exhibit 9.3).

Third Step: Follow-Up

Conduct a follow-up survey some time after the exit interview (e.g., 6 months later). Use a standardized format. Try to use a method different from the one used in the original exit interview (e.g., use another interviewer or a questionnaire).

Fourth Step: Analyze, Summarize, and Use the Data!

Exhibit 9.1. The Four-Step Exit Interview Process
SOURCE: Adapted from Giacalone and Knouse (1989).

Name of interviewer	Date	Name of departing employee

1. Have you obtained a new job?   Yes _____   No _____
   If yes, please tell us
   Employer's Name: _____   Address: _____
   If no, please tell us
   Why not: _____

2. Did you leave because of factors that were primarily controlled by your family
   (e.g., pregnancy, providing care for relatives)?   Yes _____   No _____
   If yes, specify: _____

3. Did you leave because of factors that were primarily controlled by you
   (e.g., career change, education, better pay elsewhere)? Yes _____   No _____
   If yes, specify: _____

4. Did you leave because of factors that are outside the control of anyone
   (e.g., health problems, retirement, lottery)?   Yes _____   No _____
   If yes, specify: _____

5. Did you leave because of factors that are primarily controlled by the organization you worked for (e.g., they paid too little, too little participation, too little
   opportunity for growth/promotion etc.)?   Yes _____   No _____
   If yes, specify: _____

6. Do you think that your supervisor or employment-related business decisions
   contributed to your decision to quit (e.g., recent wage cuts, conflicts, downsizing)?   Yes _____   No _____
   If yes, specify: _____

7. Please report any events in this organization that you regard as unfair. We are
   particularly interested in investigating occurrences of discrimination and
   harassment in the workplace. Please note with regard to this particular question that we have to investigate any leads that point toward illegal behaviors of
   any organizational member. As a result, we cannot guarantee confidentiality
   of your responses to this particular question.   Yes _____   No _____
   If yes, specify: _____

Exhibit 9.2. Sample Interview Administered to Departing Employees (Do Not
Administer to Employees Who Were Discharged or Laid Off)

NOTE: Administer a short form of this questionnaire also to employees who were terminated or discharged.
Please ask only question number 7 for those employees and note your name, their name, and the date of the
interview.

| Name of Supervisor | Date | Name of departing employee |

1. The employee was:

   Discharged: _____   Yes _____ No _____

   Laid off: _____   Yes _____ No _____

   Quit voluntarily: _____   Yes _____ No _____

   Explain in your own words the reason why the employee left: _____

   _____

2. If allowed by plant policy, would you reemploy the departing employee?

                                                     Yes _____ No _____

   Explain why you would/would not reemploy the departing employee: _____

   _____

3. How easy will it be to replace the departing employee?

   very easy _____   somewhat easy _____   neither easy nor difficult _____
                     somewhat difficult _____   difficult _____

4. If the employee was discharged: Did the employee act in a way that suggests
   that he or she quit internally before the actual discharge occurred (e.g., did
   not show up to work, excessive lunch breaks)?   Yes _____ No _____

   If yes, specify: _____

5. If the employee quit: Did the employee mention any family-related or other
   private reasons for quitting?   Yes _____ No _____

   If yes, specify: _____

6. If the employee quit: Did the employee mention any organizational policies or
   practices as a reason for quitting?   Yes _____ No _____

   If yes, specify: _____

7. Did the employee mention any policies or events in this organization that he
   or she regarded as unfair or otherwise discriminatory? Yes _____ No _____

   If yes, specify: _____

Exhibit 9.3. Sample Survey Administered to Supervisors of Departing Employees

Summary and Conclusions

Probably the most interesting feature of the discussion surrounding the exit interview is the large gap between research and practice. In summary, this chapter suggests the following:

1. First, although companies heavily use the exit interview to probe the reasons why employees leave, researchers pay little attention to this technique for data collection.
2. Second, although research that exists on the exit interview suggests that exit interviews are inaccurate, most executives believe that they provide useful information (Brotheron, 1996).
3. We believe that the exit interview will remain a popular organizational tool basically because it serves an important symbolic purpose in an employee-employer relationship.
4. As such, the exit interview serves as a last farewell—created to provide a formal endpoint of a relationship between the employee and the employer. Of course, there is nothing wrong with the exit interview being used for that purpose. However, our review showed that exit interviews should not be used as the main tool for determining why employees leave. Extending the use of the exit interview to this purpose requires a degree of accuracy that presently cannot be expected from that instrument.
5. Thus, we suggest that organizations should rely on employee surveys for measuring employee attitudes and linking them to turnover information.
6. Structured and cross-checked exit interviews can then be used for classifying cases of employee turnover as functional, voluntary, avoidable, or due to illegal actions of organizational members.

Appendix A

The Job Rating Form

This appendix reproduces the Job Rating Form (JRF), a companion instrument to the Job Diagnostic Survey designed to be used by supervisors of the focal job (or by outside observers) in rating job characteristics. The JRF provides measures of the key job dimensions; none of the scales measuring affective reactions to the job or work context is included. Scoring procedures for the JRF are included in Appendix C.

Job Rating Form

This questionnaire was developed as part of a Yale University study of jobs and how people react to them. The questionnaire helps to determine how jobs can be better designed by obtaining information about how people react to different kinds of jobs.

You are asked to rate the characteristics of the following job:_____

Please keep in mind that the questions refer to the job listed above and not to your own job.

On the following pages, you will find several different kinds of questions about the job listed above. Specific instructions are given at the start of each section. Please read them carefully. It should take no more than 10 minutes to complete the entire questionnaire. Please move through it quickly.

Section 1

This part of the questionnaire asks you to describe the job listed above as objectively as you can. Try to make your description as accurate and as objective as you possibly can.

A sample question is given below.

A. To what extent does this job require the job incumbent to work with mechanical equipment?

1 - - - - - - **2** - - - - - - **3** - - - - - - **4** - - - - - - - **5** - - - - - - (**6**) - - - - - **7**

| Very little; the job requires almost no contact with mechanical equipment of any kind. | Moderately | Very much; the job requires almost constant work with mechanical equipment. |

You are to circle the number that is the most accurate description of this job.

If, for example, this job requires the incumbent to work with mechanical equipment a good deal of the time—but also requires some paperwork—you might circle the number 6, as was done in the example above.

1. To what extent does this job require the incumbent to work closely with other people (either "clients" or people in related jobs in your own organization)?

1- - - - - - **2** - - - - - - **3** - - - - - - **4** - - - - - - - **5** - - - - - - - **6** - - - - - - **7**

| Very little; dealing with other people is not at all necessary in doing the job. | Moderately; some dealing with others is necessary. | Very much; dealing with other people is an absolutely essential and crucial part of doing the job. |

2. How much autonomy is there in this job? That is, to what extent does this job permit the incumbent to decide on his or her own how to go about doing the work?

1 - - - - - - 2 - - - - - - 3 - - - - - - 4 - - - - - - 5 - - - - - - 6 - - - - - 7

Very little; the job gives the employee almost no personal "say" about how and when the work is done.	Moderate autonomy; many things are standardized and not under employee control, but he or she can make some decisions about the work.	Very much; the job gives the employee almost complete responsibility for deciding how and when the work is done.

3. To what extent does this job involve doing a "whole" and identifiable piece of work? That is, is the job a complete piece of work that has an obvious beginning and end? Or is it only a small part of the overall piece of work, which is finished by other people or by automatic machines?

1 - - - - - - 2 - - - - - - 3 - - - - - - 4 - - - - - - 5 - - - - - - 6 - - - - - 7

The job is only a part of the overall piece of work; the results of worker activities cannot be seen in the final product or service.	The job is a moderate-sized "chunk" of the overall piece of work; worker contribution can be seen in the final outcome.	The job involves doing the whole piece of work, from start to finish; the results of worker activities are easily seen in the final product or service.

4. How much variety is there in this job? That is, to what extent does the job require the worker to do many different things at work, using a variety of skills and talents?

1 - - - - - - 2 - - - - - - 3 - - - - - - 4 - - - - - - 5 - - - - - - 6 - - - - - 7

Very little; the job requires the worker to do the same routine things over and over again.	Moderate variety.	Very much; the job requires the worker to do many different things, using a number of different skills and talents.

5. In general, how significant or important is this job? That is, are the results of the work likely to significantly affect the lives or well-being of other people?

1 - - - - - - 2 - - - - - - 3 - - - - - - 4 - - - - - - 5 - - - - - - 6 - - - - - 7

Not very significant; the outcomes of the work are not likely to have important effects on other people.	Moderately significant.	Highly significant; the outcomes of the work can affect other people in very important ways.

6. To what extent do managers or coworkers let the worker know how well he or she is doing in the job?

1- - - - - - -2- - - - - - 3 - - - - - - 4 - - - - - - - 5 - - - - - - - 6 - - - - - - 7

| Very little; people almost never let the worker know how well he or she is doing. | Moderately; sometimes people may give "feedback"; other times they may not. | Very much; managers or coworkers provide almost constant "feedback" about how well the worker is doing. |

7. To what extent does doing the job itself provide the worker with information about his or her performance? That is, does the actual work itself provide clues about how well he or she is doing—aside from any "feedback" coworkers or supervisors may provide?

1- - - - - - -2- - - - - - 3 - - - - - - 4 - - - - - - - 5 - - - - - - - 6 - - - - - - 7

| Very little; the job itself is set up so the worker could work forever without finding out how well he or she is doing. | Moderately; sometimes doing the job provides "feedback"; sometimes it does not. | Very much; the job is set up so that the worker get almost constant "feedback" about how well he or she is doing. |

Section 2

Listed below are a number of statements that could be used to describe a job. You are to indicate whether each statement is an accurate or an inaccurate description of this job.

Once again, please try to be as objective as you can in deciding how accurately each statement describes this job.

Write a number in the blank beside each statement, based on the following scale:

How accurate is the statement in describing this job?

1 - - - - - - 2 - - - - - - 3 - - - - - - 4 - - - - - - - 5 - - - - - - - 6 - - - - - - 7

Very Inaccurate	Mostly Inaccurate	Slightly Inaccurate	Uncertain	Slightly Accurate	Mostly Accurate	Very Accurate

_____ 1. The job requires the worker to use a number of complex or high-level skills.

_____ 2. The job requires a lot of cooperative work with other people.

_____ 3. The job is arranged so that the worker does not have the chance to do an entire piece of work from beginning to end.

_____ 4. Just doing the work required by the job provides many chances for the worker to figure out how well he or she is doing.

_____ 5. The job is quite simple and repetitive.

_____ 6. The job can be done adequately by a person working alone— without talking or checking with other people.

_____ 7. The supervisors and coworkers on this job almost never give the worker any "feedback" about how well he or she is doing in his or her work.

_____ 8. This job is one in which a lot of other people can be affected by how well the work gets done.

_____ 9. The job denies the worker any chance to use his or her personal initiative or judgment in carrying out the work.

_____ 10. Supervisors often let the worker know how well they think he or she is performing the job.

_____ 11. The job provides the worker the chance to completely finish the pieces of work he or she begins.

_____ 12. The job itself provides very few clues about whether or not the worker is performing well.

_____ 13. The job gives the worker considerable opportunity for independence and freedom in how he or she does the work.

_____ 14. The job itself is not very significant or important in the broader scheme of things.

General Information

1. What is your name? _____

2. What is your own job title? _____

3. What is your age? (Check one)
   _____ under 20   _____ 40–49
   _____ 20–29   _____ 50–59
   _____ 30–39   _____ 60 or over

4. How long have you been in your present position? (Check one)
   _____ 0–½ year   _____ 3–5 years
   _____ ½ year–1 year   _____ 5–10 years
   _____ 1–2 years   _____ 10 or more years

In the space below, please write any additional information about the job you rated that you feel might be helpful in understanding that job. Thank you for your cooperation.

Appendix B

The Job Diagnostic Survey

his questionnaire was developed as part of a Yale University study of jobs and how people react to them. The questionnaire helps to determine how jobs can be better designed, by obtaining information about how people react to different kinds of jobs.

On the following pages you will find several different kinds of questions about your job. Specific instructions are given at the start of each section. Please read them carefully. It should take no more than 25 minutes to complete the entire questionnaire. Please move through it quickly.

The questions are designed to obtain your perceptions of your job and your reactions to it.

There are no trick questions. Your individual answers will be kept completely confidential. Please answer each item as honestly and frankly as possible.

Thank you for your cooperation.

Section 1

This part of the questionnaire asks you to describe the job listed above as objectively as you can. Try to make your description as accurate and as objective as you possibly can.

A sample question is given below.

A. To what extent does your job require you to work with mechanical equipment?

1 - - - - - **2** - - - - - **3** - - - - - **4** - - - - - - **5** - - - - - - (**6**) - - - - - **7**

Very little; the job requires almost no contact with mechanical equipment of any kind.

Moderately.

Very much; the job requires almost constant work with mechanical equipment.

You are to circle the number that is the most accurate description of your job.

If, for example, your job requires you to work with mechanical equipment a good deal of the time—but also requires some paperwork—you might circle the number 6, as was done in the example above.

1. To what extent does your job require you to work closely with other people (either "clients" or people in related jobs in your own organization)?

1 - - - - - **2** - - - - - **3** - - - - - **4** - - - - - - **5** - - - - - - **6** - - - - - **7**

Very little; dealing with other people is not at all necessary in doing the job.

Moderately; some dealing with others is necessary.

Very much; dealing with other people is an absolutely essential and crucial part of doing the job.

2. How much autonomy is there in your job? That is, to what extent does your job permit you to decide on your own how to go about doing the work?

1 - - - - - **2** - - - - - **3** - - - - - **4** - - - - - - **5** - - - - - - **6** - - - - - **7**

Very little; the job gives me almost no personal "say" about how and when the work is done.

Moderate autonomy; many things are standardized and not under my control, but I can make some decisions about the work.

Very much; the job gives me almost complete responsibility for deciding how and when the work is done.

3. To what extent does your job involve doing a "whole" and identifiable piece of work? That is, is the job a complete piece of work that has an obvious beginning and end? Or is it only a small part of the overall piece of work, which is finished by other people or by automatic machines?

1 - - - - - - 2 - - - - - - 3 - - - - - - 4 - - - - - - - 5 - - - - - - - 6 - - - - - - 7

| My job is only a part of the overall piece of work; the results of my activities cannot be seen in the final product or service. | My job is a moderate-sized "chunk" of the overall piece of work; my own contribution can be seen in the final outcome. | My job involves doing the whole piece of work, from start to finish; the results of my activities are easily seen in the final product or service. |

4. How much variety is there in your job? That is, to what extent does the job require you to do many different things at work, using a variety of your skills and talents?

1 - - - - - - 2 - - - - - - 3 - - - - - - 4 - - - - - - - 5 - - - - - - - 6 - - - - - - 7

| Very little; the job requires me to do the same routine things over and over again. | Moderate variety. | Very much; the job requires me to do many different things, using a number of different skills and talents. |

5. In general, how significant or important is your job? That is, are the results of your work likely to significantly affect the lives or well-being of other people?

1 - - - - - - 2 - - - - - - 3 - - - - - - 4 - - - - - - - 5 - - - - - - - 6 - - - - - - 7

| Not very significant; the outcomes of my work are not likely to have important effects on other people. | Moderately significant. | Highly significant;the outcomes of my work can affect other people in very important ways. |

6. To what extent do managers or coworkers let you know how well you are doing in your job?

1 - - - - - - 2 - - - - - - 3 - - - - - - 4 - - - - - - - 5 - - - - - - - 6 - - - - - - 7

| Very little; people almost never let me know how well I am doing. | Moderately; sometimes people may give me "feedback"; other times they may not. | Very much; managers or coworkers provide me with almost constant "feedback" about how well I am doing. |

7. To what extent does doing the job itself provide you with information about your work performance? That is, does the actual work itself provide clues about how well you are doing—aside from any "feedback" coworkers or supervisors may provide?

1 - - - - - - 2 - - - - - 3 - - - - - - 4 - - - - - - 5 - - - - - - 6 - - - - - 7

Very little; the job itself is set up so I could work forever without finding out how well I am doing.	Moderately; sometimes doing the job provides "feedback" to me; sometimes it does not.	Very much; the job is set up so that I get almost constant "feedback" as I work about how well I am doing.

Section 2

Listed below are a number of statements that could be used to describe a job. You are to indicate whether each statement is an accurate or an inaccurate description of your job.

Once again, please try to be as objective as you can in deciding how accurately each statement describes your job regardless of whether you like or dislike your job.

Write a number in the blank beside each statement, based on the following scale:

How accurate is the statement in describing your job?

1 - - - - - - 2 - - - - - 3 - - - - - - 4 - - - - - - 5 - - - - - - 6 - - - - - 7

Very Inaccurate	Mostly Inaccurate	Slightly Inaccurate	Uncertain	Slightly Accurate	Mostly Accurate	Very Accurate

_____ 1. The job requires me to use a number of complex or high-level skills.

_____ 2. The job requires a lot of cooperative work with other people.

_____ 3. The job is arranged so that I do not have the chance to do an entire piece of work from beginning to end.

_____ 4. Just doing the work required by the job provides many chances for me to figure out how well I am doing.

_____ 5. The job is quite simple and repetitive.

_____ 6. The job can be done adequately by a person working alone—without talking or checking with other people.

_____ 7. The supervisors and coworkers on this job almost never give me any "feedback" about how well I am doing in my work.

_____ 8. This job is one in which a lot of other people can be affected by how well the work gets done.

_____ 9. The job denies me any chance to use my personal initiative or judgment in carrying out the work.

_____ 10. Supervisors often let me know how well they think I am performing the job.

_____ 11. The job provides me the chance to completely finish the pieces of work I begin.

_____ 12. The job itself provides very few clues about whether or not I am performing well.

_____ 13. The job gives me considerable opportunity for independence and freedom in how I do the work.

_____ 14. The job itself is not very significant or important in the broader scheme of things.

Section 3

Now please indicate how you personally feel about your job.

Each of the statements below is something that a person might say about his or her job. You are to indicate your own personal feelings about your job by marking how much you agree with each of the statements.

Write a number in the blank for each statement, based on this scale:

How much do you agree with the statement?

```
1 - - - - - - 2 - - - - - - 3 - - - - - - 4 - - - - - - - 5 - - - - - - - 6 - - - - - - 7
```

| Disagree Strongly | Disagree | Disagree Slightly | Neutral | Agree Slightly | Agree | Agree Strongly |

_____ 1. It's hard, on this job, for me to care very much about whether or not the work gets done right.

_____ 2. My opinion of myself goes up when I do this job well.

_____ 3. Generally speaking, I am very satisfied with this job.

_____ 4. Most of the things I have to do on this job seem useless or trivial.

_____ 5. I usually know whether or not my work is satisfactory on this job.

_____ 6. I feel a great sense of personal satisfaction when I do this job well.

_____ 7. The work I do on this job is very meaningful to me.

_____ 8. I feel a very high degree of personal responsibility for the work I do on this job.

_____ 9. I frequently think of quitting this job.

_____ 10. I feel bad and unhappy when I discover that I have performed poorly on this job.

_____ 11. I often have trouble figuring out whether I'm doing well or poorly on this job.

_____ 12. I feel I should personally take the credit or blame for the results of my work on this job.

_____ 13. I am generally satisfied with the kind of work I do in this job.

_____ 14. My own feelings generally are not affected much one way or the other by how well I do on this job.

_____ 15. Whether or not this job gets done right is clearly my responsibility.

Section 4

Now please indicate how satisfied you are with each aspect of your job listed below. Once again, write the appropriate number in the blank beside each statement.

How satisfied are you with this aspect of your job?

1- - - - - - - 2 - - - - - - 3 - - - - - - 4 - - - - - - - 5 - - - - - - - 6 - - - - - - 7

| Extremely Dissatisfied | Dissatisfied | Slightly Dissatisfied | Neutral | Slightly Satisfied | Satisfied | Extremely Satisfied |

_____ 1. The amount of job security I have.

_____ 2. The amount of pay and fringe benefits I receive.

_____ 3. The amount of personal growth and development I get in doing my job.

_____ 4. The people I talk to and work with on my job.

_____ 5. The degree of respect and fair treatment I receive from my boss.

_____ 6. The feeling of worthwhile accomplishment I get from doing my job.

_____ 7. The chance to get to know other people while on the job.

_____ 8. The amount of support and guidance I receive from my superior.

_____ 9. The degree to which I am fairly paid for what I contribute to this organization.

_____ 10. The amount of independent thought and action I can exercise in my job.

_____ 11. How secure things look for me in the future of this organization.

_____ 12. The chance to help other people while at work.

_____ 13. The amount of challenge in my job.

_____ 14. The overall quality of the supervision I receive in my work.

Section 5

Now please think of the other people in your organization who hold the same job you do. If no one has exactly the same job as you, think of the job that is most similar to yours.

Please think about how accurately each of these statements describes the feelings of those people about the job.

It is quite all right if your answers here are different from those you used when you described your own reactions to the job. People often feel quite different about the same job.

Once again, write a number in the blank for each statement, based on the scale:

How much do you agree with the statement?

1 - - - - - - - 2 - - - - - - 3 - - - - - - 4 - - - - - - - 5 - - - - - - - 6 - - - - - - 7

Disagree Strongly	Disagree	Disagree Slightly	Neutral	Agree Slightly	Agree	Agree Strongly

_____ 1. Most people on this job feel a great sense of personal satisfaction when they do the job well.

_____ 2. Most people on this job are very satisfied with the job.

_____ 3. Most people on this job feel that the work is useless or trivial.

_____ 4. Most people on this job feel a great deal of personal responsibility for the work they do.

_____ 5. Most people on this job have a pretty good idea of how well they are performing their work.

_____ 6. Most people on this job find the work very meaningful.

_____ 7. Most people on this job feel that whether or not the job gets done right is clearly their own responsibility.

_____ 8. People on this job often think of quitting.

_____ 9. Most people on this job feel bad or unhappy when they find that they have performed the work poorly.

_____ 10. Most people on this job have trouble figuring out whether they are doing a good or a bad job.

Section 6

Listed below are a number of characteristics that could be present on any job. People differ about how much they would like to have each one present in their own jobs. We are interested in learning how much you personally would like to have each one present in your job.

Using the scale below, please indicate the degree to which you would like to have each characteristic present in your job.

Note: The numbers on this scale are different from those used in previous scales.

4 - - - - - - 5 - - - - - - 6 - - - - - - 7 - - - - - - - 8 - - - - - - - 9 - - - - - - 10

Would like having this only a moderate amount (or less)	Would like having this very much	Would like having extremely much

_____ 1. High respect and fair treatment from my supervisor.

_____ 2. Stimulating and challenging work.

_____ 3. Chances to exercise independent thought and action in my job.

_____ 4. Great job security.

_____ 5. Very friendly coworkers.

_____ 6. Opportunities to learn new things from my work.

_____ 7. High salary and good fringe benefits.

_____ 8. Opportunities to be creative and imaginative in my work.

_____ 9. Quick promotions.

_____ 10. Opportunities for personal growth and development in my job.

_____ 11. A sense of worthwhile accomplishment in my work.

Section 7

People differ in the kinds of jobs they would most like to hold. The questions in this section give you a chance to say just what it is about a job that is most important to you.

For each question, two different kinds of jobs are briefly described. You are to indicate which of these jobs you personally would prefer—if you had to make a choice between them.

In answering each question, assume that everything else about the jobs is the same. Pay attention only to the characteristics listed.

Two examples are given below.

JOB A	**JOB B**
A job requiring work with mechanical equipment most of the day.	A job requiring work with other people most of the day.

1 - - - - - - - - 2 - - - - - - - - - (3) - - - - - - - - - 4 - - - - - - - - - 5

| Strongly Prefer A | Slightly Prefer A | Neutral | Slightly Prefer B | Strongly Prefer B |

If you like working with people and working with equipment equally well, you would circle the number 3, as has been done in the example.

*   *   *

Here is another example. This one asks for a harder choice—between two jobs that both have some undesirable features.

JOB A	**JOB B**
A job requiring you to expose yourself to considerable physical danger.	A job located 200 miles from your home and family.

1 - - - - - - - -(2)- - - - - - - - - - - 3 - - - - - - - - - - - 4 - - - - - - - - - - - 5

Strongly Prefer A	Slightly Prefer A	Neutral	Slightly Prefer B	Strongly Prefer B

If you would slightly prefer risking physical danger to working far from your home, you would circle number 2, as has been done in the example.

JOB A	**JOB B**
1. A job in which the pay is very good.	A job in which there is considerable opportunity to be creative and innovative.

1 - - - - - - - - 2 - - - - - - - - - - - 3 - - - - - - - - - - - 4 - - - - - - - - - - - 5

Strongly Prefer A	Slightly Prefer A	Neutral	Slightly Prefer B	Strongly Prefer B

JOB A	**JOB B**
2. A job in which you often are required to make important decisions.	A job with many pleasant people to work with.

1 - - - - - - - - 2 - - - - - - - - - - - 3 - - - - - - - - - - - 4 - - - - - - - - - - - 5

Strongly Prefer A	Slightly Prefer A	Neutral	Slightly Prefer B	Strongly Prefer B

3. A job in which greater responsibility is given to those who do the best work.

A job in which greater responsibility is given to loyal employees who have the most seniority.

1 - - - - - - - - 2 - - - - - - - - - - 3 - - - - - - - - - - 4 - - - - - - - - - - 5

| Strongly Prefer A | Slightly Prefer A | Neutral | Slightly Prefer B | Strongly Prefer B |

4. A job in an organization that is in financial trouble—and might have to close down within the year.

A job in which you are not allowed to have any say whatever in how your work is scheduled or in the procedures to be used in carrying it out.

1 - - - - - - - - 2 - - - - - - - - - - 3 - - - - - - - - - - 4 - - - - - - - - - - 5

| Strongly Prefer A | Slightly Prefer A | Neutral | Slightly Prefer B | Strongly Prefer B |

5. A very routine job.

A job in which your coworkers are not very friendly.

1 - - - - - - - - 2 - - - - - - - - - - 3 - - - - - - - - - - 4 - - - - - - - - - - 5

| Strongly Prefer A | Slightly Prefer A | Neutral | Slightly Prefer B | Strongly Prefer B |

6. A job with a supervisor who is often very critical of you and your work in front of other people.

A job that prevents you from using a number of skills that you worked hard to develop.

1 - - - - - - - - 2 - - - - - - - - - - 3 - - - - - - - - - - 4 - - - - - - - - - - 5

| Strongly Prefer A | Slightly Prefer A | Neutral | Slightly Prefer B | Strongly Prefer B |

7. A job with a supervisor who respects you and treats you fairly.

A job that provides constant opportunities for you to learn new and interesting things.

1- - - - - - - - -**2**- - - - - - - - - - - -**3**- - - - - - - - - - - -**4**- - - - - - - - - - -**5**

| Strongly Prefer A | Slightly Prefer A | Neutral | Slightly Prefer B | Strongly Prefer B |

8. A job in which there is a real chance you could be laid off.

A job with very little chance to do challenging work.

1- - - - - - - - -**2**- - - - - - - - - - - -**3**- - - - - - - - - - - -**4**- - - - - - - - - - -**5**

| Strongly Prefer A | Slightly Prefer A | Neutral | Slightly Prefer B | Strongly Prefer B |

9. A job in which there is a real chance for you to develop new skills and advance in the organization.

A job that provides lots of vacation time and an excellent fringe benefit package.

1- - - - - - - - -**2**- - - - - - - - - - - -**3**- - - - - - - - - - - -**4**- - - - - - - - - - -**5**

| Strongly Prefer A | Slightly Prefer A | Neutral | Slightly Prefer B | Strongly Prefer B |

10. A job with little freedom and independence to do your work in the way you think best.

A job in which the working conditions are poor.

1- - - - - - - - -**2**- - - - - - - - - - - -**3**- - - - - - - - - - - -**4**- - - - - - - - - - -**5**

| Strongly Prefer A | Slightly Prefer A | Neutral | Slightly Prefer B | Strongly Prefer B |

11. A job with very satisfying teamwork.   A job that allows you to use your skills and abilities to the fullest extent.

1 - - - - - - - - 2 - - - - - - - - - - 3 - - - - - - - - - - 4 - - - - - - - - - - 5

| Strongly | Slightly | Neutral | Slightly | Strongly |
| Prefer A | Prefer A | | Prefer B | Prefer B |

12. A job that offers little or no challenge.   A job that requires you to be completely isolated from coworkers.

1 - - - - - - - - 2 - - - - - - - - - - 3 - - - - - - - - - - 4 - - - - - - - - - - 5

| Strongly | Slightly | Neutral | Slightly | Strongly |
| Prefer A | Prefer A | | Prefer B | Prefer B |

Section 8
Biographical Background

1. Sex: Male _____   Female _____

2. Age (check one):
   _____ under 20   _____ 40–49
   _____ 20–29   _____ 50–59
   _____ 30–39   _____ 60 or over

3. Education (check one):
   _____ Grade School
   _____ Some High School
   _____ High School Degree
   _____ Some Business College or Technical School Experience
   _____ Some College Experience (other than business or technical school)
   _____ Business College or Technical School Degree
   _____ College Degree
   _____ Master's or Higher Degree

4. What is your brief job title? _____

Appendix C

Scoring Key for the Job Diagnostic Survey and the Job Rating Form

---

The scoring manual for the Job Diagnostic Survey (JDS) and the Job Rating Form (JRF) is presented below. For each variable measured by the JRF and JDS, the questionnaire items are averaged to yield a summary score for the variable are listed.

Sections 1 and 2 (the measures of the job characteristics) are identical for the JDS and the JRF; therefore, the same scoring key is used for both instruments.

I. Job Characteristics (for both the JDS and the JRF)

A. *Skill variety.* Average the following items:
   Section 1: No. 4
   Section 2: No. 1
                   No. 5 (reversed scoring—i.e., subtract the number entered by the respondent from 8)

B. *Task identity.* Average the following items:
Section 1:   No. 3
Section 2:   No. 11
              No. 3 (reversed scoring)

C. *Task significance.* Average the following items:
Section 1:   No. 5
Section 2:   No. 8
              No. 14 (reversed scoring)

D. *Autonomy.* Average the following items:
Section 1:   No. 2
Section 2:   No. 13
              No. 9 (reversed scoring)

E. *Feedback from the job itself.* Average the following items:
Section 1:   No. 7
Section 2:   No. 4
              No. 12 (reversed scoring)

F. *Feedback from agents.* Average the following items:
Section 1:   No. 6
Section 2:   No. 10
              No. 7 (reversed scoring)

G. *Dealing with others.* Average the following items:
Section 1:   No. 1
Section 2:   No. 2
              No. 6 (reversed scoring)

II. Experienced Psychological States

Each of the three constructs is measured both directly (Section 3) and indirectly via projective-type items (Section 5) (from JDS).

A. *Experienced meaningfulness of the work.* Average the following items:
Section 3:   No. 7
              No. 4 (reversed scoring)
Section 5:   No. 6
              No. 3 (reversed scoring)

B. *Experienced responsibility for the work.* Average the following items:

Section 3:   No. 8, No. 12, No. 15

No. 1 (reversed scoring)

Section 5:   No. 4, No. 7

C. *Knowledge of results.* Average the following items:

Section 3:   No. 5

No. 11 (reversed scoring)

Section 5:   No. 5

No. 10 (reversed scoring)

III. Affective Outcomes

The first two constructs (general satisfaction and internal work motivation) are measured both directly (Section 3) and indirectly (Section 5); growth satisfaction is measured only directly (Section 4) (from JDS).

A. *General satisfaction.* Average the following items:

Section 3:   No. 3, No. 13

No. 9 (reversed scoring)

Section 5:   No. 2

No. 8 (reversed scoring)

B. *Internal work motivation.* Average the following items:

Section 3:   No. 2, No. 6, No. 10

No. 14 (reversed scoring)

Section 5:   No. 1, No. 9

C. *Growth satisfaction.* Average the following items:

Section 4:   No. 3, No. 6, No. 10, No. 13

IV. Context Satisfactions

Each of these short scales uses items from JDS Section 4 only.

A. *Satisfaction with job security.* Average the following items:

Section 4:   No. 1 and No. 11

B. *Satisfaction with compensation (pay).* Average the following items:

Section 4:   No. 2 and No. 9

    C. *Satisfaction with coworkers.* Average the following items:
Section 4:   No. 4, No. 7, and No. 12

    D. *Satisfaction with supervision.* Average the following items:
Section 4:   No. 5, No. 8, and No. 14

V. Individual Growth Need Strength

The JDS questionnaire yields two separate measures of growth need strength, one from Section 6 (the *would like* format) and one from Section 7 (the *job choice* format).

    A. *Would like* format *(Section 6).* Average the six items from Section 6 listed below. Before averaging, subtract 3 from each item score; this will result in a summary scale ranging from 1 to 7. The items are No. 2, No. 3, No. 6, No. 8, No. 10, and No. 11.

    B. *Job choice* format *(Section 7).* Each item in Section 7 yields a number from 1 to 5 (i.e., *Strongly prefer A* is scored 1, *Neutral* is scored 3, and *Strongly prefer B* is scored 5). Compute the need strength measure by averaging the 12 items as follows:
No. 1, No. 5, No. 7, No. 10, No. 11, No. 12 (direct scoring)
No. 2, No. 3, No. 4, No. 6, No. 8, No. 9 (reversed scoring—i.e., subtract the respondent's score from 6)

Note: To transform the job choice summary score from a 5-point scale to a 7-point scale, use this formula: $Y = 1.5X - .5$

    C. *Combined growth need strength score.* To obtain an overall estimate of growth need strength based on both *would like* and *job choice* data, first transform the job choice summary score to a 7-point scale (using the formula given above), and then average the *would like* and the *transformed job choice* summary scores.

VI. Motivation Potential Score

Motivating Potential Score (MPS) = [Skill Variety + Task Identity + Task Significance ÷ 3] × Autonomy × Feedback From the Job

Appendix D

Job Characteristics Overall National Norms

Job Characteristics

Skill variety	4.7
Task identity	4.7
Task significance	5.5
Autonomy	4.9
Feedback from job	4.9
Feedback from agents	4.1
Dealing with others	5.6
Motivating Potential Score	128

NOTE: Based on the responses of 6,930 employees working in 876 different jobs in 56 organizations. The norms were computed by averaging the scores of employees who work on each of the 876 jobs and by computing overall means across those jobs (from Oldham, Hackman, & Stepina, 1979).

References

Abbott, A. D. (1988). *The system of professions.* Chicago: University of Chicago Press.

Abelson, M. A. (1987). Examination of avoidable and unavoidable turnover. *Journal of Applied Psychology, 72,* 382-386.

Abelson, M. A., & Baysinger, B. D. (1984). Optimal and dysfunctional turnover: Toward an organizational level model. *Academy of Management Review, 9,* 331-341.

Alexander, J., Bloom, J., & Nuchols, B. (1994). Nursing turnover and hospital efficiency: An organization-level analysis. *Industrial Relations, 33,* 505-520.

Alexander, S. (1998). Keeping workers happy. *Info World, 20*(50), 91-92.

Allen, D. G., Renn, R. W., & Griffeth, R. W. (1999, August). *An individual level model of telecommuting.* Paper presented at the Academy of Management meeting, Chicago.

Andersen, S. L. (1989). The nurse advocate project. *Journal of Nursing Administration, 19,* 22-26.

Aquino, K., Griffeth, R. W., Allen, D. G., & Hom, P. W. (1997). An integration of justice constructs into the turnover process: Test of a referent cognitions model. *Academy of Management Journal, 40,* 1208-1227.

Arvey, R. D., Bouchard, T. J., Segal, N. L. & Abraham, L. M. (1989). Job satisfaction: Environmental and genetic components. *Journal of Applied Psychology, 74,* 187-192.

Arvey, R. D., & Faley, R. H. (1988). *Fairness in selecting employees.* Reading, MA: Addison-Wesley.

Aryee, S., Luk, V., Stone, R. (1998). Family-responsive variables and retention-relevant outcomes among employed parents. *Human Relations, 51,* 73-87.

Ashforth, B., & Saks, A. (1996). Socialization tactics: Longitudinal effects on newcomer adjustment. *Academy of Management Journal, 39,* 149-178.

Aversa, J. (1999, September 4). Unemployment falls to 4.2%. *Associated Press.* Retrieved September 6, 1999, from the World Wide Web: http://www.azcentral.com/business/0904economy.shtml

Babin, B. J., & Boles, J. S. (1998). Employee behavior in a service environment: A model and test of potential differences between men and women. *Journal of Marketing, 62,* 77-91.

Baker, S., Lee, D., & Coy, P. (1991, July 1). Assembly lines start migrating from Asia to Mexico. *Business Week,* 43.

Bannister, B., Kinicki, A. DeNisi, A., & Hom, P. (1987). A new method for the statistical control of rating error in performance ratings. *Educational and Psychological Measurement, 47,* 583-596.

Bannister, B., & Peña, L. (1993). Turnover in the maquiladora industry in Mexico: A challenge of transferring high technology production processes to developing countries. In L. Gomez-Mejia & M. Lawless (Eds.), *Global management of high technology* (Vol. 6, pp. 199-217). Greenwich, CT: JAI.

Barrick, M. R., & Mount, M. K. (1991). The big five personality dimensions and job performance: A meta-analysis. *Personnel Psychology, 44,* 1-26.

Barrick, M. R., & Mount, M. K. (1996). Effects of impression management and self-deception on the predictive validity of personality constructs. *Journal of Applied Psychology, 81,* 261-272.

Bauer, T., Morrison, E., & Callister, R. (1998). Organizational socialization: A review and directions for future research. In G. Ferris (Ed.), *Research in personnel and human resources management* (Vol. 16, pp. 149-214). Greenwich, CT: JAI.

Bennett, N., Blum, T. C., Long, R. G., & Roman, P. M. (1993). A firm-level analysis of employee attrition. *Group and Organization Management, 18,* 482-499.

Bernardin, H. J. (1987). Development and validation of a forced choice scale to measure job-related discomfort among customer service representatives. *Academy of Management Journal, 30,* 162-173.

Bernardin, H., & Russell, J. (1998). *Human resource management: An experiential approach.* New York: McGraw-Hill.

Bernstein, A. (1991, June 3). Family leave may not be that big a hardship for business. *Business Week,* 28.

Bernstein, A. (1998, June). We want you to stay. Really. *Business Week,* 67-68, 70, 72.

Bernstein, A., Weber, J., & Driscoll, L. (1991, November 25). *Business Week,* 234-237.

Bhagat, R., McQuaid, S., Lindholm, H., & Segovis, J. (1985). Total life stress: A multimethod validation of the construct and its effects on organizationally valued outcomes and withdrawal behaivors. *Journal of Applied Psychology, 70,* 202-214.

Black college graduates in today's labor market. (1991, February 18). *Fair Employment Practices,* p. 15.

Blakemore, A., Low, S., & Ormiston, M. (1987). Employment bonuses and labor turnover. *Journal of Labor Economics, 5,* 124-135.

Blanchard, S. L. (1983). The discontinuity between school and practice. *Nursing Management, 14,* 41-43.

Bogdanich, W. (1991, November 1). Danger in white: The shadowy world of "temp" nurses. *Wall Street Journal,* p. B1.

Bohl, D. (1999, March/April). Competition for hot talent: How companies are responding. *Compensation and Benefits Review, 31,* 29-35.

Bovee, T. (1991, September 20). Black, white pay unequal, study says. *Arizona Republic,* p. C1.

Bowen, D. E., & Schneider, B. (1988). Services marketing and management: Implications for organizational behavior. In B. Staw & L. Cummings (Eds.), *Research in organizational behavior* (Vol. 10, pp. 43-80). Greenwich, CT: JAI.

Brayfield, A. H., & Crockett, W. H. (1955). Employee attitudes and employee performance. *Psychological Bulletin, 52,* 396-424.

Breaugh, J. A. (1983). Realistic job previews: A critical appraisal and future research directions. *Academy of Management Review, 8,* 612-619.

Breaugh, J. A. (1992). *Recruitment: Science and practice.* Boston: PWS-Kent.

Breaugh, J. A., & Dossett, D. L. (1989). Rethinking the use of personal history information: The value of theory-based biodata for predicting turnover. *Journal of Business and Psychology, 3,* 371-385.

Bretz, R. D., & Judge, T. A. (1998). Realistic job previews: A test of the adverse self selection hypothesis. *Journal of Applied Psychology, 83,* 330-337.

Bridges, W. (1994, September 19). The end of the job. *Fortune,* 62-68.

Brief, A. P., Burke, M. J., George, J. M., Robinson, B. S. & Webster, J. (1988). Should negative affectivity remain an unmeasured variable in the study of job stress? *Journal of Applied Psychology, 73,* 193-198.

Brimelow, P., & Spencer, L. (1993, February 15). When quotas replace merit, everybody suffers. *Forbes,* 80-102.

Brotheron, P. (1996). Exit interviews can provide a reality check. *HR Magazine, 41*(8), 45-50.

Buckley, M. R., Fedor, D. B., Veres, J., Wiese, D., & Carraher, S. M. (1998). Investigating newcomer expectations and job-related outcomes. *Journal of Applied Psychology, 83,* 452-461.

Burns, D. (1984). *Intimate connections.* New York: William Morrow.

Burns, D. (1999a). *Feeling good: The new mood therapy.* New York: William Morrow.

Burns, D. (1999b). *The feeling good handbook.* New York: Plume.

Butler, P. (1981). *Talking to yourself: Learning the language of self-support.* New York: Harper & Row.

Caldwell, D. F., & O'Reilly, C. A. (1990). Measuring person-job fit with a profile-comparison process. *Journal of Applied Psychology, 75,* 648-657.

Campion, M. (1991). Meaning and measurement of turnover: Comparison of alternative measures and recommendations for research. *Journal of Applied Psychology, 76,* 199-212.

Campion, M. A., Palmer, D. K., & Campion, I. E. (1997). A review of structure in the selection interview. *Personnel Psychology, 50,* 655-702.

Cappelli, P. (2000, January/February). A market-driven approach to retaining talent. *Harvard Business Review, 78,* 103-111.

Career evolution. (1999, January 29). *The Economist,* pp. 89-92.

Carson, P. P., Carson, K. D., Griffeth, R. W., & Steel, R. P. (1993). Promotion and employee turnover: Critique, meta-analysis, and implications. *Journal of Business and Psychology, 8,* 245-256.

Carsten, J. M., & Spector, P. E. (1987). Unemployment, job satisfaction, and employee turnover: A meta-analytic test of the Muchinsky model. *Journal of Applied Psychology, 72,* 374-381.

Cascio, W. F. (1976). Turnover, biographical data, and fair employment practice. *Journal of Applied Psychology, 61,* 576-580.

Cascio, W. F. (2000). *Costing human resources.* Cincinnati, OH: South-Western.

Catanzarite, L. M., & Strober, M. H. (1993). The gender recomposition of the maquiladora workforce in Ciudad Juarez. *Industrial Relations, 32,* 133-147.

Chao, G., O'Leary-Kelly, A., Wolf, S., Klein, H., & Gardner, P. (1994). Organizational socialization: Its content and consequences. *Journal of Applied Psychology, 79,* 730-743.

Chatman, J. A. (1991). Matching people and organizations: Selection and socialization in public accounting firms. *Administrative Science Quarterly, 36,* 459-484.

Choi, T., Jameson, H., Brekke, M. L., Podratz, R. O., & Mundahl, H. (1986). Effects on nurse retention: An experiment with scheduling. *Medical Care, 24,* 1029-1043.

Clark, K. (1999, November 1). Why it pays to quit. *U.S. News & World Reports.* Retrieved December 2, 1999, from the World Wide Web: www.usnews.com/usnews/issue991101/nycu/quit.htm

Cleveland, J. N., & Kerst, M. E. (1993). Sexual harassment and perceptions of power: An underarticulated relationship. *Journal of Vocational Behavior, 42,* 49-67.

Cohen, A. (1999). Turnover among professionals: A longitudinal study of American lawyers. *Human Resource Management, 38,* 61-75.

Cohen, D. J., Griffeth, R. W., & Barksdale, K. (1994, November). Evaluating the effectiveness of an on-site employer sponsored child care center: Human resource implication. *Proceedings of the Southern Management Association,* 164-166.

Colarelli, S. M. (1984). Methods of communication and mediating processes in realistic job previews. *Journal of Applied Psychology, 69,* 633-642.

Conlin, M., Coy, P., Palmer, T., & Saveri, G. (1999, December 6). *Business Week,* 38-42, 44.

Cook, A. H. (1989). Public policies to help dual-earner families meet the demands of the work world. *Industrial and Labor Relations Review, 42,* 201-215.

Cose, E. (1993). *The rage of a privileged class.* New York: HarperCollins.

Cotton, J. L., & Tuttle, J. M. (1986). Employee turnover: A meta-analysis and review with implications for research. *Academy of Management Review, 11,* 55-70.

Cox, T. (1991). Organizational culture, stress, and stress management. *Work and Stress, 5,* 1-4.

Cox, T. H., & Blake, S. (1991). Managing cultural diversity: Implications for organizational competitiveness. *Academy of Management Executive, 5,* 45-56.

Cox, T. H., Lobel, S. A., & McLeod, P. L. (1991). Effects of ethnic group cultural differences on cooperative and competitive behavior on a group task. *Academy of Management Journal, 34,* 827-847.

Cundiff, V. A. (1993). How to conduct an exit interview: An intellectual property law perspective. *Employee Relations Law Journal, 19,* 159-168.

Cusumano, M. (1995). *Microsoft secrets: How the world's most powerful software company creates technology, shapes markets, and manages people.* New York: Free Press.

Dalton, D. R., Hill, J. W., & Ramsay, R. J. (1997). Women as managers and partners: Context specific predictors of turnover in international public accounting firms. *Auditing: A Journal of Practice and Theory, 16,* 29-50.

Dalton, D. R., Krackhardt, D. M., & Porter, L. W. (1981). Functional turnover: An empirical assessment. *Journal of Applied Psychology, 66,* 716-721.

Dalton, D. R., & Mesch, D. J. (1990). The impact of flexible scheduling on employee attendance and turnover. *Administrative Science Quarterly, 35,* 370-387.

Dalton, D. R., & Todor, W. D. (1979). Turnover turned over: An expanded and positive perspective. *Academy of Management Review, 4,* 225-235.

Dansereau, F., Graen, G., & Haga, W. J. (1975). A vertical dyad linkage approach to leadership within formal organizations. *Organizational Behavior and Human Performance, 13,* 46-78.

Darmon, R. Y. (1990). Identifying sources of turnover costs: A segmental approach. *Journal of Marketing, 54,* 46-56.

Davy, J. A., Kinicki, A. J., & Scheck, C. L. (1991). Developing and testing a model of survivor responses to layoffs. *Journal of Vocational Behavior, 38,* 302-317.

Dean, R. A., Ferris, K. R., & Konstans, C. (1988). Occupational reality shock and organizational commitment: Evidence from the accounting profession. *Accounting, Organizations and Society, 13,* 235-250.

Dean, R. A., & Wanous, J. P. (1984). Effects of realistic job previews on hiring bank tellers. *Journal of Applied Psychology, 69,* 61-68.

Dear, M. R., Weisman, C. S., & O'Keefe, S. (1985). Evaluation of a contract model for professional nursing practice. *Health Care Management Review, 10,* 65-77.

Deci, E. (1975). *Intrinsic motivation.* New York: Plenum.

Deutschman, A. (1991, November 4). Dealing with sexual harassment. *Fortune,* 145.

Dillman, D. A. (1978). *Mail and telephone surveys: The Total Design Method.* New York: John Wiley.

Dipboye, R. L. (1982). Self-fulfilling prophecies in the selection-recruitment interview. *Academy of Management Review, 7,* 579-586.

Dittrich, J. E., & Carrell, M. R. (1979). Organizational equity perceptions, employee job satisfaction, and departmental absence and turnover rates. *Organizational Behavior and Human Performance, 24,* 29-40.

Donovan, M., Drasgow, F., & Munson, L. (1998). The perceptions of fair interpersonal treatment scale: Development and validation of a measure of interpersonal treatment in the workplace. *Journal of Applied Psychology, 83,* 683-692.

Dougherty, J, & Holthouse, D. (1998, July 9). Bordering on exploitation. *Phoenix New Times, 29,* 10-25.

Drost, D. A., O'Brien, F. P., & Marsh, S. (1987). Exit interviews: Master the possibilities. *Personnel Administrator, 32,* 104-110.

Dugoni, B. L., & Ilgen, D. R. (1981). Realistic job previews and the adjustment of new employees. *Academy of Management Journal, 24,* 579-591.

Duleep, H. O., & Sanders, S. (1992). Discrimination at the top: American-born Asian and white men. *Industrial Relations, 31,* 416-432.

Dunham, R., & Smith, F. (1979). *Organizational surveys.* Glenview, IL: Scott, Foresman.

Ehrlich, E. (1989). The mommy track. *Business Week,* 126.

Embrey, W. R., Mondy, R. W., & Noe, R. M. (1979, May). Exit interview: A tool for personnel development. *The Personnel Administrator,* 43-48.

Ettorre, B. (1997, May). How are companies keeping the employees they want. *Management Review,* 49-53.

Farh, L., Werbel, J., & Bedeian, A. (1988). An empirical investigation of self-appraisal based performance evaluation. *Personnel Psychology, 41,* 141-156.

Farquharson, M. (1991, September). Maquila conundrum: Keeping maquila workers without increasing labor costs. *Business Mexico, 1,* 18-19.

Farr, J. L., O'Leary, B. S., & Bartlett, C. J. (1973). Effect of work sample test upon self selection and turnover of job applicants. *Journal of Applied Psychology, 58,* 283-285.

Farrell, D., & Rusbult, C. E. (1981). Exchange variables as predictors of job satisfaction, job commitment, and turnover: The impact of rewards, costs, alternatives, and investments. *Organizational Behavior and Human Performance, 28,* 78-95.

Feldman, D. C. (1988). *Managing careers in organizations.* Glenview, IL: Scott, Foresman.

Feldman, D., & Gainey, T. (1997). Patterns of telecommuting and their consequences: Framing the research agenda. *Human Resource Management Review, 4,* 369-388.

Feldman, D. C., & Klaas, B. S. (1999). The impact of exit questionnaire procedures on departing employees' self-disclosure. *Journal of Managerial Issues, 11,* 13-25.

Ferguson, E., & Hatherly, D. (1991). The work environment in the accountancy firm: A comparison of student expectations and trainee perceptions. *British Accounting Review, 23,* 123-132.

Fernandez, J. P., with Barr, M. E. (1993). *The diversity advantage.* Lexington, MA: Lexington Books.

Ferris, G. R. (1985). Role of leadership in the employee withdrawal process: A constructive replication. *Journal of Applied Psychology, 70,* 777-781.

Fisher, A. B. (1992, September 21). When will women get to the top? *Fortune,* 44.

Fitzgerald, L., Gelfand, M., & Drasgow, F. (1995). Measuring sexual harassment: Theoretical and psychometric advances. *Basic and Applied Social Psychology, 17,* 425-445.

Fitzgerald, L. F., & Shullman, S. L. (1993). Sexual harassment: A research analysis and agenda for the 1990s. *Journal of Vocational Behavior, 42,* 5-27.

Flamholtz, E. (1985). *Human resource accounting.* San Francisco: Jossey-Bass.

Fleishman, E., & Harris, E. (1962). Patterns of leadership behavior related to employee grievances and turnover. *Personnel Psychology, 15,* 43-56.

Folger, R., & Cropanzano, R. (1998). Organizational justice and human resource management. Thousand Oaks, CA: Sage.

Folger, R., & Konovsky, M. A. (1989). Effects of procedural and distributive justice on reactions to pay-raise decisions. *Academy of Management Journal, 32,* 115-130.

Folger, R., Konovsky, M., & Cropanzano, R. (1992). A due process metaphor for performance appraisal. In B. Staw & L. Cummings (Eds.), *Research in organizational behavior* (Vol. 14, pp. 129-177). Greenwich, CT: JAI.

Fottler, M. D., Crawford, M. A., Quintana, I. B., & White, I. B. (1995). Evaluating nurse turnover: Comparing attitude surveys and exit interviews. *Hospital and Health Service Administration, 40,* 278-295.

Frayne, C. A., & Latham, G. P. (1987). Application of social learning theory to employee self-management of attendance. *Journal of Applied Psychology, 72,* 387-392.

Frone, M., Russell, M., & Cooper, M. (1992). Antecedents and outcomes of work-family conflict: Testing a model of the work-family interface. *Journal of Applied Psychology, 77,* 65-75.

Frone, M., Yardley, J., & Markel, K. (1997). Developing and testing an integrative model of the work-family interface. *Journal of Vocational Behavior, 50,* 145-167.

Galen, M. (1993, June 28). Work and family. *Business Week,* 80.

Garland, S. B. (1991, August 19). Throwing stones at the "glass ceiling." *Business Week,* 29.

Garretson, P., & Teel, K. S. (1982). The exit interview: Effective tool or meaningless gesture? *Personnel, 4,* 70-77.

Gates, D. (1993, March 19). White male paranoia. *Newsweek,* 48.

Gatewood, R. D., & Feild, H. S. (1998). *Human resource selection.* Hinsdale, IL: Dryden.

George, J. M. (1989). Mood and absence. *Journal of Applied Psychology, 74,* 317-324.

George, J. M. (1990). Personality, affect, and behavior in groups. *Journal of Applied Psychology, 75,* 107-116.

Gerhart, B., & Rynes, S. (1991). Determinants and consequences of salary negotiations by male and female MBA graduates. *Journal of Applied Psychology, 76,* 256-262.

Gerson, K. (1985). *Hard choices.* Berkeley: University of California Press.

Gerstner, C., & Day, D. (1997). Meta-analytic review of leader-member exchange theory: Correlates and construct issues. *Journal of Applied Psychology, 82,* 827-844.

Ghiselli, E. E. (1974). Some perspectives for industrial psychology. *American Psychologist, 80,* 80-87.

Giacalone, R. A., & Duhon, D. (1991). Assessing intended employee behavior in exit interviews. *Journal of Psychology, 125,* 83-90.

Giacalone, R. A., & Knouse, S. B. (1989). Farewell to fruitless exit interviews. *Personnel, 66*(9), 60-62.

Giacalone R. A., Knouse, S. B., & Ashworth, D. N. (1991). Impression management and exit interview distortion. In R. A. Giacalone & P. Rosenfeld (Eds.), *Applied impression management—How image making affects managerial decision.* Newbury Park, CA: Sage.

Giacalone, R. A., Knouse, S. B., & Montagliani, A. (1997). Motivation for and prevention of honest responding in exit interviews and surveys. *Journal of Psychology, 131,* 438-448.

Giacalone, R. A., Stuckey, L., & Beard, J. W. (1996). Conditions influencing biased responding in exit interviews and surveys. *Organization Development Journal, 14,* 27-39.

Glass, J. L., & Riley, L. (1998). Family responsive policies and employee retention following childbirth. *Social Forces, 76,* 1401-1435.

Gleckman, H., Smart, T., Dwyer, P., Segal, T., & Weber, J. (1991, July 8). Race in the workplace. *Business Week,* 50.

Glover, S., & Crooker, K. (1995). Who appreciates family-responsive human resource policies: The impact of family-friendly policies on the organizational attachment of parents and non-parents. *Personnel Psychology, 48,* 271-288.

Goff, S. J., Mount, M. K., & Jamison, R. L. (1990). Employer supported child care, work/family conflict, and absenteeism: A field study. *Personnel Psychology, 43,* 793-809.

Goldberg, L. R. (1999). A broad-bandwidth, public-domain, personality inventory measuring the lower-level facets of several five-factor models. In I. Mervielde, I. Deary, F. De Fruyt, & F. Ostendorf (Eds.), Personality psychology in Europe (Vol. 7, pp. 728). Tilburg, The Netherlands: Tilburg University Press.

Gomersall, E., & Myers, M. (1966, July-August). Breakthrough in on-the-job training. *Harvard Business Review,* 62-72.

Gomez-Mejia, L. R., & Balkin, D. B. (1987). The determinants of managerial satisfaction with the expatriation and repatriation process. *Journal of Management Development, 6,* 7-17.

Gomez-Mejia, L., & Balkin, D. (1992). *Compensation, organizational strategy, and firm performance.* Cincinnati, OH: South-Western.

Gomez-Mejia, L. R., Balkin, D. B., & Milkovich, G. T. (1990). Rethinking your rewards for technical employees. *Organizational Dynamics, 18,* 62-75.

Graen, G. B., & Ginsburgh, S. (1977). Job resignation as a function of role orientation and leader acceptance: A longitudinal investigation of organizational assimilation. *Organizational Behavior and Human Performance, 19,* 1-17.

Graen, G. B., Liden, R., & Hoel, W. (1982). Role of leadership in the employee withdrawal process. *Journal of Applied Psychology, 67,* 868-872.

Graen, G., Novak, M., & Sommerkamp, P. (1982). The effects of leader-member exchange and job design on productivity and satisfaction: Testing a dual attachment model. *Organizational Behavior and Human Performance, 30,* 109-131.

Greene, R. (1998, November/December). Effectively coping with chaotic labor markets. *ACA News, 41,* 31-33, 35.

Greenhaus, J. H., Collins, K. M., Singh, R., & Parasuraman, S. (1997). Work and family influences on departure from public accounting. *Journal of Vocational Behavior, 50,* 249-270.

Griffeth, R. W. (1985). Moderation of the effects of job enrichment by participation: A longitudinal field experiment. *Organizational Behavior and Human Decision Processes, 35,* 73-93.

Griffeth, R., & Fink, L. (1992). *The Turnover Events Scale.* Unpublished manuscript, Department of Management, Georgia State University, Atlanta.

Griffeth, R. W., & Hom, P. W. (1988a). A comparison of different conceptualizations of perceived alternatives in turnover research. *Journal of Organizational Behavior, 9,* 103-11.

Griffeth, R. W., & Hom, P. W. (1988b). Locus of control and delay of gratification as moderators of employee turnover. *Journal of Applied Social Psychology, 13,* 1318-1333.

Griffeth, R., Hom, P., & Gaertner, S. (2000). A meta-analysis of antecedents and correlates of employee turnover: Update, moderator tests, and research implications for the next millennium. *Journal of Management, 26,* 463-488.

Grimsley, K. (1999, June 5). With jobs plentiful, workers take their pick; South Dakota firms use executive perks to fill basic jobs. *Washington Post.* Retrieved August 26, 1999, from the World Wide Web: http://proquest.umi.com/pqdweb

Gross, S. (1998, November/December). What's a compensation manager to do in era of full employment? *ACA News, 6-8.*

Gutek, B. A., & Koss, M. P. (1993). Changed women and changed organizations: Consequences of and coping with sexual harassment. *Journal of Vocational Behavior, 42,* 28-48.

Hackman, J. R., & Oldham, G. R. (1976). Motivation through the design of work: Test of a theory. *Organizational Behavior and Human Performance, 16,* 250-259.

Hackman, J. R., & Oldham, G. R. (1980). *Work redesign.* Reading, MA: Addison-Wesley.

Hammonds, K. (1996, September 16). Balancing work and family. *Business Week,* 74-80.

Hanisch, K. A., & Hulin, C. L. (1990). Job attitudes and organizational withdrawal: An examination of retirement and other voluntary withdrawal behaviors. *Journal of Vocational Behavior, 37,* 60-78.

Hanisch, K., Hulin, C., & Roznowski, M. (1998). The importance of individuals' repertoires of behaviors: The scientific appropriateness of studying multiple behaviors and general attitudes. *Journal of Organizational Behavior, 19,* 463-480.

Harris, M., & Schaubroeck, J. (1988). A meta-analysis of self-superior, self-peer, and peer-supervisor ratings. *Personnel Psychology, 41,* 43-62.

Harrison, D. A., Virick, M., & William, S. (1996). Working without a net: Time, performance, and turnover under maximally contingent rewards. *Journal of Applied Psychology, 81,* 331-345.

Hecht, L., & Morici, P. (1993). Managing risks in Mexico. *Harvard Business Review, 71*(4), 32-39.

Heilman, M. E. (1983). Sex bias in work settings: The lack of fit model. *Research in Organizational Behavior, 5,* 269-298.

Heilman, M. E., Rivero, J. C., & Brett, J. F. (1991). Skirting the competence issue: Effects of sex-based preferential selection on task choices of women and men. *Journal of Applied Psychology, 76,* 99-105.

Heneman, H. G. (1985). Pay satisfaction. In K. M. Rowland & G. R. Ferris (Eds.), *Research in personnel and human resources management* (Vol. 3, pp. 115-40). Greenwich, CT: JAI.

Heneman, R. L. (1990). Merit pay research. In G. R. Ferris & K. M. Rowland (Eds.), *Research in personnel and human resources management* (Vol. 8, pp. 203-263). Greenwich, CT: JAI.

Himmelberg, M. (1999, March 3). Older workers may be offered incentives to stay. *Orange County Register.* Retrieved March 3, 1999, from the World Wide Web: http://www.azcentral.com/news/0303aging.shtml

Hinrichs, J. R. (1975). Measurement of reasons for resignation of professionals: Questionnaire versus company and consultant exit interviews. *Journal of Applied Psychology, 60,* 530-532.

Hochschild, A. (1997). *The time bind: When work becomes home and home becomes work.* New York: Metropolitan.

Hoffman, C., Nathan, B., & Holden, L. (1991). A comparison of validation criteria: Objective versus subjective performance measures and self-versus supervisor ratings. *Personnel Psychology, 44,* 601-619.

Holloran, S. D., Mishkin, B. H., & Hanson, B. L. (1980). Bicultural training for new graduates. *Journal of Nursing Administration, 10,* 17-24.

Holmes, T., & Rahe, R. (1967). The social readjustment rating scale. *Journal of Psychosomatic Research, 11,* 213-218.

Hom, P. W. (1979). Effects of job peripherality and personal characteristics on the job satisfaction of part-time workers. *Academy of Management Journal, 22,* 551-565.

Hom, P. W. (1980). Expectancy predictions of reenlistment in the National Guard. *Journal of Vocational Behavior, 16,* 235-248.

Hom, P. W. (1992). *Turnover costs among mental health professionals.* Unpublished manuscript, College of Business, Arizona State University, Tempe.

Hom, P. W., Bracker, J. S., & Julian, G. (1988, October). In pursuit of greener pastures. *New Accountant, 4,* 24.

Hom, P., DeNisi, A., Kinicki, A., & Bannister, B. (1982). The effectiveness of performance feedback from behaviorally anchored rating scales. *Journal of Applied Psychology, 67,* 568-576.

Hom, P. W., & Griffeth, R. (1991). Structural equations modeling test of a turnover theory: Cross-sectional and longitudinal analyses. *Journal of Applied Psychology, 76,* 350-366.

Hom, P., & Griffeth, R. (1995). *Employee turnover.* Cincinnati, OH: South-Western.

Hom, P., Griffeth, R., Palich, L., & Bracker, J. (1998). An exploratory investigation into theoretical mechanisms underlying realistic job previews. *Personnel Psychology, 51,* 421-451.

Hom, P. W., & Hulin, C. L. (1981). A competitive test of the prediction of reenlistment by several models. *Journal of Applied Psychology, 66,* 23-39.

Hom, P., & Kinicki, A. (2000). *Toward a more comprehensive and integrated understanding of how job affect initiates turnover.* Unpublished manuscript, Department of Management, Arizona State University, Tempe.

Hom, P., Palich, L., & Bracker, J. S. (1990, August). *Realistic job previews for accountants: Psychological mediating processes.* Paper presented at the annual meeting of the Academy of Management, San Francisco.

Horner, S. O., Mobley, W. H., & Meglino, B. M. (1979). *An experimental evaluation of the effects of a realistic job preview on Marine recruit affect, intentions, and behavior* (Tech. Rep. 9). Columbia, SC: Center for Management and Organizational Research.

Hough, L. M., Eaton, N. K., Dunnette, M. D., Kamp, J. D., & McCloy, R. A. (1990). Criterion-related validities of personality constructs and the effect of response distortion on those validities. *Journal of Applied Psychology, 75,* 581-595.

House, R., Schuler, R., & Levanoni, E. (1983). Role conflict and amiguity scales: Reality or artifacts. *Journal of Applied Psychology, 68,* 334-337.

How employees perceive sexual harassment. (1992, March-April). *Harvard Business Review, 23.*

Howard, G. S., Dailey, P. R., & Gulanick, N. A. (1979). The feasibility of informed pretests in attenuating response-shift bias. *Applied Psychological Measurement, 3,* 481-494.

Huey, F. L., & Hartley, S. (1988). What keeps nurses in nursing. *American Journal of Nursing, 88,* 181-188.

Hulin, C. L. (1991). Adaptation, persistence, and commitment in organizations. In M. D. Dunnette & L. M. Hough (Eds.), *Handbook of industrial and organizational psychology* (2nd ed., Vol. 2). Palo Alto, CA: Consulting Psychologists Press.

Hulin, C. L., Roznowski, M., & Hachiya, D. (1985). Alternative opportunities and withdrawal decisions: Empirical and theoretical discrepancies and an integration. *Psychological Bulletin, 97,* 233-250.

Hunter, J. E., Gerbing, D. W., & Boster, F. J. (1982). Machiavellian beliefs and personality: Construct validity of the Machiavellianism dimension. *Journal of Personality and Social Psychology, 43,* 1293-1305.

Hunter, J. E., & Hunter, R. F. (1984). Validity and utility of alternative predictors of job performance. *Psychological Bulletin, 96,* 72-88.

Hunter, J. E., & Schmidt, F. L. (1990). *Methods of meta-analysis.* Newbury Park, CA: Sage.

Ippolito, R. A. (1991). Encouraging long-term tenure: Wage tilt or pension? *Industrial & Labor Relations Review, 44,* 520-535.

Igbaria, M, & Guimaraes, T. (1999, Summer). Exploring differences in employee turnover intentions and its determinants among telecommuters and non-telecommuters. *Journal of Management Information Systems, 16,* 147-164.

Jackofsky, E. F. (1984). Turnover and job performance: An integrated process model. *Academy of Management Review, 9,* 74-83.

James, F. E. (1988, June 7). More blacks quitting white-run firms. *Wall Street Journal,* p. B1.

Jarman, M. (1999, April 16). Creative benefits help hold workers. *Arizona Republic.* Retrieved April 16, 1999, from the World Wide Web: www.azcentral.com/news/0416jobs.shtml

Johnson, A. A. (1990). Parental leave—Is it the business of business? *Human Resource Planning, 13,* 119-131.

Johnson, A. A. (1995). The business case for work-family programs. *Journal of Accountancy,* 53-57.

Johnston, M., Parasuraman, A., Futrell, C., & Black, W. (1990, August). A longitudinal assessment of the impact of selected salespeople's organizational commitment during the early employment. *Journal of Marketing Research,* 333-344.

Jones, E., Kantak, D., Futrell, C., & Johnston, M. (1996). Leader behavior, work attitudes, and turnover of salespeople. *Journal of Personal Selling and Sales Management, 16,* 13-23.

Jones, G. (1986). Socialization tactics, self-efficacy, and newcomers' adjustments to organizations. *Academy of Management Journal, 29,* 262-279.

Jones, J. M. (1972). *Prejudice and racism.* Reading, MA: Addison-Wesley.

Joplin, J. R. W., & Daus, C. S. (1997). Challenges of leading a diverse workforce. *Academy of Management Executive, 11,* 32-47.

Judge, T. A. (1992). The dispositional perspective in human resources research. In G. R. Ferris & K. M. Rowland (Eds.), *Research in personnel and human resources management* (Vol. 10, pp. 31-72). Greenwich, CT: JAI.

Judge, T. A. (1993). Does affective disposition moderate the relationship between job satisfaction and voluntary turnover? *Journal of Applied Psychology, 78,* 395-401.

Judge, T. A., & Hulin, C. L. (1993). Job satisfaction as a reflection of disposition: A multiple source causal analysis. *Organizational Behavior and Human Decision Processes, 56,* 388-421.

Judge, T. A., & Locke, E. A. (1993). Effect of dysfunctional thought processes on subjective well-being and job satisfaction. *Journal of Applied Psychology, 78,* 475-490.

Kantor, R. M. (1977). *Men and women of the corporation.* New York: Basic Books.

Katerberg, R., Hom, P. W., & Hulin, C. L. (1979). Effects of job complexity on the reactions of part-time workers. *Organizational Behavior and Human Performance, 24,* 317-332.

Keeping secrets. (1997, April 10). *USA Today,* pp. 1B-2B.

Kinicki, A., Lockwood, C., Hom, P., & Griffeth, R. (1990). Interview predictions of applicant qualifications and interviewer validity: Aggregate and individual analyses. *Journal of Applied Psychology, 75,* 477-486.

Klein, H., & Weaver, N. (2000). The effectiveness of an organizational-level orientation training program in the socialization of new hires. *Personnel Psychology, 53,* 47-66.

Ko, J., Price, J., & Mueller, C. (1997). Assessment of Meyer and Allen's three component model of organizational commitment in South Korea. *Journal of Applied Psychology, 82,* 961-973.

Konrad, W. (1990, August 6). Welcome to the woman-friendly company where talent is valued and rewarded. *Business Week,* 48.

Korsgaard, M. A., Roberson, L., & Rymph, R. D. (1998). What motivates fairness? The role of subordinate assertive behavior on managers' interactional fairness. *Journal of Applied Psychology, 83,* 731-744.

Kossek, E. E. (1990). Diversity in child care assistance needs: Employee problems, preferences, and work-related outcomes. *Personnel Psychology, 43,* 769-791.

Kossek, E. E., & Grace, P. (1990). Taking a strategic view of employee child care assistance: A cost-benefit model. *Human Resource Planning, 13,* 189-202.

Kossek, E., & Nichol, V. (1992). The effects of on-site child care on employee attitudes and performance. *Personnel Psychology, 45,* 485-509.

Kossek, E., & Ozeki, C. (1998). Work-family conflict, policies, and the job-life satisfaction relationship: A review and directions for organizational behavior-human resources research. *Journal of Applied Psychology, 83,* 139-149.

Krackhardt, D., McKenna, J., Porter, L., & Steers, R. (1981). Supervisory behavior and employee turnover: A field experiment. *Academy of Management Journal, 24,* 249-259.

Krackhardt, D., & Porter, L. (1986). The snowball effect: Turnover embedded in communication networks. *Journal of Applied Psychology, 71,* 50-55.

Kramer, M. (1974). *Reality shock: Why nurses leave nursing.* St. Louis, MO: C. V. Mosby.

Kramer, M. (1977). Reality shock can be handled on the job. *RN, 63,* 11.

Kramer, M., Schmalenberg, C. (1977). *Paths to biculturalism.* Wakefield, MA: Contemporary.

Krooth, R. (1995). Mexico, NAFTA, and the hardships of progress. Jefferson, NC: McFarland & Company.

Lach, D. H., & Gwartney-Gibbs, P. A. (1993). Sociological perspectives on sexual harassment and workplace dispute resolution. *Journal of Vocational Behavior, 42,* 102-115.

Laird, D. D. (1983). Supplemental nursing agencies—A tool for combatting the nursing shortage. *Health Care Management Review, 8,* 61-67.

La Lopa, J. (1999, August 26). *Benefits for fast-food workers improve bottom line.* Retrieved September 16, 1999, from the World Wide Web: http://www.newswise.com/articles/1999/8/turnover.pur.html

La Lopa, J., Felli, A., & Kavanaugh, R. (1999). *The effect of wage and benefit incentives on turnover of part-time employees working at Indiana's franchised quickservice hamburger chain restaurants.* Unpublished manuscript, Purdue University, Department of Restaurant, Hotel, Institutional, and Tourism Management, West Lafayette, IN.

Langdon, J. (1999, July 27). *Employers sweeten benefit pots, poll says.* Gannett News Service. Retrieved July 7, 1999 from www.azcentral.com/business/0727BENEFITS27.shtml

Lardner, J. (1999, December 20). World-class workaholics. *U.S. News & World Report,* 42-53.

Lawler, E. E. (1990). *Strategic pay.* San Francisco: Jossey-Bass.

Leblanc, P. V. (1991). Skill-based pay case number 2: Northern Telecom. *Compensation and Benefits Review, 23,* 39-56.

Ledford, G. E., & Bergel, G. (1991). Skill-based pay case number 1: General Mills. *Compensation and Benefits Review, 23,* 24-38.

Ledford, G. E., Tyler, W. R., & Dixey, W. B. (1990). Skill-based pay case number 3: Honeywell ammunition assembly plant. *Compensation and Benefits Review,* 57-77.

Lee, T. W., & Maurer, S. D. (1997). The retention of knowledge workers with the unfolding model of voluntary turnover. *Human Resource Management Review, 7,* 247-275.

Lee, T. W., & Mitchell, T. R. (1994). An alternative approach: The unfolding model of voluntary employee turnover. *Academy of Management Review, 19,* 51-89.

Lee, T., Mitchell, T., Holtom, B., McDaniel, L., & Hill, J. (1999). The unfolding model of voluntary turnover: A replication and extension. *Academy of Management Journal, 42,* 450-462.

Lee, T. W., Mitchell, T. R., Wise, L., & Fireman, S. (1996). An unfolding model of voluntary employee turnover. *Academy of Management Journal, 39,* 5-36.

Lefkowitz, J., & Katz, M. L. (1969). Validity of exit interviews. *Personnel Psychology, 22,* 445-455.

Leventhal, G. S. (1980). What should be done with equity theory? In K. Gergen, M. S. Greenberg, & R. H. Willis (Eds.), *Social exchange.* New York: Plenum.

Lobel, S. A. (1993). Sexuality at work: Where do we go from here? *Journal of Vocational Behavior, 42,* 136-152.

Locke, E. A., Sirota, D., & Wolfson, A. D. (1976). An experimental case study of the successes and failures of job enrichment in a government agency. *Journal of Applied Psychology, 61,* 701-711.

Lopez, J. (1993, July 9). Firms use contracts and cash to prevent talent raids by departing executives. *Wall Street Journal,* pp. B1, B8.

Louis, M. R., Posner, B. Z., & Powell, G. N. (1983). The availability and helpfulness of socialization practices. *Personnel Psychology, 36,* 857-866.

Luthans, F., Rosenkrantz, S. A., & Hennessey, H. W. (1985). What do successful managers really do? An observation study of managerial activities. *Journal of Applied Behavioral Science, 21,* 255-270.

Lytle, R., Hom, P., & Mokwa, M. (1998). SERV*OR: A managerial measure of organizational service-orientation. *Journal of Retailing, 74,* 455-489.

Managing diversity: Successes and failures. (1991, August 5). *Fair Employment Practices,* p. 90.

Mandel, M. J., & Farrell, C. (1992, July 13). The immigrants. *Business Week,* 114.

Manz, C. C. (1992). Self-leading work teams: Moving beyond self-management myths. *Human Relations, 45,* 1119-1140.

Manz, C. C., & Neck, C. P. (1999). *Mastering self-leadership: Empowering yourself for personal excellence.* Upper Saddle River, NJ: Prentice Hall.

Manz, C. C., & Sims, H. P. (1989). *Super leadership.* Englewood Cliffs, NJ: Prentice Hall.

Marano, H. (1995, September-October). When the boss is a bully. *Psychology Today, 28,* 58-61.

Maslach, C. (1982). *Burnout: The cost of caring.* Englewood Cliffs, NJ: Prentice Hall.

Mathieu, J. E., & Zajac, D. (1990). A review and meta-analysis of the antecedents, correlates, and consequences of organizational commitment. *Psychological Bulletin, 108,* 171-194.

Mattis, M. C. (1990). New forms of flexible work arrangements for managers and professionals: Myths and realities. *Human Resource Planning, 13,* 133-146.

McDaniel, M. A., Whetzel, D. L., Schmidt, F. L., & Maurer, S. D. (1994). The validity of employment interview: A comprehensive review and meta analysis. *Journal of Applied Psychology, 79,* 599-616.

McEvoy, G. M., & Cascio, W. F. (1985). Strategies for reducing employee turnover: A meta-analysis. *Journal of Applied Psychology, 70,* 342-353.

McMahan, G. C., Bell, M. P., & Virick, M. (1998). Strategic human resource management: Employee involvement, diversity, and international issues. *Human Resource Management Review, 8,* 193-214.

Medved, M. (1982). *Hospital.* New York: Pocket Books.

Meglino, B. M., & DeNisi, A. S. (1987). Realistic job previews: Some thoughts on their more effective use in managing the flow of human resources. *Human Resource Planning, 10,* 157-167.

Meglino, B. M., DeNisi, A. S., & Ravlin, E. C. (1993). Effects of previous job exposure and subsequent job status on the functioning of a realistic job preview. *Personnel Psychology, 46,* 803-822.

Meglino, B. M., DeNisi, A. S., Youngblood, S. A., & Williams K. J. (1988). Effects of realistic job previews: A comparison using an enhancement and a reduction preview. *Journal of Applied Psychology, 73,* 259-266.

Mercer, M. W. (1988, December). Turnover: Reducing the costs. *Personnel,* 36-42.

Meyer, J., & Allen, N. (1997). *Commitment in the workplace.* Thousand Oaks, CA: Sage.

Meyer, J. P., Allen, N. J., & Gellatly, I. R. (1990). Affective and continuance commitment to the organization: Evaluation of measures and analysis of concurrent and time-lagged relations. *Journal of Applied Psychology, 75,* 710-720.

Meyer, J., Allen, N., & Smith, C. (1993). Commitment to organizations and occupations: Extension and test of a three-component conceptualization. *Journal of Applied Psychology, 78,* 538-551.

Milkovich, G. T., & Gomez, L. (1976). Day care and selected employee work behavior. *Academy of Management Journal, 19,* 111-115.

Milkovich, G. T., & Newman, J. M. (1999). *Compensation.* Burr Ridge, IL: Irwin.

Miller, J., Hom, P., & Gomez-Mejia, L. (1999). *The high costs of low wages: Do maquiladora compensation practices reduce turnover among Mexican production workers?* Unpublished manuscript, University of Wisconsin, Department of Management, Milwaukee, Wisconsin.

Miller, T. I. (1984). The effects of employer-sponsored child care on employee absenteeism, turnover, productivity, recruitment or job satisfaction: What is claimed and what is known. *Personnel Psychology, 37,* 277-289.

Mitchell, O. S. (1983). Fringe benefits and the cost of changing jobs. *Industrial and Labor Relations Review, 37,* 70-78.

Mobley, W. H. (1977). Intermediate linkages in the relationship between job satisfaction and employee turnover. *Journal of Applied Psychology, 62,* 237-240.

Mobley, W. H. (1982). *Employee turnover: Causes, consequences, and control.* Reading, MA: Addison-Wesley.

Mobley, W. H., Griffeth, R. W., Hand, H. H., & Meglino, B. M. (1979). Review and conceptual analysis of the employee turnover process. *Psychological Bulletin, 86,* 493-522.

Morita, J. G., Lee, T. W., & Mowday, R. T. (1993). The regression-analog to survival analysis: A selected application to turnover research. *Academy of Management Review, 36,* 1430-1464.

Morrison, A. M., & Von Glinow, M. A. (1990). Women and minorities in management. *American Psychologist, 45,* 200-208.

Morrison, E. F. (1993). Newcomer information seeking: Exploring types, modes, sources, and outcomes. *Academy of Management Journal, 36,* 557-589.

Morrow, P. C., & Wirth, R. E. (1989). Work commitment among salaried professionals. *Journal of Vocational Behavior, 34,* 40-56.

Motorola sues Intel. (1999, March 12). *Associated Press.* Retrieved March 12, 1999, from the World Wide Web: http://wire.ap.org/FRONTID=TECHNOLOGY&PACKAGEID= BIZCOMPUTERS

Moving past affirmative action to managing diversity. (1990, September 17). *Fair Employment Practices,* p. 109.

Mowday, R. T., Porter, L. W., & Steers, R. M. (1982). *Employee-organization linkages.* San Diego, CA: Academic Press.

Mowday, R. T., Porter, L. W., & Stone, E. F. (1978). Employees characteristics as predictors of turnover among female clerical employees in two organizations. *Journal of Vocational Behavior, 12,* 321-332.

Muchinsky, P. M. (1979). The use of reference reports in personnel selection: A review and evaluation. *Journal of Occupational Psychology, 52,* 287-297.

Muchinsky, P. M., & Tuttle, M. L. (1979). Employee turnover: An empirical and methodological assessment. *Journal of Vocational Behavior, 14,* 43-77.

Mueller, C. W., & Price, J. L. (1989). Some consequences of turnover: A work unit analysis. *Human Relations, 42,* 389-402.

Murnane, R. J., Singer, J. D., & Willett, J. B. (1989). The influences of salaries and "opportunity costs" on teachers' career choices: Evidence from North Carolina. *Harvard Educational Review, 59,* 325-346.

Naffziger, D. W. (1985, August). BARS, RJPs, and recruiting. *Personnel Administrator,* 85-96.

Neck, C. (1992). *Thought self-leadership: The impact of mental strategies training on employee cognitions, behaviors, and emotions.* Doctoral dissertation, Arizona State University, Tempe.

Neck, C., & Manz, C. (1996). Thought self-leadership: The impact of mental strategies training on employee cognition, behavior, and affect. *Journal of Organizational Behavior, 17,* 445-467.

Netermeyer, R. G., Boles, J. S., & McMurrian, R. (1996). Development and validation of work-family conflict and family-work conflict scales. *Journal of Applied Psychology, 81,* 400-410.

Netermeyer, R. G., Johnston, M. W., & Burton, S. (1990). An analysis of role conflict and role ambiguity in a structural equations framework. *Journal of Applied Psychology, 75,* 148-157.

Newby, J. M. (1980, September 1). Study supports hiring more part-time RNs. *Hospitals, 1,* 71-73.

Nkomo, S. M. (1992). The emperor has no clothes: Rewriting "Race in Organizations." *Academy of Management Review, 17,* 487-513.

OFCCP's glass ceiling initiative. (1991, September 2). *Fair Employment Practices,* p. 102.

Oldham, G. R. (1988). Effects of changes in workspace partitions and spatial density on employee reactions: A quasi-experiment. *Journal of Applied Psychology, 73,* 253-258.

Oldham, G. R., Hackman, J. R., & Stepina, L. P. (1979). Norms for the Job Diagnostic Survey. *JSAS Catalog of Selected Documents in Psychology, 9,* 14. (Ms. No. 1819)

Olson, M. H., & Primps, S. B. (1984). Working at home with computers: Work and nonwork issues. *Journal of Social Issues, 40,* 97-112.

One company's approach to valuing workforce diversity. (1991, April 25). *Fair Employment Practices,* p. 48.

O'Reilly, B. (1992, May 18). How to take care of aging parents. *Fortune,* 108-112.

O'Reilly, C. A., Caldwell, D. F., & Barnett, W. P. (1989). Work group demography, social integration, and turnover. *Administrative Science Quarterly, 34,* 21-37.

O'Reilly, C. A., & Chatman, J. (1986). Organizational commitment and psychological attachment: The effects of compliance, identification, and internalization. *Journal of Applied Psychology, 71,* 492-499.

O'Reilly, C. A., Chatman, J., & Caldwell, D. F. (1991). People and organizational culture: A profile comparison approach to assessing person-organization fit. *Academy of Management Journal, 34,* 487-516.

Orlick, T. (1986). *Psyching for sport: Mental training for athletes.* Champaign, IL: Leisure Press.

Parus, B. (1999, February). Designing a total rewards program to retain critical talent in the new millennium. *ACA News, 42,* 20-23.

Pay equity makes good business sense. (1990, September 3). *Fair Employment Practices,* p. 103.

Pelled, L. H., & Xin, K. R. (1999). Down and out: An investigation of the relationship between mood and employee withdrawal behavior. *Journal of Management, 6,* 875-895.

Phillips, J. M. (1998). Effects of realistic job previews on multiple organizational outcomes: A meta-analysis. *Academy of Management Journal, 41,* 673-690.

Picou, A., & Peluchon, E. (1995). The Texas-Mexico maquila industry: Expectations for the future. *Journal of Borderland Studies, 10,* 75-86.

Pierce, J. L., & Dunham, R. B. (1992). The 12-hour work day: A 48-hour, eight-day week. *Academy of Management Journal, 35,* 1086-1098.

Poe, A. (1998, March). Retention bonuses prove effective for companies in transition. *HRMagazine, 43,* 53-59.

Porter, L. W., & Steers, R. M. (1973). Organizational, work, and personal factors in employee turnover and absenteeism. *Psychological Bulletin, 80,* 151-176.

Premack, S., & Wanous, J. (1985). A meta-analysis of realistic job preview experiments. *Journal of Applied Psychology, 70,* 706-719.

Premack, S., & Wanous, J. (1987, August). *Evaluating the met expectations hypothesis.* Paper presented at the national meeting of the Academy of Management, New Orleans, LA.

Price, J. L. (1977). *The study of turnover.* Ames: Iowa State University Press.

Price, J. L., & Mueller, C. W. (1981). A causal model of turnover for nurses. *Academy of Management Journal, 24,* 543-565.

Price, J. L., & Mueller, C. W. (1986). *Absenteeism and turnover of hospital employees.* Greenwich, CT: JAI.

Promoting women to upper management. (1990, July 19). *Fair Employment Practices,* p. 86.

Pryor, J. B., LaVite, C. M., & Stoller, L. M. (1993). A social psychological analysis of sexual harassment: The person/situation interaction. *Journal of Vocational Behavior, 42,* 68-83.

Ragaglia, B. M. (1991, September). Raise your retention rate. *Managers Magazine,* 17-19.

Ralston, D. A., & Flanagan, M. F. (1985). The effect of flexitime on absenteeism and turnover for male and female employees. *Journal of Vocational Behavior, 26,* 206-217.

Raphael, M. A. (1975). Work previews can reduce turnover and improve performance. *Personnel Journal, 54,* 97-98.

Reilly, R. R., Tenopyr, M. L., & Sperling, S. M. (1979). Effects of job previews on job acceptance and survival of telephone operator candidates. *Journal of Applied Psychology, 64,* 218-220.

Reingold, J., & Brady, D. (1999, September 20). *Business Week,* 112-126.

Robinson, G., & Dechant, K. (1997) Building a business case for diversity. *Academy of Management Executive, 11,* 21-31.

Rokeach, M. (1973). *The nature of human values.* New York: Free Press.

Rosse, J. G. (1988). Relations among lateness, absence, and turnover: Is there a progression of withdrawal? *Human Relations, 41,* 517-531.

Roth, P., & Roth, P. (1995, September 1). Reduce turnover with realistic job previews. *CPA Journal, 65,* 68-69.

Royalty, A. B. (1998). Job-to-job and job-to-nonemployment turnover by gender and educational level. *Journal of Labor Economics, 16,* 392-443.

Russell, J. A., & Carroll, J. M. (1999). On the bipolarity of positive and negative affect. *Psychological Bulletin, 125,* 3-30.

Rynes, S. L. (1990). Recruitment, job choice, and post-hire consequences: A call for new research directions. In M. D. Dunnette & L. Hough (Eds.), *Handbook of industrial and organizational psychology* (2nd ed., pp. 399-444). Palo Alto, CA: Consulting Psychologists Press.

Sackett, P. R., DuBois, C. L., & Noe, A. W. (1991). Tokenism in performance evaluation: The effects of work group representation on male-female and white-black differences in performance ratings. *Journal of Applied Psychology, 76,* 263-267.

Saks, A., & Ashforth, B. (1996). Proactive socialization and behavioral self-management. *Journal of Vocational Behavior, 48,* 301-323.

Saks, A., & Ashforth, B. (1997). Organizational socialization: Making sense of the past and present as a prologue for the future. *Journal of Vocational Behavior, 51,* 234-279.

Salancik, G. R., & Pfeffer, J. (1978). A social information processing approach to job attitude and task design. *Administrative Science Quarterly, 23,* 224-253.

Scandura, T. A., & Graen, G. B. (1984). Moderating effects of initial leader-member exchange status on the effects of a leadership intervention. *Journal of Applied Psychology, 69,* 428-436.

Schlesinger, L. A., & Heskett, J. L. (1991, September-October). The service-driven service company. *Harvard Business Review, 69,* 71-81.

Schmidt, N., Gooding R. Z., Noe, R. D., & Kirsch, M. (1984). Meta-analyses of validity studies published between 1964 and 1982 and the investigation of study characteristics. *Personnel Psychology, 37,* 407-422.

Schmidt, F., & Rader, M. (1999). Exploring the boundary conditions for interview validity: Meta-analytic validity findings for a new interview type. *Personnel Psychology, 52,* 445-464.

Schmitt, N., & Klimoski, R. (1991). *Research in methods in human resources management.* Cincinnati, OH: South-Western.

Schneider, B. (1985). Organizational behavior. *Annual Review of Psychology, 36,* 573-611.

Schuster, J., & Zingheim, P. (1992). *The new pay.* Lexington, MA: Lexington Books.

Schwab, D. P. (1991). Contextual variables in employee performance-turnover relationships. *Academy of Management Journal, 34,* 966-975.

Schwartz, F. N. (1989, January-February). Management women and the new facts of life. *Harvard Business Review,* 65-76.

Secret, M., Sprang, G., & Bradford, J. (1998). Parenting in workplace. *Journal of Family Issues, 19,* 795-815.

Segal, U. A. (1992). Values, personality and career choice. *Journal of Applied Social Sciences, 16,* 143-159.

Shaw, J. D., Delery, J. E, Jenkins, G. D., & Gupta, N. (1998). An organizational-level analysis of voluntary and involuntary turnover. *Academy of Management Journal, 41,* 511-525.

Shellenbarger, S. (1992, December 7). Managers navigate uncharted waters trying to resolve work-family conflicts. *Wall Street Journal,* p. B1.

Sheridan, J. E. (1992). Organizational culture and employee retention. *Academy of Management Journal, 35,* 1036-1056.

Smith, F. J., & Kerr, W. A. (1953). Turnover factors as assessed by the exit interview. *Journal of Applied Psychology, 37,* 352-355.

Smith, R. (1999, November). *Turnover: A workforce planner's perspective.* Presentation to Chicago Industrial Organizational Psychologists, Chicago.

Society for Industrial and Organizational Psychology, Inc. (1987). *Principles for the validation and use of personnel selection procedure* (3rd ed.). College Park, MD: Author.

Solomon, C. M. (1991, September). Are white males being left out? *Personnel Journal,* 88.

Spector, P. E. (1997). *Job satisfaction.* Thousand Oaks, CA: Sage.

Spiers, J. (1992, February 10). The baby boom is for real. *Fortune* 101.

Staw, B. M. (1980). The consequences of turnover. *Journal of Occupational Behavior, 1,* 253-273.

Staw, B. M., Bell, N., & Clausen, J. A. (1986). The dispositional approach to job attitudes: A life time longitudinal test. *Administrative Science Quarterly, 31,* 56-77.

Steel, R. P. (1996). Labor market dimensions as predictors of the reenlistment decisions of military personnel. *Journal of Applied Psychology, 81,* 421-428.

Steel, R. P., & Griffeth, R. W. (1989). The elusive relationship between perceived employment opportunity and turnover behavior: A methodological or conceptual artifact? *Journal of Applied Psychology, 74,* 846-854.

Steel, R. P., & Ovalle, N. K. II. (1984). A review and meta-analysis of research on the relationship between behavioral intentions and employee turnover. *Journal of Applied Psychology, 69,* 673-686.

Steen, M. (1999). Readers don't all agree with HR's suggestion for exit-interview etiquette. *Info World, 21*(34), 85.

Stinson, J. 1989, November. Maquiladoras challenge human resources. *Personnel Journal, 68*(90), 92-93.

Stockdale, M. S. (1993). The role of sexual misperceptions of women's friendliness in an emerging theory of sexual harassment. *Journal of Vocational Behavior, 42,* 84-101.

Stroh, L. K., Brett, J. M., & Reilly, A. H. (1992). All the right stuff: A comparison of female and male managers' career progression. *Journal of Applied Psychology, 77,* 251-260.

Stroh, L., Brett, J., & Reilly, A. (1996). Family structure, glass ceiling, and traditional explanations for the differential rate of turnover of female and male managers. *Journal of Vocational Behavior, 49,* 99-118.

Sundstrom, E., De Meuse, K. P., & Futrell, D. (1990). Work teams: Applications and effectiveness. *American Psychologist, 45*(2), 120-33.

Survey confirms high cost of turnover. (1998, August 17). *Puget Sound Business Journal.* Retrieved from the World Wide Web: www.bizjournals.com/seattle/stories/1998/08/17/focus6.html

Suszko, M., & Breaugh, J. A. (1986). The effects of RJPs on applicant self-selection and employee turnover, satisfaction, and coping ability. *Journal of Management, 12,* 513-523.

Tang, T., Kim, J., & Tang, D. (2000). Does attitude toward money moderate the relationship between intrinsic job satisfaction and voluntary turnover. *Human Relations, 53,* 213-245.

Tannenbaum, J. A. (1999, January 12). Small companies find new way to retain employees—payroll-deduction plans springing up to pay for things like car insurance. *Wall Street Journal,* p. B3.

Taylor, M. S. (1985). The role of occupational knowledge and vocational self-concept crystallization in students' school-to-work transition. *Journal of Counseling Psychology, 32,* 539-550.

Taylor, M. S. (1988). Effects of college internship on individual participants. *Journal of Applied Psychology, 73,* 393-401.

Taylor, M., Tracy, K., Renard, M., Harrison, J., & Carroll, S. (1995). Due process in performance appraisal: A quasi-experiment in procedural justice. *Administrative Science Quarterly, 40,* 495-523.

Teagarden, M. B., Butler, M. C., & Von Glinow, M. A. (1992). Mexico's maquiladora industry: Where strategic human resource management makes a difference. *Organizational Dynamics, 20*(3), 34-47.

Telecommuting can save employers $10,000 per worker. (2000). *ACA News, 43,* p. 14.

Tepper, B. (2000). Consequences of abusive supervision. *Academy of Management Journal, 43,* 178-190.

Terborg, J. R., & Lee, T. W. (1984). A predictive study of organizational turnover rates. *Academy of Management Journal, 27,* 793-810.

Tett, R. P., Jackson, D. N., & Rothstein, M. (1991). Personality measures as predictors of job performance: A meta-analytic review. *Personnel Psychology, 44,* 703-742.

Tett, R. P., & Meyer, J. P. (1993). Job satisfaction, organizational commitment, turnover intention, and turnover: Path analyses based on meta-analytic findings. *Personnel Psychology, 46,* 259-293.

Thibaut, J. W., & Kelly, H. H. (1959). *The social psychology of groups.* New York: John Wiley.

Thomas, D. A. (1993). Racial dynamics in cross-race developmental relationships. *Administrative Science Quarterly, 38,* 169-194.

Thomas, L. T., & Ganster, D. C. (1995). Impact of family-supportive work variables on work-family conflict and strain: A control perspective. *Journal of Applied Psychology, 80,* 6-15.

Title VII's overseas reach; upward mobility for women. (1991, September 16). *Fair Employment Practices,* p. 105.

Trenk, B. S. (1990 September). Future moms, serious workers. *Management Review,* 33-37.

Trevor, C., Gerhart, B., & Boudreau, J. (1997). Voluntary turnover and job performance: Curvilinearity and the moderating influences of salary growth and promotions. *Journal of Applied Psychology, 82,* 44-61.

Tsui, A., & Ashford, S. (1994). Adaptive self-regulation: A process view of managerial effectiveness. *Journal of Management, 20,* 93-121.

Tsui, A. S., Egan, T. D., & O'Reilly, C. A. (1992). Being different: Relational demography and organizational attachment. *Administrative Science Quarterly, 37,* 549-579.

Tsui, A. S., & O'Reilly, C. A. (1989). Beyond simple demographic effects: The importance of relational demography in superior-subordinate dyads. *Academy of Management Journal, 32,* 402-423.

Tyler, T. (1990). *Why people obey the law.* New Haven, CT: Yale University Press.

Ulrich, D., Halbrook, R., Meder, D., Stuchlik, M., & Thorpe, S. (1991). Employee and customer attachment: Synergies for competitive advantage. *Human Resource Planning, 14,* 89-103.

Van Dierendonck, D., Schaufeli, W., & Buunk, B. (1998). Evaluation of an Individual Burnout Intervention Program: The Role of Inequity and Social Support. *Journal of Applied Psychology, 83,* 392-407.

Van Eerde, W., & Thierry, H. (1996). Vroom's expectancy models and work-related criteria: A meta-analysis. *Journal of Applied Psychology, 81,* 575-586.

Van Maanen, J. (1978). People processing: Strategies of organizational socialization. *Organizational Dynamics, 7,* 19-36.

Van Maanen, J., & Barley, S. R. (1984). Occupational communities. In B. Staw & L. Cummings (Eds.), *Research in organizational behavior* (Vol. 6, pp. 287-365). Greenwich, CT: JAI.

Van Maanen, J., & Schein, E. H. (1979). Toward a theory of organizational socialization. In B. Staw (Ed.), *Research in organizational behavior* (Vol. 1, pp. 209-264). Greenwich, CT: JAI.

Villanova, P., Bernardin, H., Johnson, D., & Dahmus, S. (1994). The validity of a measure of job compatibility in the prediction of job performance and turnover of motion picture theater personnel. *Personnel Psychology, 47,* 73-90.

Von Glinow, M. A. (1988). *The new professionals.* Cambridge, MA: Ballinger.

Vroom, V. H. (1964). *Work and motivation.* New York: John Wiley.

Wallace, J. E. (1995). Organizational and professional commitment in professional and nonprofessional organizations. *Administrative Science Quarterly, 40,* 230-255.

Wandelt, M. A., Pierce, P. M., & Widdowson, R. R. (1981). Why nurses leave nursing and what can be done about it. *American Journal of Nursing, 81,* 72-77.

Wanous, J. P. (1978). Realistic job previews: Can a procedure to reduce turnover also influence the relationship between abilities and performance? *Personnel Psychology, 31,* 249-258.

Wanous, J. P. (1980). *Organizational entry: Recruitment, selection and socialization of newcomers.* Reading, MA: Addison-Wesley.

Wanous, J. P. (1989). Installing a realistic job preview: Ten tough choices. *Personnel Psychology, 42,* 117-134.

Wanous, J. P. (1992). *Organizational entry: Recruitment, selection, orientation, and socialization of newcomers* (2nd ed.). Reading, MA: Addison-Wesley.

Wanous, J. P., & Colella, A. (1989). Organizational entry research: Current status and future directions. In G. Ferris & K. Rowland (Eds.), *Research in personnel and human resources management* (pp. 59-120). Greenwich, CT: JAI.

Wanous, J., Keon, T., & Latack, J. (1983). Expectancy theory and occupational/organizational choices: A review and test. *Organizational Behavior and Human Performance, 32,* 66-86.

Wartson, W. E., Kumar, K., & Michaelsen, L. K. (1993). Cultural diversity's impact on interaction process and performance: Comparing homogeneous and diverse task groups. *Academy of Management Journal, 36,* 590-602.

Waung, M. (1995). The effects of self-regulatory coping orientation on newcomer adjustment and job survival. *Personnel Psychology, 48,* 633-650.

Weiss, H. M., & Adler, S. (1984). Personality and organizational behavior. In B. M. Staw & L. L. Cummings (Eds.), *Research in organizational behavior* (Vol. 6, pp. 1-50). Greenwich, CT: JAI.

Weiss, S. J. (1984). The effect of transition modules on new graduate adaptation. *Research in Nursing and Health, 7,* 51-59.

Weitz, J. (1952). A neglected concept in the study of job satisfaction. *Personnel Psychology, 5,* 201-205.

Wernimont, P., & Campbell, J. (1968). Signs, samples, and criteria. *Journal of Applied Psychology, 52,* 372-376.

West, M. (2000). *Employee turnover in the maquiladora industry of Mexico: A cultural investigation of causes.* Unpublished doctoral dissertation, Arizona State University, Tempe.

Whiting, L. (1989). *Turnover costs: A case example.* Columbus: Ohio Department of Mental Health.

Williams, C. R., & Livingstone, L. P. (1994). A second look at the relationship between performance and voluntary turnover. *Academy of Management Journal, 37,* 269-298.

Wilson, N., & Peel, M. J. (1991). The impact on absenteeism and quits of profit-sharing and other forms of employee participation. *Industrial and Labor Relations Review, 44,* 454-468.

Wilson, T. (2000, May). Brand imaging: Five steps to developing a retention program. *ACA News, 43,* 44-48.

Winkler, R., & Hays, W. (1975). *Statistics: Probability, inference, and decision.* New York: Holt, Rinehart & Winston.

Workers switch jobs for sake of families. (2000, January 11). *Detroit Free Press.* Retrieved from the World Wide Web: *www.freep.com/business/wise11_2000111.htm*

Wright, P. M., & McMahan, G. C. (1992). Theoretical perspectives for strategic human resource management. *Journal of Management, 18,* 295-320.

Yalow, E. (1990, June). Corporate child care helps recruit and retain workers. *Personnel Journal,* 48-55.

Yang, C., Palmer, A., Browder, S., & Cuneo, A. (1996, November 11). Low-wage lessons. *Business Week,* 108-116.

Youngblood, S. A., & Chambers-Cook, K. (1984). Child care assistance can improve employee attitudes and behavior. *Personnel Administrator, 29,* 45.

Youngblood, S. A., Mobley, W. H., & Meglino, B. M. (1983). A longitudinal analysis of the turnover process. *Journal of Applied Psychology, 68,* 507-516.

Zarandona, J. L., & Camuso, M. A. (1985). A study of exit interviews: Does the last word count? *Personnel, 62*(3), 47-48.

Zedeck, S., Jackson, S. E., & Summers, E. (1983). Shift work schedules and their relationship to health, adaptation, satisfaction, and turnover intention. *Academy of Management Journal, 26,* 297-310.

Zedeck, S., & Mosier, K. L. (1990). Work in the family and employing organization. *American Psychologist, 45,* 240-251.

Zingheim, P., & Schuster, J. (1999, March/April). Dealing with scarce talent: Lessons from the leading edge. *Compensation and Benefits Review, 31,* 36-44.

Index

Absenteeism, reducing, 81-82, 197, 199
Accountants:
    realistic job previews, 23-24, 49-53
    self-management training, 79-80
    See also Public accounting firms
Adverse self-selection, 57
Aetna Life & Casualty, 22, 192, 195
Affective commitment, 129
Affective disposition measures, 110,
    111-112
Affirmative action programs, 187, 189, 192
African Americans:
    bias in performance appraisals of, 184
    turnover rates, 183
    See also Minorities
Allen, D. G., 200-201
Aon Corp., 157
Applications:
    biodata questionnaires, 95, 102-103
    See also Weighted application blanks
Arizona Council of Human Service Provid-
    ers, 8, 25
Arizona mental health industry:
    compensation strategies, 176
    turnover costs, 2
    turnover rates, 8

Arizona Society of Certified Public Accoun-
    tants, 49, 53
Ashforth, B., 81
AT&T, 195
Auditors. *See* Public accounting firms
Autonomy, 32, 37-38, 39, 42
Avoidable turnover, 6

Balkin, D., 176
Bank tellers, 90-92, 102
Barksdale, K., 197
Barrick, M. R., 107
BARS. *See* Behaviorally Anchored Rating
    Scale
Baxter International, 192
Behaviorally Anchored Rating Scale
    (BARS), 55
Belief systems, 77-80
Benchmarking:
    turnover costs, 24-25
    turnover rates, 8-9, 177
Bernardin, H. J., 102, 113-114
Bhagat, R., 141
Bicultural training, 71-73
Big Five Personality Scale, 107, 108-109
Biodata questionnaires, 95, 102-103

Boston University Center on Work and Family, 164
Breaugh, J. A., 102
Bretz, R. D., 57
Broad-banding, 159
Bruce, Stephen D., 214
Buckley, M. R., 63
Bureau of Labor, 66
Burns, D., 78, 79
Buunk, B., 83

Campbell Soup Company, 196
Campion, M., 219
Camuso, M. A., 207, 215
Career ladders, 155
Carraher, S. M., 63
Catalyst, 166
Ceridian Corp., 168
Child care services, 196-197
Chrysler Corporation, 29
Circuit City, 103
Clients:
    customer service, 26-27
    direct relationships with employees, 41-42, 43
Cognitive restructuring, 84-85
Cohen, D. J., 197
Colarelli, S. M., 59
College instructors, 55
Commitment, organizational. *See* Organizational commitment
Compensation:
    attracting and retaining employees with, 154-155
    bonuses, 159-160, 162-163
    broad-banding, 159
    career ladders, 155
    counteroffers, 162
    deferred, 159-160, 162-163
    fair distribution, 170-175
    fringe benefits, 163-164, 166-168
    in maquila industry, 168-170
    internal equity, 154, 157-158
    market pricing, 157-158, 159
    merit increases, 159
    new forms of base pay, 155-159
    of unskilled workers, 166-168
    of women and minorities, 185
    optional benefits, 168
    recommendations, 179
    research on, 154, 160-161, 167-168
    skill-based or knowledge-based, 155-157, 159
    stock options, 159-160
    strategies for reducing turnover, 175-177
    variable pay, 159-162
    See also Family-friendly policies; Salary surveys
Competitors:
    business lost to, 27-28
    perceived job opportunities with, 132-136
    See also Salary surveys
Computers:
    interviews using, 105
    surveys using, 150
ConAgra Refrigerated Foods, 166-167
Consistency principle, 95
Consulting firms, surveys by, 150-151, 217, 218
Coopers & Lybrand, 163
Corning Glass, 183
Costs. *See* Turnover costs
Cox, T., 191-194
Critical incidents, 54
Critical psychological states, 32, 33
Culture. *See* Organizational culture
Customer service, 26-27
Customers. *See* Clients

Dating, workplace, 191
Day care services, 196
Deferred compensation, 159-160, 162-163
Deloitte Consulting, 166
DeNisi, A. S., 58-59
Diagnostic model of turnover, 3
Difficulty-to-recall perspective, 210-211
Digital, 193
Discrimination:
    as turnover cause, 183-184
    combating, 193
    issues with biodata questionnaires, 103
    reverse, 189
    sources, 183-184
Diversity:
    as competitive advantage, 182-183
    definition, 182
    increase in, 188-189
    managing, 192-194

training, 192, 193
valuing, 182, 192
See also Minorities; Women
Dossett, D. L., 102
Dow Chemical, 28
Due process of law, 173-174
DuPont, 6, 191
Dysfunctional turnover:
  definition, 5-6
  managing, 143-145, 159, 160-162
  predicting, 143-145, 151

EAP. *See* Employee assistance programs
Eddie Bauer, 6
ELP. *See* Expectation Lowering Procedure
Employee assistance programs (EAPs), 24
Employee selection:
  affective disposition measures, 110, 111-
    112
  biodata questionnaires, 95, 102-103
  personality measures, 105-110, 113-114
  person-environment fit, 112-113
  person-job fit, 57, 113-115
  See also Interviews; Realistic job pre-
    views; Weighted application blanks
Employees:
  binding to job, 59, 140
  discouraging retirements, 166
  high performers, 143-145, 160-162
  new labor force entrants, 60
  peer influences, 187-188
  perceived job alternatives, 132-136
  turnover costs, 139-140, 163
  unskilled, 166-168
  visible high performers, 161-162
  See also Minorities; Women
Employment contracts, 59, 140
Ethnic groups. *See* Minorities
Exit interviews:
  accuracy measurements, 207, 215-216,
    219, 222
  alternatives to, 216-219
  avoiding repercussions, 214-215
  confidentiality, 214, 218
  confrontations avoided by employees, 7-8,
    204, 208-210
  costs, 10-12
  identifying turnover reasons, 7-8, 35, 205,
    206

improving, 212-216
  inaccuracies in, 206-211
  measuring turnover types, 219
  problems with, 7-8, 204-205, 206-212
  process, 219, 220
  purposes, 205-206, 223
  sample form, 219, 221
  selecting interviewer, 205, 214
  semi-structured, 212-213
  skills needed, 211, 213
  structured, 212, 213
  training for, 211, 213
  using information from, 216
Expectancy theory of motivation, 133, 135-
  137
Expectation Lowering Procedure (ELP), 63-65
Expectations of new employees. *See* Realistic
  job previews (RJPs)
Eyre, Richard, 194

Facet satisfaction, 124
Families. *See* Family-friendly policies; Role
  stress
Families and Work Institute, 164, 194
Family and Medical Leave Act, 194-195
Family-friendly policies:
  alternative work schedules, 197-198
  child and dependent care services, 196-197
  family leave, 195-196
  flexible spending accounts, 196
  impact, 202
  index of, 194-195
  reducing role stress, 165-166
  research on, 166, 202
  roles of supervisors, 88
  telecommuting, 42, 198-201
  turnover reduction as purpose, 6, 165-166
Fast-food restaurants, 166, 167-168
Fedor, D. B., 63
Feedback to employees, 32-33, 35, 37-38,
  39, 43
  See also Performance appraisals
Feldman, D., 199-200
Feldman, D. C., 210, 214
Fink, L., 141-142
Flexible spending accounts, 196
Forced-choice personality inventory, 113-114
Ford Motor Company, 8
Fottler, M. D., 218

Frayne, C. A., 81
Fringe benefits, 163-164, 166-168
  See also Family-friendly policies
Functional turnover, 2, 5

Gainey, T., 199-200
Gates, Bill, 155
Gender. *See* Men; Women
General Electric, 28
General Motors, 28
Gomez-Mejia, L., 176
Graen, G. B., 86
Greenhalgh, Leonard, 210-211
Griffeth, R., 119-121, 129, 133, 141-142,
  143-144
Griffeth, R. W., 197
Gripe index, 111-112

Hackman, J. R., 32, 35, 37, 38, 39, 40,
  42, 43
Health care. *See* Nurses
Hiring. *See* Employee selection; Interviews
Hom, P., 121, 131, 132, 138
Hom, P. W., 119-121, 129, 133, 143-144, 176
Honeywell, 193
Hospitals. *See* Nurses
Human services professionals, 83-84, 163

Iacocca, Lee, 29
Info World, 208
Informix, 28
Intel, 2, 28
Intellectual property, 28
Interest inventories, 105
Internet, surveys using, 150
Interviews:
  costs, 17
  interviewer errors, 104
  probing questions, 212-213
  selection, 17, 103-105, 212
  semi-structured, 212-213
  structured, 105, 212, 213
  technology used in, 105
  See also Exit interviews
Involuntary turnover, 4, 187, 219

JE. *See* Job enrichment
Job attraction, 131-132, 136
Job Compatibility Questionnaire, 114-117

Job Diagnostic Survey, 35-36, 230-243
  national norms, 36, 248
  scoring key, 244-247
Job enrichment (JE):
  example, 44-45
  identifying areas for improvement, 36-38
  redesigning work, 38-45
  reducing turnover through, 31-32
  research on, 33-34
  See also Task characteristics model
Job Rating Forms (JRFs), 34-35, 224-229,
  244-247
Job satisfaction:
  affective disposition measures, 111, 112
  as turnover cause, 120, 126-129, 144
  causal antecedents, 120, 184
  facet satisfaction, 124, 144
  of women and minorities, 184, 185-186
  survey questions, 124-129
Job sharing, 197-198
Journal of Accountancy, 20
JRF. *See* Job Rating Forms
Judge, T. A., 57, 111, 112
Justice:
  distributive, 170
  interactional, 171-173
  procedural, 170-171

Kinicki, A., 121, 131, 132, 138
Klaas, B. S., 210, 214
Klein, H., 70
Knowledge-based pay, 155-157, 159
Korsgaard, M. A., 174-175
Krackhardt, D., 90, 91
Kramer, M., 71

Latham, G. P., 81
Leader-member exchanges (LMX), 86-87
Leadership, 86-87
  See also Supervisors
Life insurance industry, 60
Likelihood to Sexually Harass (LSH) Scale,
  190
Lindholm, H., 141
LMX. *See* Leader-member exchanges
Locke, E. A., 112
Lopez de Arriortua, J. Ignacio, 29
LSH. *See* Likelihood to Sexually Harass
  (LSH) Scale

Managers. *See* Supervisors
Manz, C. C., 74, 75, 76, 77
Maquila industry, 8, 168-170
Market pricing of compensation, 157-158, 159
Marriott Corporation, 27, 159, 166
McDonald's, 166, 192
McKenna, J., 90, 91
McQuaid, S., 141
Meglino, B. M., 58-59
Men:
    workplace dating, 191
    See also Minorities; Sexual harassment;
        White men
Mental health industry. *See* Arizona mental
    health industry
Merck & Company, 22
Metropolitan Life Insurance, 199
Mexico, maquila industry, 8, 168-170
Microsoft, 155, 160
Minorities:
    affirmative action programs, 187, 189, 192
    compensation, 185
    concerns with use of biodata, 103
    in workforce, 182
    informal networks, 193
    lack of promotions, 186-187
    lack of research on turnover, 183
    organizational commitment, 184
    performance appraisals, 184, 188
    reducing turnover, 201-202
    tokenism, 186
    turnover causes, 184
    turnover rates, 29, 183
    unsupportive coworkers, 187-188
    See also Diversity
Mirage Resorts, 167
Monsanto, 183, 192
Motivating Potential Score, 37-38
Motivation:
    expectancy theory, 133, 135-137
    natural and extrinsic rewards, 77
    pursuing job alternatives, 133-137
    self-, 32, 75, 76-77
    See also Task characteristics model
Motorola, 28
Mount, M. K., 107

NAFTA. *See* North American Free Trade
    Agreement

Natural work units, 40-41
Neck, C., 82
Neck, C. P., 76, 77
Newsweek, 189
North American Free Trade Agreement
    (NAFTA), 169
Northern Telecom, 157, 193
Norwest Bank, 179
Nurses:
    alternative job opportunities, 133-135,
        136, 158, 178
    dysfunctional turnover, 143-144
    job satisfaction surveys, 125-127, 128-129
    organizational commitment, 129
    orientation programs, 71-73
    quit reasons, 4-5, 6-7
    realistic job previews, 54
    surveys, 218

OCP. *See* Organizational Culture Profiles
Oldham, G. R., 32, 35, 37, 38, 39, 40,
    42, 43
Opportunity thinking, 77, 80, 82
Oracle, 28
Organizational commitment:
    affective, 129
    as turnover cause, 120-121
    as turnover predictor, 129
    causal antecedents, 120-121, 184
    definition, 129
    effects of unfair policies, 171, 175
    measures, 129
    of women and minorities, 184
    person-environment fit and, 113
    survey questions, 129
Organizational culture, 112-113
Organizational Culture Profiles (OCP), 112-
    113
Orientation programs:
    bicultural training, 71-73
    Expectation Lowering Procedure (ELP),
        63-65
    realistic, 71-85
    ROPES (Realistic Orientation Programs for
        new Employee Stress), 73-74
    self-management training, 74-85
    socialization learning, 70
    See also Realistic job previews

Pacific Bell, 193
PaineWebber, 28
Part-time work, 197-198
Peer influences, 187-188
Pelled, L. H., 112
Pepsico, 192
Performance appraisals:
  bias in, 184
  fairness, 171, 172, 173
  of women and minorities, 184, 188
  self-ratings related to, 143
  training for employees, 174-175
  training for supervisors, 173-174
Performaworks, 150
Personality measures:
  Big Five Personality Scale, 107
  forced-choice personality inventory, 113-114
  turnover predicted by, 105-107
Person-environment fit, 112-113
Person-job fit:
  Job Compatibility Questionnaire, 114-117
  personality measures, 113-114
  realistic job previews and, 57
Porter, L., 90, 91
PriceWaterhouseCoopers, 165-166
Productivity losses, 14, 20
Promotions:
  career ladders, 155
  obstacles for minorities and women, 186-187
Prudential, 54
Public accounting firms:
  compensation systems, 156
  realistic job previews, 23-24, 49-53
  self-management training, 79-80
  turnover costs, 21
Purdue University, 167-168

Quit decisions, 121-124, 211
Quitting. *See* Voluntary turnover
Qwest, 193

Racial groups. *See* Minorities
Rational distortion perspective, 208-210
Realistic job previews (RJPs):
  alternatives to, 63-65
  booklets, 48, 49-55
  content, 49, 54-55

cost savings, 23-24
delivered by job incumbents, 59-60
designing, 49-55
effects on departure timing, 58-59
for accountants, 23-24, 49-53
for nurses, 54
job performance improvements, 63
media, 48-49, 63
purposes, 47
research on effectiveness, 34, 48, 51-53, 61
timing, 57-58
turnover predicted by, 106
types of jobs, 62-63
types of recipients, 60-63
work samples, 60
Realistic Orientation Programs for
  new Employee Stress (ROPES), 73-74
References, 214-215
Religious minorities. *See* Minorities
Research designs, 23
Resignations. *See* Voluntary turnover
Retail employees, 132, 138
Retention:
  cost-benefit analysis of strategies, 22-24
  employee selection methods, 117
  of potential retirees, 166
  See also Turnover reduction methods
Retirement, postponing, 166
Revenues, lost, 12, 21, 27-28
Reverse discrimination, 189
RewardsPlus of America Corp., 168
RJP. *See* Realistic job previews
Robert Half International, 206
Role stress:
  as turnover cause, 137-139, 164-165, 194
  increase in, 164
  reducing, 87-88, 194, 197, 199
  survey questions, 138-139
  See also Family-friendly policies
ROPES (Realistic Orientation Programs for
  new Employee Stress), 73-74
Ryder Truck Rental, 2

Saks, A., 81
Salaries. *See* Compensation
Salary surveys:
  compensation strategy questions, 175-177
  frequency, 179
  implementation problems, 158

purpose, 175
relevant competitors, 177-179
Saratoga Institute, 1
Schaufeli, W., 83
Schedule of Recent Experiences, 141
Schmalenberg, C., 71
Sears, 27
Security Pacific, 193
Segovis, J., 141
Self-management:
  belief systems and, 77-80
  cognitive restructuring, 84-85
  reducing absenteeism, 81-82
  reducing burnout, 83-84
  research on, 80-85
  strategies, 75-77
  thought self-leadership, 82-83
  training, 74, 80-85
Seligman, Martin, 77
Semi-structured interviews, 212-213
Service quality, 26-27
Sexual Experience Questionnaire, 189-190
Sexual harassment:
  as turnover cause, 188
  grievance procedures, 191
  measures, 189-190
  reasonable woman standard, 191
  reducing, 189-191
Shocks, as turnover cause, 121, 141-142
Sioux Falls (South Dakota), 179
Skill-based pay, 155-157, 159
Social information processing theory, 28
Socialization:
  inadequate, 66
  individualized, 67-69
  institutionalized, 67-69
  learning, 69-70
  orientation programs, 63-65, 70, 71-85
  proactive, 74
  research on, 69-70, 80-85
  self-management training, 74-85
  tactics, 67-69
Statistical tests, 127-129
Steers, R., 90, 91
Stock options, 159-160
Stress:
  coping skills, 71-74
  See also Role stress
Structured interviews, 105, 212, 213

Supervisors:
  abusive, 88-90
  as turnover cause, 85-86
  biases, 184
  data-based intervention, 90-93
  evaluation with survey data, 147
  loyalty-inducing leadership practices, 86-87
  reducing role stress of employees, 87-88, 197
  relationships with subordinates, 86-87, 171-173
  training, 86-87
  verifying accuracy of exit interviews, 215, 219, 222
  See also Performance appraisals
Surveys:
  administration, 145-150
  as alternative to exit interviews, 216-217
  benefits, 217-219
  by consulting firms, 150-151, 217, 218
  cautions, 217
  confidentiality, 146-147, 150, 217, 218
  demographic questions, 146-147, 149
  job attraction questions, 131-132
  job satisfaction questions, 124-129
  lengths, 146
  managing dysfunctional turnover with, 143-145
  organizational commitment questions, 129
  participation, 145-146
  perceived job alternatives questions, 132-136
  quit intention questions, 121-124
  recommendations, 152
  role conflict questions, 138-139
  samples, 148-150
  statistical tests, 127-129
  turnover causes, 119, 124, 126
  turnover costs questions, 139-140
  turnover predictions, 118, 119, 123-124, 129, 150
  uses, 118, 147
  See also Salary surveys

Task characteristics model:
  autonomy, 32, 37-38, 39, 42
  definitions, 39
  feedback, 32-33, 35, 37-38, 39, 43
  identifying areas for improvement, 36-38

implementing principles, 38-43
internal motivation principles, 32
job analysis, 34-38
overview, 32-33
redesigning jobs, 38-45
skill variety, 32, 37, 39
task identity, 32, 37, 39
task significance, 32, 36, 37, 39
Teachers, 55
Telecommuting, 42, 198-201
Thomas, Clarence, 191
Thought self-leadership (TSL), 82-83
Tokenism, 186, 190-191
Total Quality Management, 43
Training:
  bicultural, 71-73
  costs, 10, 18-21
  diversity, 192, 193
  for exit interviews, 211, 213
  for performance appraisals, 173-175
  leadership, 86-87
  self-management, 74-85
  See also Orientation programs
Travelers Insurance, 199
Truck drivers, 107
TSL. *See* Thought self-leadership
Turnover:
  among new employees, 66
  assessing severity of problem, 29-30
  avoidable, 6
  benchmarking, 8-9, 177
  current levels, 1
  diagnostic model, 3, 119-121
  dysfunctional, 5-6, 143-145, 151, 159,
    160-162
  effects on organizational effectiveness, 2
  functional, 2, 5
  identifying unwanted, 3
  involuntary, 4, 187, 219
  jobs with high, 63
  unavoidable, 6, 7, 121, 141-142
  voluntary, 4-5, 219
Turnover causes:
  for minorities and women, 184, 194
  for white men, 188-189
  identifying in exit interviews, 7-8, 35, 205,
    206
  job attraction, 131-132
  job dissatisfaction, 120, 126-129, 144

model, 119-121
  organizational commitment, 120-121
  perceived job alternatives, 132-136
  role stress, 137-139, 164-165, 194
  sexual harassment, 188
  shift rotation, 197
  shocks (events), 121, 141-142
  supervision, 85-86
  surveys on, 119, 124, 126
Turnover costs:
  benchmarking, 24-25
  business lost to competitors, 27-28
  increased turnover rate, 28-29
  lost revenues, 12, 21
  monitoring, 2
  per incidence, 1-2, 22
  replacement, 10, 14-17
  separation, 10-14
  service quality, 26-27
  to employee, 139-140, 163
  training, 10, 18-21
Turnover predictions:
  demographic traits, 149
  dysfunctional turnover, 143-145, 151
  interviews used for, 104
  personality measures, 105-107
  realistic job previews, 106
  surveys used for, 118, 119, 121-124, 129,
    150
  unavoidable turnover, 141-142
  with weighted application blanks, 95-100
Turnover reduction methods. *See* Compensation; Family-friendly policies; Job
  enrichment; Realistic job previews;
  Retention; Socialization; Supervisors

Unavoidable turnover, 6, 7, 121, 141-142
U.S. Department of Labor, 194
U.S. Navy, 191
U.S. West, 193

Van Dierendonck, D., 83
Veres, J., 63
Volkswagen, 28, 29
Voluntary turnover:
  definition, 5
  measuring, 219
  reasons, 4-5

WAB. *See* Weighted application blanks
Wages. *See* Compensation
Wanous, J. P., 73
Waung, M., 84
Weaver, N., 70
Weighted application blanks (WAB):
  bias in, 101
  problems, 100-102
  screening applicants with, 100
  turnover predictions, 95-100
Weitz, J., 111
West, M., 169-170
White men:
  relations with minority coworkers, 187-188
  reverse discrimination, 189
  turnover causes, 188-189
Wiese, D., 63
William M. Mercer consultants, 2
Women:
  alternative work schedules, 197-198
  bias in performance appraisals, 184
  bias in weighted application blanks, 101
  compensation, 185
  in workforce, 182
  lack of promotions, 186-187
  lack of research on turnover, 183
  mothers, 194

  organizational commitment, 184
  performance appraisals, 184, 188
  reducing turnover, 201-202
  sexual harassment, 188, 189-191
  tokenism, 186, 190-191
  turnover causes, 184, 194
  turnover rates, 29, 183
  unsupportive coworkers, 187-188
  workplace dating, 191
  See also Diversity; Family-friendly policies; Role stress
Work outcomes, 32
Work samples, 60
Work schedules:
  alternative, 197-198
  compressed, 197-198
  job sharing, 197-198
  part-time, 198
  rotating shifts, 197
Work-family conflicts. *See* Family-friendly policies; Role stress

Xerox, 192, 193
Xin, K. R., 112

Yankelovich Clancy Shulman, 193-194

Zarandona, J. L., 207, 215

About the Authors

Rodger W. Griffeth is Professor of Management in the J. Mack Robinson College of Business at Georgia State University. He earned his PhD from the University of South Carolina, his MEd at Georgia State University and his BS at Old Dominion University. His primary interests are in the areas of organizational behavior and employee turnover. He has investigated how job enrichment can reduce turnover among part-time employees and how realistic job previews can improve retention among new professionals. Dr. Griffeth also has comprehensively reviewed the turnover literature using meta-analysis, examined how employee impressions of the job market influence their turnover decisions, and developed and tested turnover theories. Professor Griffeth authored a landmark article on turnover in *Psychological Bulletin* (with William Mobley) and won the 1992 Scholarly Achievement Award from the Human Resource Division of the Academy of Management for best published article (on testing turnover models with Peter Hom). He coauthored *Employee Turnover* with Peter Hom and has published in numerous journals, including the *Journal of Applied Psychology, Personnel Psychology,* and the *Academy of Management Journal.* He currently serves as editor of *Human Resources Management Review.*

Peter W. Hom is Professor of Management in the College of Business at Arizona State University (Tempe). He received his PhD from the University of Illinois (Champaign–Urbana) in Industrial/Organizational Psychology. He has investigated theories of employee turnover in various occupations (industrial salesmen, retail sales personnel, and national guardsmen), designed realistic job previews to reduce reality shock and early quits among new nurses and accountants, estimated the economic costs of turnover for mental health agencies, and examined psychological commitment to new products in cross-functional design teams. Currently, he is studying the causes of turnover among Swiss bank personnel and Mexican factory workers. He has authored scholarly articles in the *Academy of Management Journal,* the *Journal of Applied Psychology, Organizational Behavior and Human Decision Processes,* and *Personnel Psychology.* He also coauthored *Employee Turnover* with Rodger Griffeth. He and Dr. Griffeth won the 1992 Scholarly Achievement Award from the Human Resources Division of the Academy of Management for best published academic article in the field of human resources management. Dr. Hom has served on editorial boards for the *Academy of Management Journal, Journal of Applied Psychology,* and *Journal of Management.*